REDISCOVERED MASTERPIECES

A SERIES BY
GÉRALD BERJONNEAU AND JEAN-LOUIS SONNERY

REDISCOVERED MASTERPIECES
OF AFRICAN ART

Producers: Gérald Berjonneau, Jean-Louis Sonnery and
Fondation Dapper

ISBN 2-905 351-06-3

CONTENTS

PREFACE

Picasso's reply to a question concerning a subject to which he had obviously given thought is often quoted: 'African art? Don't know anything about it!'

How many cultivated people today however could repeat the same words on their own account, not in jest but as an admission.

With the exception of some researchers and collectors, the sculptures of the black continent remain the victim of tenacious prejudices. For too large a proportion of public opinion, both inside and outside the continent, Africa is seen, consciously or unconsciously, as a land that 'spawns monsters', a universe of barbarity, peopled by savages incapable of sensitivity or artistic creation. Have attempts not been made to find the invaders to whom Nigeria would appear to owe the Benin bronzes? Can one not read here and there of certain suspicious links between a pottery decoration, or a weave design from Central Africa and the protogeometric or geometric style of ancient Greece?

Yet here is an art which, when discovered by Europe, touched and overwhelmed the sensitivity of a certain number of the most significant artists of the turn of the century. The emotion it aroused obsessed them and fertilised their imaginations, leaving clear marks on their own canvases and sculptures.

Whenever possible, the general public in Europe, taken by surprise, renders due hommage to these works. This was to be seen recently at the Grand Palais during the exhibition of Benin bronzes. The classicism of their forms upset and dispelled many a prejudice.

Yet sculpture in wood deserves no less interest.

The selection presented here allows one to grasp the major components of a multi-facetted art form, ranging through stylisation to the abstract, whereby the connoisseur can, through certain specific details, determine the origin of the item. The Bakuba coffee grain eyes, the baroque flowering of the Bamoun and the Tshokwe. Impossible to confuse a Muluba mask with one of Senufo origin, or a Baoule and a Mukongo mother figure. Finally, what a great distance exists between a mask of the Mossendjo Batekes, a statue of a Kota ancestor and a Bambara chiwara. There is not one African civilisation, but several African civilisations — whence the varied sculptural identities.

However, as in the case of the black African societies taken overall, there is in this statuary, over and above the characteristic individualities of the various cultural zones, one language, a symbolic code characteristic of the continent south of the Sahara: body poses, the place accorded to certain limbs, the look that questions the far beyond, always with the same impassivity, is not just a common place. It corresponds to a tangible reality.

Yet we ourselves, Africans, do we really know the true value of these treasures scattered throughout the world in public and private collections? Are we aware that these works form a vital part of our folk memory? That they constitute the expression of an identity that is still as much threatened as are our ways of singing, dancing, or praying?

It is high time that we looked at these works no longer through the eyes of the ethnologist or the anthropologist, but rather with a view towards the discovery of our aesthetics.

May the evocative power of the photographs gathered here, whose quality brings a new dimension to the art of these divine, albeit nameless, sculptors, give us the desire to know more, to touch and caress these works of art, witnesses of a heritage that alone can help us keep our soul!

May the magical pages of this museum fertilise the imagination of the artists of an Africa that is searching for both its present and its past. Not to repeat ancient creations, but to create this vision of the universe that nature had not prepared us for, and of which our elders never dreamed. They are free to create in the tradition of the ancient forms, or to react against this heritage, provided they take it as their starting point!

Henri LOPES

FOREWORD

When Gérald Berjonneau and Jean-Louis Sonnery made their proposal of an association to publish the second volume of their 'Rediscovered Masterpieces' collection, we gave in to temptation.

The great talent of the photographer plus the experience of prior jointly produced catalogues formed an ideal combination. However two elements in their project carried the decision:

— Unpublished items: By enlarging an aesthetic and scientific panorama, often too familiar to researchers and art lovers, this book was intended to contribute to the studies of the former and the pleasure of the latter.

— The quality of the items: When confronting all the items, the book could include in each category only those items which appeared to be the best: a selection committee was created to take this procedure in hand; furthermore, none of the items presented were to be for sale.

Such were the high ambitions of this enterprise — let the reader judge how far these objectives have been attained.

Nevertheless, with this dual requirement, that works be of high quality and yet unpublished, it was obvious that certain major artistic creations could not be featured; for example, all the major works of Ife classical sculpture have already been published (but where is it possible to discover an unknown expression of Greek statuary?). We also knew how formidable the method of confrontation could be for items that slipped through the selection process by mistake.

All due credit must be given to the team for their energy and perseverance, leading for the first time to the completion of such a vast inventory of the artistic wealth of Africa — over time and space.

Actually getting to the works of art, in order to build up a corpus of representative items, was no easy matter since an inventory existed only for a few peoples and all that was readily accessible had already been seen; it is difficult to imagine how jealously these works are guarded when it comes to photographing them — and not only in private collections.

Often the possession of these objects is shrouded in mystery. Could it be that they retain some strange power that secretes the taste of mystery? This conspiracy of silence is likely to grow since there are ancient works buried in the soil of Africa waiting to be discovered. Due to the insufficiency of African budgetary aid swamped by other priorities, the items revealed according to satisfactory procedures are truly exceptions — undoubtedly less than one item in ten. Thus the archeological studies — however great their interest — only leave us with but partial information. A major part of the historical environment is being subjected to irreversible destruction and only rapid and urgent safeguard action can perhaps still yet prevent all being lost. This concerns in particular the finest items, yet the problem is so serious and so difficult that people often do not care to bring up the subject.

The African terra cotta items could thus have been left out of this book. However, in a presentation of Greek Art, it would seem absurd to decide to omit the Venus de Milo on account of the circumstances under which it was 'acquired'. This masterpiece is today one of those that draws the most visitors to the Louvre.

Will this book help to convince that certain major African masterpieces of black Africa merit the same place?

Fondation Dapper

INTRODUCTION

'OBJECTS, LIKE MEN,
ONLY HAVE VALUE WHEN COMPARED TO OTHERS'

André MALRAUX, during a conversation two days before his death

André Malraux still lives and is very much of our time. This book we are presenting to you is centred around his notion of comparison.

The concept of confrontation of works of art, which was a fundamental preoccupation of the author of 'Les Voix du Silence' (Voices of Silence), has been the guiding principle for our classification of this book on the rediscovered masterpieces of black Africa.

In it, we compare objects made of the same materials: terra cotta, metal, ivory, wood. This division is in no way arbitrary but is linked to the creative process.

For the wood items, we compare shape with shape: masks, statues, everyday objects. From this comparison springs the stimulating confrontation that reveals feeling and creativity. Here, we are not talking of an 'Imaginary Museum', but of an 'Imaginary Exhibition' — inconceivable since it consists of photographs of objects discovered in several different continents; over three hundred specimens which, in our eyes, deserve to be called masterpieces. By what criteria, you may ask? Compared to art in general? According to their antiquity? Or by their plastic beauty as seen through our Western eyes replete with Grecian culture or modern art?

Not at all. We have followed the only criteria that satisfied us: the rational selection and cultural choice known as 'taste'. Taste has the particularity of being generally termed bad by some (those who do not share your opinion) and excellent by others (those who do). We have examined many thousands objects. The first fact to be noted is the sheer volume of production of African artefacts, and thus the need to learn how to steer a clear path through them.

Aided by a team of specialists, we carried out a selection of 4,600 items that form the core of this book. First we had to authentificate them, so as to weed out any modern items. We always used scientific methods when possible, in particular the thermoluminescence tests for the terra cotta items. Then we confronted them again and again. This comparative dialogue gave birth to the selection that we offer you. Coming back briefly to the supposed subjectivity of artistic taste, we became aware that certain items are unanimously appreciated. We must therefore conclude that they are major items. Secondly, discussion arises when there is the possibility of choice between criteria. For example, should an extremely rare item be ranked higher simply because it is so rare? Should a very ancient item be ranked higher just on the ground of its age? All these tricky criteria can provoke endless discussion. We have adopted the principle that rarity in itself is not a criterion of aesthetic value, and also that the 'romantic' appearance of a wooden item eaten away by termites or weather-worn is not a synonym of quality. Thus, while the method of selection was intended to be rational, the final choice was not: it was the choice of a team trusting in its taste and culture.

Masterpieces perhaps, but let us not lose sight of our prime objective: REDISCOVERY.

Like most art lovers, we thirst after new images, unknown iconography. We became somewhat weary of albeit finely produced books that always showed the same 'masterpieces' that are recognised as the showpieces of various museums, and decided to take up the challenge. However, we had to be realistic and in order to encompass this notion of rediscovery, we set ourselves a rule which is not totally restrictive and which is intended to give satisfaction to our readers.

We compared ourselves with other art books dealing with the same subject, and state that 'a rediscovery is something that has not been published in an art book within the last 20 years'. However, we have not excluded those items which have already appeared in exhibition pamphlets, or art gallery, museum or auction catalogues.

But every rule has its exception, to which some of the Tshokwe figures bear witness.

Now we feel it is high time to lead you into our imaginary exhibition. In room after room, under each object, you will find its reference number, ethnic group and dimensions. This information is succint, but if you seek further details, the number of the photograph will refer you to the chapter with explanatory notes on page 289. How have we spelt the names of the ethnic groups? In the simplest possible manner, and always using U for the phoneme OU.

If you are searching for objects from a particular ethnic group, just consult the index of ethnic groups appearing in the book on page 76 and facing page, and you will find the numbers of the photographs to help you organise your encounters.

Just a few more words to tell you how the book is divided up. You start with *terra cotta,* shown in by a Nok head leading you through to an amazing Djenne mask.

For the *metalwork,* you will go through Djenne and Benin bronzes and Ashanti gold.

For the *ivory items,* a panorama of Lega heads, a Kongo sceptre and even an astonishing fan with Janus figures. *Then comes the wood section* which starts with masks and also includes headdresses and reliquary figures.

Confront and compare! From surrealism to cubism, from figurative to abstract.

You will then discover the statuary. You may well be surprised to see specimens several centuries old: the Dogon/Djenne.

Just as for the masks, we have endeavoured to follow the usual geographical progression of books about Africa, by moving from west to east, then south. The last pages are given over to environmental objects: cups, spears, pullies, spoons, etc. These objects convey the joy of the African sculptor working with total freedom. Although of perhaps a minor genre, they are nevertheless of high quality. There can be no aesthetic discrimination between a Luba statue and a Luba walking stick, or between a Dogon 'telem' and a Dogon door.

Welcome to our imaginary exhibition, and may the scholars forgive our telescoping time and space, all for the pleasures of confrontation. Our intent is above all to highlight aesthetic values, and not to update knowledge. We have accomplished this in this book in more than 200 pages of photographs over which we have taken particular care. On the rare occasions when we could not ourselves travel, we dispatched a photographer in order to catch the best possible expression of the object. We have always tried to capture just the right light to allow the masterpiece full expression.

The texts in this publication are the reflection of our principle of rediscovered art.

Bernard de Grunne introduces the various chapters of the book, situating the objects you are about to discover in their overall context, and, for the first time in an art book, expounds what is known today about terra cotta. Robert Farris Thompson brings in fresh data and an original view of the Yorubas and the Kongos.

Finally, if you see a photograph about which you require

detailed information, consult the notes. The main commentaries are written by Dr. Pierre Harter.

Come into a world of discovery! Let your emotions flow freely. You will not need to look for the signature at the bottom of a work to know whether it is beautiful or not — there is no signature. To the God of all the arts, our heartfelt thanks!

Gérald BERJONNEAU, Jean-Louis SONNERY

In hommage to André Malraux, we invite you to reread these prophetic sentences drawn from 'Les Voix du Silence' (pages 541 to 568). Editions N.R.F. La Galerie de la Pléiade, 1951.

'... For fetishes to enter into the Imaginary Museum with their full meaning, the white man, and not just one or other group of artists or amateurs, would have to relinquish the determination that ever since Rome has defined it for the whole world. He would have to accept to elect within himself his share of profundity.

Elect and not annex. For then it would no longer be a question of what is the place of these art forms; while they are no longer those of shapes fuelled by another world (of shapes nonetheless); if they give full voice to their sermon, they do not invade the Museum — they set it ablaze...'

'... Obviously there is no such thing as Negro art, but African *arts*. Leaving aside prehistory, one of these arts developed in a vein that is well known to us: not only in Benin or Ife, but also to a lesser extent with the Bakuba, in the figures of the Bushongo kings; whatever the material of this ornate architectural stylisation, evoking Byzantine art but without Christ, it calls for bronze. Its art which at times represents its kings, readily catches whatever surrounds and stylises our XVIth century adventurers with a Caucasian vigour. And then there are what are improperly called fetishes, i.e. masks and figures of ancestors: the art of a collective subjectivity, where the artist conquers interior, yet recognised structures: the means of possessing not what one can see, but that which one cannot. On the one hand, the ivories and bronzes created in Benin, a kingdom where velvet was woven; on the other hand, the fabled hunter of cave painters, and all that art could offer him: in the half-light where the antelope-man and the panther-man come to life, behold the mask with which the sorcerer with the bird skull necklace goes to search out the saturnine times...

What does the African artist strive to achieve? Actual resemblance is often of no import to him. Expressiveness? Yes, if we see it as being as specific as that of music. Negro art has rarely sought suggestion by realism, even via caricature or passion, except when it has been submitted to the influence of foreign models. The African mask is not the representation of a human expression, it is an apparition... The sculptor is not geometrising a phantom unknown to him — he is summoning it forth by his geometry; his mask acts all the more powerfully insofar as it does not resemble man; the animal masks are not animals; the antelope mask is not an antelope, but the Antelope Spirit, and it is its style that renders it Spirit. For the black sculptor, it is said that the best mask is the most effective; where else can its effectiveness come from, if not from the fullness of its style...?

Negroes are artists because they are creators of another world, they are also quite simply true *artists;* like the Prophets, they create the shapes that determine the style of their tribe for centuries, and also that as sculptors, they create those forms that will determine it for years. Even when the African style is the passionate call of geometry to the supernatural, one can follow, or at least guess, the avenues it has taken to conquer. The design of the Antelope Spirit is not simply an emblem. The limbs of Europeanised fetishes look like limbs, those of ancestral figures indicate them but do not resemble them: they are pure invention. The genius of certain black sculptors leads them to arrange their figures at the limit of a style: yet Poussin 'beautified' each arm to suit his picture, just as the African reduces it to essentials, or invents it to confer upon his sculpture an invulnerable unity. Both are seeking to eliminate all extraneous elements from their work: the writing on the Pongwe mask, which evokes Klee, links up with the most violent Dogon figure, with the most architectural Guinean ancestor, by the proclamation of an imperious presence in each of these works. Clearly that of the artist...'

FROM PRIME OBJECTS TO MASTERPIECES

The study of African aesthetics has demonstrated the essential relationship between beauty and goodness. For the Africans, art provides not only aesthetic pleasure but simultaneously upholds moral values. A masterpiece in African terms will then offer a balanced fusion of formal beauty and moral content.

From a western point of view, masterpieces, in addition to the emotions they provoke, are useful concepts for art historians. George Kubler, in his theoretical art historical study *The Shape of Time,* defines prime objects as inventions possessing prime traits and denoting the entire system of replicas, copies, reductions, transfers and derivations floating in the wake of an important work of art.[1] These prime objects are extremely few and, like black holes in astrophysics, are known solely by the large mass of derivative stuff left in their path.

In a recent conversation with him at Yale, Professor Kubler added several nuances. Accordingly, objects were called prime after prime numbers in mathematics. Prime numbers are infinite and their occurence most unusual and unpredictable. By extension, prime objects are undetermined, unforseeable and unpredictable.

Prime objects occur at rare moments when all combinations and permutations of the formal game are in front of an artist. Prime objects could then be understood as works of art of the highest quality whose influence in art history are directly proportional to their aesthetic achievement. Prime objects can be compared to the holotype in biology, the single specimen designated by an author as the *type* of a species at the time of establishing that species.

Kubler cites the Parthenon as an example of a prime object. Although it is built upon an archaic formula (a peripteral temple) surviving in Periclean time, the Parthenon is recognized as prime by direct comparison with other temples of lesser quality and by the presence of many refinements lacking in other temples of its series. In time, inventions (prime objects) evolve into replicas. This replicas then generate change through variation. Variations are of long or short life. They change slowly or quickly.

The mythology of the Tabwa, an ethnic group from Southeast Zaire can enable us to analyze the concept of prime object. Kyomba, the cultural hero of all Tabwa clans is said to have carried in his hair the essential inventions of Tabwa cultures, i.e. the seeds of the necessary plants, the fire (symbol of his political power), and the special basket to collect taxes (the symbol of his economic powers). Furthermore, by shaking his head and planting his hair he initiated agriculture. Kyomba is considered in Tabwa thought to be the ideal father, the ideal chief, the perfect lover and husband.[2] By extension, he is also the ideal artistic model for every Tabwa artist asked to carve a new statue of a chief or an important ancestor. Kyomba is thus the archetypal model both on the mythical and artistic level. Each Tabwa statue representing chiefs of different Tabwa clans such as Tanga, Kiubwe, Tumbwe and Manda or other important ancestors can be analyzed as a more or less distant replica of Kyomba which has changed through numerous variations in the flow of time. The importance of Kyomba's coiffure in Tabwa mythic thought may explain the wealth and variety of hair styles on Tabwa statuary. An accurate chronology of the birth and flourishing of these various chiefdoms (a dynastic clock) can produce a useful time scale for the different styles.

For Tabwa art, the archetype (prime object) would ideally be the most complete statue of Kyomba. Although this object no longer exists, the statues of the Kunga royal clan among the Boyo, just north of the Tumbwe, can illustrate this concept. Indeed, this famous group of statues may actually be early witnesses of a mixed Proto-Luba/Tabwa style which have been miraculously preserved.[3] In the photo, (left-side photo) the owner of the statues has placed them in order of both their genealogical importance and chronology. The largest statue on the extreme left is the oldest and could then be a portrait of a mythical founding figure like Kyomba. Two other statues by the same artist, not represented in this photo and brought back to an Italian museum around 1900,[4] and the third statue from the left on the photo, are very close replicas of the oldest statue (the prime object). The four other statues in this photo, probably made by another hand, are more remote replicas of the prime object.

We will come back to the concept of prime object later in our analysis of human statuary. Our essay will be devided in five parts, analyzing firstly, objects in different materials such as terracotta, metal and ivory. In the second part of this essay, the use and function of masks, statues and the decorative arts such as household items, jewelry and furniture objects will be described.

1. THE ART OF TERRACOTTA SCULPTURE

In Picasso's portrait of Gertrude Stein, one recognizes immediately the person represented despite the fact that Picasso painted her face like a hieratic mask. Mrs Stein's face which both resembles her and is a conventionalized image was painted both by having the model pose over ninety times and by a truthful reconstruction of her face from memory. In fact, Picasso repainted the entire face from memory a few months after finishing the portrait. Memory plays also a crucial role for African artists. The terracotta heads and statues from Nok, Ife, Akan and the Inland Niger Delta in Mali, depict human beings ranging from the highly naturalistic Ife heads to the extremely conventionalised Akan terracotta heads. The features of the sculptures tend to correlate with the physical features from each specific ethnic group represented because artists abstract from the physical types which surround them.

ANCESTOR STATUES OF THE ROYAL KUNDA CLAN. BOYO DYNASTY
(PHOTO BY LUC DE HEUSCH).

GROUP OF FIVE TABWA STATUES. MANDA CHIEFDOM.

16

It is fascinating to note that even among the most schematized heads of some of the Inland Niger Delta statues, there is still a likeness to present-day inhabitants from the Inland Delta.

The question arises of whether these terracotta sculptures were meant to be true portraits or representations of conventionalized types? Akan artists worked like Picasso. The terracotta heads were made from memory some time after the death of the person whose portrait was commisioned. Sculptors modeled a close likeness of dead royalty by first observing his or her image during their lifetime, memorizing it and then evoking it by gazing into a pan of water or palm oil. Because the plasticity of clay enables it to be modeled into any shape, it also gives the artist total freedom from his material. It is not by pure chance that some of the most realistic portraits ever made in the history of art, the Ife heads, are made in clay. This short essay will analyze the artistic production in terracotta of four major centres of Black creativity, the Nok, Inland Niger Delta, Bankoni and Akan.

THE ART OF NOK

The Nok culture, which spanned more than one millenium from 500 B.C. to about 1000 A.D., was named after the small village of Nok where the first object was found in 1943, coincidentally the same year the French archeologist T. Monod published the first terracotta statue from the Inland Niger Delta. The Nok statuary is the oldest tradition of full-size figurative sculpture in Africa, with the exception of the Egyptian civilization. The most frequent formal characteristic of Nok art is the treatment of the eyes which generally form the segment of a circle as well the piercing of the eyes, ears, nostrils and lips. The artists of the Nok culture were very skilled, making nearly life-size human sculptures in terracotta, a remarkable technical accomplishment.

The geographical distribution of statues in the Nok style in an area of more than 40,000 square miles implies that the artists who shared similar formal vocabulary must have lived in a structured society with a common focus of both political and religious power. The Nok people were also the earliest smelters of iron as well as sophisticated farmers. They were also noted for their complex coiffures, adorning themselves with large quantities of beads, bracelets and anklets.

Frank Willet has described some of the formal similarities between the Nok, Ife and modern Yoruba traditions. One fascinating artistic convention shared by both Nok art and the modern Yoruba styles is the manner in which the eye is treated. The roughly semi-circular pierced Nok eye is an artistic convention which survived two thousand years to be used by contemporary Yoruba artists to design the eyes of Gelede masks.[5] Since the Gelede mask is worn as a helmet on top of a dancer's head and does not cover it, there is no reason for the Yoruba artist to design pierced eyes. Other artistic conventions such as the detail of the costumes, hair styles and jewelry in addition to subject matters such as Janus heads were transmitted from Nok artists to Ife sculptors.

No data exists to describe the function of Nok statues. However, working backwards by analogy from data on Ife art, one could suggest that Nok people used nearly life-size figures as portraits of important persons in a similar fashion to that documented for Ife life-size statuary. Ife bronze heads were attached to wooden bodies and the crown of the dead monarch was put on top of the head in order to be carried in a second burial ceremony similar to the rituals of the kings of France and England in the late Middle Ages. The purpose of the ceremony was to show that although the King was dead, the power of his office still continued. This funerary custom was subsequently transmitted to Benin royalty for the secondary funeral ceremony of the King as well as in the Kingdom of Owo, one hundred miles east of Ife.[6] A similar practice can be suggested for the larger Nok statues. Unfortunately, we can only speculate as to the use of smaller statues.

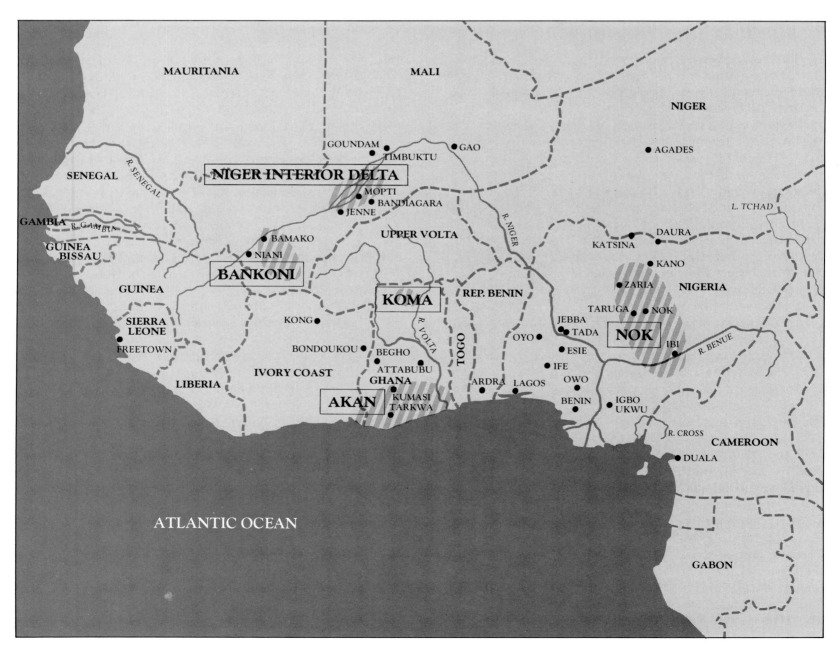

THE INLAND NIGER DELTA STATUARY

The careful study of the results of archeological excavations as well as my own research in Mali have now demonstrated that the corpus of terracotta statues previously called 'Jenne statuary' originates from the entire Inland Niger Delta region, and is not focused specifically on the city of Jenne or its predecessor Jenne-Jeno. Hence, the denomination of 'Jenne statuary' is incorrect and the appellation of Inland Niger Delta statuary is more accurate pending further research. To date, no human figures in terracotta have been documented outside the Inland Niger Delta, that is north of lake Debo, west of Diafarabe, south of San or east of Sevaré. The unifying factor of this particular art style appears to be ecological in the first place, rather than ethnic or linguistic.

The Inland Niger Delta in Mali is a large alluvial floodplain of approximately 30,000 square kilometers fed by two major arteries, the Niger River and its major tributary, the Bani.[7] This region played a crucial role in the ancient history of West Africa. Wild rice was first domesticated in the Inland Niger Delta, more than 2000 years ago. Excavations at the now abandoned site of Old Jenne (also called Jenne-Jeno) has shown the earliest trace of carbonized steel in West Africa, a remarkable technical invention. Clay from the Inland Niger Delta is also famous for its quality.

The most striking characteristic of the large corpus of statues from the Inland Niger Delta is the variety of sixty-six different gestures documented. This corpus is the largest source of sacred gestures documented for one artistic style in Africa. A careful study of more than two hundred complete statues reveals that within this remarkable variety, the most frequent gesture is a kneeling attitude. Within the larger category of kneeling figures, the most common gesture is kneeling with the bust straight, arms placed along the side and hands on kneecaps, a gesture attributed to 42 % of all statues in a kneeling attitude. The second most prevalent attitude is sitting, followed by riding. Both kneeling and sitting attitudes can each be broken down into as many as twenty-four differ-ent gestures of the limbs and the head.[8]

The dates of manufacture of these objects span the 8th to the 18th century A.D. with a strong concentration in the 14th-15th century. Since fired clay, unlike wood, does not deteriorate with time, it is possible that any terracotta statue could have survived for many centuries before being broken or destroyed. Therefore, any seriation of this art style into early, middle and late periods is probably meaningless. A statue made in the 13th century could very well have been used as a model for another artist in the 17th century. This may explain why any statue from the Inland Niger Delta is immediately recognizable and similar to many others, regardless of its age. The ethnic groups whose ancestors made the terracotta statuary in our study are the Sorogo, also called the Bozo, great hunters, fishermen, architects and masons. Other groups include different waves of Soninke such as the Nono and Dogon who came from northeast Mali as early as the 11th century A.D. Other groups of Soninke migrated after the 13th century from the Mande region in southern Mali.

My fieldwork in the Inland Niger Delta consistently demonstrated that this terracotta statuary represents the gods of the ancient inhabitants of the Inland Niger Delta. The statues were made by the blacksmiths or their wives and were used by all ethnic and socio-professional groups such as the Sorogo, Soninke, Marka-Nono, Rimaïbe, Fulani, Sugulube and blacksmiths. Some of these gods are considered to be deifeid ancestors of famous founding kings and queens in the region. Terracotta statues were venerated in special houses which were the first houses to be built when a new village was founded. Some of the statues were hung on the walls of these houses, while others were placed in a small niche or on the floor. Statues were also kept on altars in private houses. Both men and women were permitted to venerate them. A special guardian was appointed to take charge of the sanctuary where the statues were kept. Another person would make the sacrifices required by the gods.

De Heusch, at the end of his structuralist analysis of sacrifice in Africa, emphasizes that men have two essential means for establishing communication with their gods: sacrifice and possession.[9] Possession unites human and divine beings within the body of the possessed person, but without destroying it. Sacrifice, on the other hand, reestablishes a new cosmological and social order between men and gods by destroying the means of communication, the sacrificial victim. Both sacrifice and ritual possession were used by worshippers to communicate with the terracotta gods from the Inland Niger Delta.

Kubler speaks of the tragic other side of any aesthetic experience.[10] Although the art of the Inland Niger Delta cannot qualify as an 'art of tragic necessity based on human sacrifice', as Kubler wrote of Aztec art, sacrifice is an integral part of its aesthetic experience. The rituals attributed to the terracotta statuary included prayers and the offering of sacrifices. My fieldwork has established that the sacrificial victim can be human, animal or vegetable. Sacrificial victims were reported to include human beings, bulls, sheep, chickens, goats, and horses. The preferred human sacrifice was an albino. The blood of the sacrificial victim was poured on the terracotta statues while they were being venerated. When performing these ritual sacrifices, the worshipper adopted the same position as the statue in front of him.

Since the worshipper adopted an attitude similar to the one represented by the statue of the god in front of him, one could conclude that the aim of these gestural prayers was for the worshipper to experience himself as divine. By adopting these poses, he became ritually possessed by the spirit of the god inhabiting the statue. The terracotta statues were sacred images used as tools to induce a mystical state where the worshipper experienced the fusion between himself and his god. One of the main formal characteristics of the statuary, the bulging eyes and the ecstatic angle of the head may symbolize this state of possession, in the same way that the large bulging eyes on the Yoruba Ogboni figures also represent a state of possession.[11]

If, as Mauss has remarked, man's first and most natural instrument is his body, it is also his first and most natural source of symbols and his foremost means of communication not only with his peers but with his gods. The sacred gestures of the devotees of the Inland Niger Delta are like *mudras*, symbolic gestures of the hands which act as seals between the deity and the worshipper in Buddhist religion. The divine gestures of these earthly gods are the only surviving signs of a great mystical religion.

The theme of the equestrian statue deserves a special mention in the study of Inland Niger delta statuary. Horses are generally associated with wealth, speed, elegance and elevation. They represent power: political, military, legal and mystical. A large group of terracotta horsemen composed of six complete statues plus fragments of at least twenty more have been dated to 1240-1460 A.D. In addition, a large wooden horseman now in the collection of the Minneapolis Institute of Art, is very similar and probably belongs to a related workshop.[12] Scarifications composed of rows of small bumps found in relief on the temples of ten of these statues can be attributed to the Kagoro.[13] This typical scarification alludes to the Kagoro clan's most important crop, the *voandzou* or bambara nut. According to D. Zahan, the Kagoro's name, on a metonymical level, signifies 'insides bumps', an allusion to the small relief scarifications used by the members of the Kagoro clan, which resemble small bumps. These small, spherical bumps were reminders of the other 'small, round cultivated protuberance', the bambara nut, the Kagoro's most important crop. Because several statues show this typical scarification, it can be concluded that the persons represented by these marks are indeed Kagoro Soninke, probably of the Kamara clan.

According to oral tradition, the Kamara are one of the sixteen noble clans of archers, allies of Sunjata in his war to liberate Mande. They were the chiefs of their group of villages, owners of the land as well as warriors. They were at the same time kings, priests, diviners, healers and master hunters.[14] Hence they were considered to be representatives of God on earth. They had both political, religious, magical and healing powers. The equestrian figures probably represent these Kamara Kagoro sacred ancestors who were at the same time clan founders, powerful rulers, master hunters and important religious figures. This hypothesis is confirmed by the bows and quivers found on each statue, the prerogative of the clans of archers.

Sacrifices of animals as rare as horses may seem implausible. In the Inland Niger Delta, I collected data on the sacrifice of horses to these terracotta equestrian statues in order to obtain help from the divinities represented by the statues. Archeologically documented evidence reveals the existence of the sacrifice and ritual burial of horses on the tombs of royal persons, in the northern part of the Inland Niger Delta, sometime before 1000 A.D. These ritual sacrifices are contemporary with the Soninke empire of Wagadu. These discoveries confirm oral traditions which claimed that the Soninke introduced the horse to the Malinke.[15]

In the well-known epic of the founding of the Soninke Empire, sacrifices of horses are among the crucial founding acts of the Empire. A recent version portrays the annual sacrifice of the most beautiful girl in the kingdom along with a pregnant mare as the founding act of Soninke kingship. Forty mares were offered to the sacred vulture who helped Jaaba, the founder of one of the Soninke kingdoms. Another reference mentions the annual sacrifice of both a young virgin and a pregnant mare to the snake Wagadu Bida, the twin brother of Jaaba, in order to insure the continuity of the Soninke Empire of Wagadu.[16] All these elements seem to confirm my findings on the ritual importance of horses in the ancient inland Niger delta region.

THE BANKONI TERRACOTTA STATUARY FROM SOUTHERN MALI

The corpus of terracotta statuary from the Inland Niger Delta is not the only one found in Mali. Indeed, there is another large group of terracotta figurines which originated in southern Mali. This other group is stylistically very different from the objects found in the Inland Delta. This style has been called the Bankoni style because Bankoni is the first site where one of these statues has been documented archeologically.[17] The geographical distribution of the entire southern corpus of statues is based on three statues excavated from small mounds of stone in Bankoni, a site now part of Bamako, as well as other statues found in the Baninko region near the town of Bla, southeast of Bamako.[18] The principal formal characteristics of the corpus of Bankoni statues includes the cylindrical treatment of the different parts of the body and an exaggerated elongation of the proportions of the torso to the rest of the body. The statues vary in height from twenty to seventy centimeters. The clay, generally brown-orange in color with large quartz inclusions, is rather crude and lacks the refined texture of the Inland Niger Delta clay.

A majority of the Bankoni statues represent human figures kneeling with hands placed on the kneecaps or arms raised with hands on the head. A few statues are also seated with their legs crossed or bent sideways, while others represent standing figures. Horsemen, as well as unidentified animals are found among the statuary of this region, in addition to figures representing pregnant women. Twenty-seven terracotta statuettes, similar to those found in Bankoni, were dated by thermoluminescence. The dates are clustered in the 15th-16th century A.D.

There is no data on the use or function of Bankoni style statues. The statues are found on mounds of stones called pseudotumuli by archeologists because they show no signs of inhumation or habitation. This characteristic contrasts with the Inland Niger Delta statuary which is found in sanctuaries or private houses. It can be suggested that these terracotta figurines were used by the members to the Jo and Gwan initiatory societies who also built these mounds of stone during their initiation ceremonies. Other similar stone tumuli in close proximity to those where the terracotta statues were found cover underground domed burial chambers several meters long where the head priests of Jo and Gwan initiation societies are buried. In addition, the geographical distribution of both the terracotta statuary and the Jo and Gwan initiation societies is roughly identical.

The Jo and Gwan initiation societies also used wooden statues, both near life-size human figures and smaller figures some of which show formal similarities to the terracotta statuary.[19] Five of these larger wooden statues dated by the C-14 method are clustered in the 14th-16th centuries, thus contemporary with this southern terracotta style.[20] These dates demonstrate that the Jo initiation societies and the statues used in their cults existed at the same time the Bankoni terracotta statues were made. The smaller wooden statues with elongated torsoes, large palm-like hands and scarifications similar to the terracotta ones were used mainly by another initiation society, the blacksmith society, which was related to the Jo and Gwan societies. The young initiates from the blacksmith society dance with the small wooden statues in the performances which celebrate the end of their initiation period. All these elements suggest a ritual use of Bankoni terracotta statuary during initiatory rites.

One reason for the flourishing of human statuary in the Baninko region in southern Mali is its remoteness from the main centers of political power. Indeed, according to Dominique Zahan, the Bani river, the northern border of the Bankoni style, served as a cultural and political boundary from northern invaders.[21] A similar situation occurred in the Inland Niger Delta, a region inaccessible during the months of annual flooding and also outside of the large political structures such as the islamized court of the Malian Empire. The Bandiagara Cliff provides another example of a region with strong natural defenses where human statuary was used in various rituals by the Dogon.

AKAN TERRACOTTA STATUES

Available archeological and ethnographical evidence as well as the reports of early European travellers suggests that by 1640 A.D., a pan-Akan funerary tradition of clay portraiture of royalty was practiced in the southern part of Ghana. The tradition of terracotta statues dated to before the creation of the Ashanti confederacy in 1701. However, funeral customs as described by 17th and 18th century travellers, resemble the traditions found by contemporary ethnographic research in the 20th century. This artistic tradition of terracotta statuary has thus changed very little in the past 300 years.

Among the Akan, terracotta statuary is the plastic realization of the inseparable linked spiritual force of each Akan chief, his deceased predecessors and his future successors. According to Professor Preston, evidence indicates that the terracotta funerary tradition had an origin in the true Twi-speaking heartland of the southern kingdoms of Adanse, Twifo and Assin.[22] From there it diffused to the southeast Ivory Coast with the migrations of the Krinnjyabo Anyi and Sanwi Anyi and then to the plains of Afram with the Kwahu. The variation of styles was caused both by the migration of various groups as well as artists who sculpted the works of art sporadically in their artistic careers. Artists were also summoned to city states other than their own to make these clay portraits. Professor Sieber points out that in Kwahu, for example, there were no sculptors of terracotta images. Instead, potters, male or female, were commissioned as needed.[23] Each style can be attributed to an individual style or the style of a workshop with one master potter whose work spans one or two generations. The Akan people who sculpted the terracotta statues spoke different dialects of the Akan-Twi language such as Adanse, Twifo, Akwamu, Kwahu, Aowin. Each dialect represented politically independent city-states with a long history of cultural cross-fertilization between cities. The terracotta figures and heads are a more exclusively royal prerogative. A royal clan is made of the matrilineal descendants of the founders of a village or state, going back to the first queenmother of the state. The chief or king had both political, jural and priestly functions attached to him. The sculptural program of the Akan artistic production often mirrors the social hierarchy of each Akan society with one central figure, the ruler, surrounded by attendants. Terracotta statues and heads representing the founding ruler of the lineage, her daughter, a court member, an elder, a hunter, his servant and a slave were discovered among the Aowin at the site of Nkwanta.[24]

Akan terracotta statues and heads are intended to be portraits of the deceased. A successful portrait is considered *paa,* meaning at the same time both good and beautiful.[25] However, the formal variety of styles span from the near naturalism of the Twifo Hemang to the highly stylized representation of the head in a disk form among the Kwahu. Each sculpture is personalized by details of coiffure, clothing and regalia. The Akan generally disdain the practice of scarification.[26] There is even an injunction against the scarification of royalty. Mutilation in any form, a hernia, any proeminent asymmetry or any serious alteration of the body were grounds for the dismissal of a chief or would prevent his nomination. The Akan aesthetic canon called for a regularly formed ovoid head. This form was obtained by modelling the skull of newborn babies in order to confer this canon upon each infant. This practice would produce a broader forehead with a flattened sharp angle, a characteristic observed on many of the terracotta heads.[27]

The Akan terracotta statues were made for formal funerary ceremonies some time after death, apart from the actual burial of the body. The statues, fully dressed in their regalia, were carried throughout the town in a large procession with musicians praising the recently departed. They than sat in state serving as surrogates of the king or queen they represent. A week later the statues were removed to their final destination called the *asensie,* or place of pots. This place of pots is outside the village but is not an actual cemetery. It is considered to be the village of the dead. The statues were then ritually washed with different colors of paint each of which had a symbolic meaning. Food offerings were made to the statues as well as sacrifices, both human and animal. As early as 1702 A.D., missionaries reported the sacrifice of the wives and slaves of a recently deceased king at his funeral.[28] There are even reports of pouring the blood of the sacrificial victim on the statues themselves in a practice similar to the Inland Niger Delta statuary.

Recent research among the Aowin, the Kwahu and the Nzema Akan has recorded another use of terracotta heads among the Akan.[29] Among these groups, a priestess could be possessed by the spirit of the ancestor represented by the terracotta statue. The terracotta heads were used not only in the funerary ceremonies of famous medium-priests but also as tools to induce the state of trance through which the god or spirit would speak through the possessed priest of the cult. The terracotta heads became shrine pieces kept in the house of the priest. A similar explanation has been offered for the Inland Niger Delta terracotta statuary.

At this time, it is not possible to prove any direct connection or influence between the Southern Akan terracotta artistic tradition and the ones much further north in the Inland Niger Delta and Bankoni. However, the recent discovery and publication of a large corpus of terracotta statuettes tentatively dated to the 15th-16th century A.D. from the site of Yikpabongo among the Koma in Northern Ghana may provide a first proof of a link[30]. This group of statues from northern Ghana was found on ritual mounds surrounded by stone circles. Some of these mounds were used as burial places, others as sacred ritual places where sacrifices were performed These ritual mounds appear to be similar to those on which the Bankoni terracotta statuary from southern Mali was found.

Further proof of possible connections between the Akan and the Inland Niger Delta region in Mali are found in two important but little cited articles by ethnographer Germaine Dieterlen in which she underlines the ancient and ritually important relations between the Inland Niger Delta, the Bandiagara cliff, the Mande region and sacred areas among the Akan in Ghana.[31] Sacred pilgrimages were undertaken by Dogon, Sorgo and Soninke blacksmiths and priests as part of their initiation. Their itinerary passed through Wagadugu, Kumassie, Lake Bosumtwi and ended at Accra on the shores of the Golf of Guinea. Dieterlen demonstrates that these pilgrimages have occurred for at least a thousand years and were probably initiated by the Soninke for economic reasons tied to the gold trade. Subsequently, other ethnic groups such as the Sorko, Malinke, and Dogon would also undertake this initiatory voyage. One of the places where these pilgrims would stop is a town called Navronga, a few miles from the sites where the Koma terracotta statues from northern Ghana were recently excavated.

A final element to substantiate some kind of relationship between the Akan and other ethnic groups is the presence of scarifications made of a series of four to six low relief parallel grooves found on the temples of some Akan heads. These scarifications, called *donko* by the Akan, refer to enslaved Mossi people who worked for the Akan.[32] These scarifications, somewhat similar to those found on Soninke Kagoro equestrian figures from Mali raise more questions on the historical relationship between the Akan and other neighboring populations, such as the Mossi, Dogon and Soninke.

Among the Nok, Akan, Inland Niger Delta and Bankoni art styles, gods are represented by terracotta images of their worshippers. Human statuary thus exemplifies a religious and artistic closeness between men and their gods. The anthropomorphism of deities among these ethnic groups can partially be explained by the fact that the statues represent the antiquity and strength of the founders of dynasties, personified as deified ancestors. The bodies of the gods even fuse with that of the worshippers during ritual possession induced by worshipping the works of art. This deification of the human body is one of two major trends in the iconography of African religions. The other major trend which we shall mention only briefly, is towards elevating natural objects to a divine status, an excellent example of which is the Bamana *boli*.[33]

Boli are religious objects in which large quantities of *nyama* are concentrated. *Nyama* is a dynamic principle of divine forces which can be used in a positive or negative way. A *boli* is any religious object made of a central core, sometimes a small nugget of gold, surrounded by multicolored threads of cotton as well as various bits and pieces of organic and mineral origin. The entire object is wrapped in layers of white cotton which become black from absorbing the blood of the numerous sacrifices made to the *boli*. *Boli* are generally shaped like large spherical balls but can also represent human beings, generally young children or animals such as cows. The most powerful *boli* are very large objects covered by layers and layers of coagulated blood from the many sacrifices accomplished to stimulate the divinity which inhabits it. This second major trend towards a non-anthropomorphic and often totally abstract representation of the divinity is found concomitantly in many African religions.

Each religion and its multiple artistic manifestations appears to be split between the desire of a divine presence directly accessible to mankind —the deified human body— and the necessity to prevent divinities from entrapment within a physical world in which they must remain apart in order to preserve their divine status. Both traditions coexist but only one enables us to appreciate the artistic creativity found in these works of art.

2. THE ART OF METALWORK

Variety and virtuosity are two of the outstanding features of African metal working. Such remarkable metallic objects as the life-size so-called Tsoede bronzes from Nigeria, the elegant miniature pure copper masks from the Inland Niger Delta, the Bamana iron staffs in Mali and the elaborate Igbo Ukwu metal castings demonstrate a high degree of artistic and technical virtuosity in mastering not only an incredible spectrum of metals and metallic alloys but also an excellent sense of using each material to produce beautiful forms.

The history of metals is a long one and we shall give only the briefest outline of it. For the first few millennia, the history of metallurgy was the history of copper.[34] It all started in western Asia some time after 8000 B.C. with the discovery of annealing, that is alternately heating and coldhammering copper in order to smith the first tools and weapons. Annealing needed only a few hundred degrees of heat but one needs 1038° C. to melt copper which can only be accomplished with a forced draft. The next step, the smelting of ores, probably occurred sometimes around 4000 B.C. The history of this complex discovery is linked to pottery making. Kilns to fire pottery were capable of reaching temperatures of more than 1100° C. In West Africa, the potters are the wives of the blacksmiths, since both knew soils and minerals and how to manipulate heat. Finally, the techniques of smelting and forging iron were invented by the Hittites around 1500 B.C.

In sub-Saharan Africa, recent archeological discoveries suggest that a copper age began around 2000 B.C. in the Agadès region of Niger. Ironworking spread unevenly over broad areas of the African continent from about 500 B.C. to 500 A.D., with the earliest dates at the Nok site of Taruga in Nigeria and sites east of Agadès in Niger.[35] The old theory proposed by the linguist Guthrie on the association of iron with the dispersion of the Bantu-speaking people is now increasingly challenged. The current view is that ironworking reached West Africa from Carthage through the chariot routes across the Sahara while an early cradle in East Africa came from Southern Arabia, through the Bab-el-Mandab straits to Ethiopia during the fifth century B.C. When the first Europeans arrived in Africa during the fifteenth century, the use of metal was universal except among the Pygmies of the equatorial forest and the San of South Africa.

Among the numerous types of metal cast in Africa, copper and gold predominate. Less traditional metals include tin Senufo masks or silver Mamprussi jewelry. Copper was combined with tin to produce true bronze, or with zinc to produce brass. Both brass and bronze need to be distinguished from one another, although the two alloys have not been systematically distinguished in the literature. There are relatively few sources of copper in West Africa. Mines are located in Akjoujt in western Mauritania, Azelick and Agadès in Niger, and at Nioro in Mali. However, central and southern Africa are much richer in copper, with sites in the Kongo kingdom, the copper mines of Katanga, as well as those of Zimbabwe, Zambia, Mozambique and Transvaal.

Since copper was so precious in Africa, it was always reserved for the production of prestige objects such as sumptuous ornaments, jewelry, or royal portraits. Copper and its alloys was associated with major political centers and kingdoms under royal and state patronage such as the kingdoms of Ife and Benin in Nigeria. The earliest workers of copper and its alloys in West Africa were the artists of Igbo-Ukwu who smithed pure copper. For casting they used leaded bronze which flows better in moulds. The style of Igbo-Ukwu is very unusual, its outstanding feature being the great elaboration of surface decoration. The artists of Ife also used pure copper to cast objects. The famous Obalufon mask from Ife is a flawless casting in copper. Five other heads from the Wunmonije compound represent another remarkable technical achievement in copper casting. Frank Willet has suggested that the art of Ife developed in terracotta and was then translated into metal which reinforces the idea of the technical links between potters and blacksmiths.[36]

The art of Benin is clearly a royal art. Both bronze and ivory sculpture could only be used by the king, unless he granted special permission. According to traditions, each time a king of Benin died, his head was sent back to the city of Ife and in return, the king of Ife would send back a bronze head to be placed on his ancestral shrine in Benin. During the reign of Oguala, sixth king of Benin in the 14th century, the king of Ife accepted to send a craftsman to the city of Benin in order to teach the inhabitants how to make bronze heads. The first memorial heads date from that period. Heads of Queen Mothers were introduced during the reign of Esigie (ca. 1550 A.D.), while the rectangular bronze plaques which were nailed on the columns of the Royal palace at Benin are provisionally dated to the early sixteenth century through the seventeenth century.[37]

Other centers of bronze work in Nigeria include cult objects for the Yoruba Ogboni society, the lower Niger bronze bells with a complex iconography but very few reliable dates, the Cross River bronze figures made by itinerant Igbo groups and used in ritual contexts related to sacred chieftanship.[38] Other centers of copper metallurgy include the ceremonial vessels and jewelry dated between the 12th and the 17th centuries among the ancient populations around lake Chad and in the Inland Niger Delta in Mali.

Iron played an important role in many populations but certain groups are more prominent, such as the Dogon and Bamana iron staffs, the Kuba, Songye and Azande weapons famous for their quality throughout central Africa. The ancient kingdoms of Ghana and Mali were famous for their gold which they traded for salt which they considered to be more precious. The only culture from which we still possess several gold objects are the gold masks from the Akan kingdoms. A beautiful gold earring was recently discovered by American archeologists on the site of Old Jenne in Mali, a rare witness of a vanished art form.

3. IVORY

Until recently, elephants could be found in most of sub-Saharan Africa; and ivory was carved by many ethnic groups. Nevertheless, several centers of ivory carving have produced remarkable ivory objects. The coasts of Sierra Leone and Benin are known for the 'Afro-Portuguese' saltcellars and horns, the Yoruba kingdoms for their tappers used by Ifa divination priests, the kingdoms of Kongo for their powerful chief's staffs and the Lega for their massive ivory heads and masks used by high-ranking members of the Bwami society.

Two important characteristics of ivory are its durability and its color. Objects made of ivory withstand time, climate and deterioration long enough to have been recovered by archeologists and used by art historians. Afro-Portuguese saltcellars dated to the fifteenth century are very useful in reconstructing the art history of styles among the Sherbo-Bullom in Sierra Leone and enable us to assign a similar date to *nomoli* soapstone statues.

African ivory was treated by a number of different substances to enhance certain colors or patinas. Carved Benin tusks placed on the royal altars in Benin are bleached with citrus juice or coated with chalk to enhance their whiteness.[39] The inner surfaces of bracelets or the backs of pendants take a yellow-brown hue through the constant rubbing against the human skin while other ivories become dark-brown or deep red color through coating with palm oil and camwood. Often African artists would use the natural curve of the tusk in their sculptures exemplified by Luba miniature pendants, representing women supporting their breasts in a gesture of greeting and respect.[40] In African states, the possession and trade of ivory was the prerogative of the ruler. The king of Benin had a monopoly on ivory while among the Kuba, ivory tusks were used as tributes from each local chief to the king. Ivory objects were also used as a means of communication with the ancestors. Lega ivories are the insignia of two of the highest levels of the Bwami association. These masks and heads not only represent moral qualities such as generosity, strength and peacefulness for which the bwami is known, but symbolize the continuity of these qualities through each member who owned these objects. These ivories are thus charged with healing power, both moral and physical.[41]

4. MASKS

Masks in Africa are living statues. By wearing a mask, a dancer listens to the specific music of the initiation or secret society, dances the steps prescribed by the tradition, making his body a metaphor for ethics and morality which ultimately link him to the gods. Several types of masks are commonly found in Africa: three-dimensional sculpture such as the helmet mask of the Mende Sande/Bondo society in Sierra Leone, the Gelede masquerades of the Yoruba, the Ejagham/Efik skin covered heads from the Cross river region in Nigeria, and the face masks of the Dan in Liberia and Ivory coast. Masks are part of the sacred objects belonging to secret societies. They are used in initiation rites for young men or women and can also play an important judicial role as well. Each type of mask has its own costumes, musical instruments and specific rhythms and will only appear in specific circumstances.

Sande, the women's ceremonial organization among the Mende in southern Sierra Leone and northwestern Liberia uses a helmet mask called Sowo, the only known example of wooden mask danced by women in Africa. All others masks documented are danced by men. As Sylvia Boone explains: 'Sowo is the embodiment of the Sande society, a presentation which Sande has designed to ennoble its members and strengthen the larger community. In Sowo, the world can see what canons Sande cherishes, what values it upholds. Sowo is an exemplar, a water deity, a goddess, a Mende metaphor in motion.'[42]

To be accepted by the Sande society, each Sowo mask must meet eight important aesthetic criteria:

1. The mask must be complete and correct in all its parts: full, striated neck, small face with closed mouth, lowered eyes, large forehead, plaited hairdo.
2. The mask must be comfortable to wear; it must sit evenly on the dancer's head, its horizontal planes level.
3. The mask must be shiny black; it must glow by repeated applications of black dye until the hue has soaked deep into the wood.
4. The mask must be perfectly smooth with no bumps or rough spots.
5. It must be well balanced and symmetrical with straight vertical and horizontal planes.
6. The individual features of the mask must be clearly defined and not blurred.
7. The mask must appear fresh, new, crisp and youthful.
8. The physical features of the mask must be delicate and the details fine.[43]

Sowo masks are the embodiment of Mende aesthetic canons and moral ideals. Indeed, the criteria used to analyze the Sowo mask can be applied directly to any Mende woman. Cosmetic efforts are applied at the earliest age on Mende babies, when bones are still soft enough to be molded into perfect shape. Daily baths of young children are considered beauty sessions in which the mother tries to shape the child's physical features to resemble those prescribed by the accepted aesthetic canons. On a moral level, Sande society is a rigorous school where young women learn the epitome of Mende con-

duct. The ideal Mende woman should be intelligent, correct and fair, show physical strength, a sense of social responsability, courage, persistence, swiftness of action and the ability not to speak without purpose.[44] These moral qualities correspond to the aesthetic criteria used for each Sowo mask.

Gelede masquerades among the Yoruba in Nigeria are artistic expressions of the belief that elderly women possess extraordinary powers equal to or greater than that of the gods and ancestors. Unlike the Sande dancers, however Gelede dancers are men, not women. By dancing the Gelede, the Yoruba believe that the forces of the cosmos can be tamed for the well-being of the entire society in order to maintain social control. These performances are living commentary on the role of men and women in society, on fashion, innovation, and antisocial behavior. The Gelede spectacle is composed of two different performances: the nightime Efè and the daytime Gelede which are performed annually at the first rainfalls, for funeral commemorations and at times of social disasters such as famines.

Great ancestral mothers are considered to be the gods of the Gelede. These powerful women can be founding foremothers of towns or lineages, ancestors which have slowly become deified. They are considered even more powerful than the Yoruba gods like Ogùn or Esù. As one informant stated:

'No orisha(god) can do good without the mothers. Therefore Shango cannot help his worshippers without the permission of the mothers. (...) Oro and Egun cannot kill without the mother. (...) Without their sanction no healing can take place, rain cannot fall, plants cannot bear fruits and children cannot come into the world.'[45]

Both the night Efè and the daytime Gelede masquerades are elaborate ceremonies with many different types of masks appearing in succession, some accompanied only by drums, others with a choir singing specific songs. The most spectacular mask of the Efè ceremony is the mask of the Great Mother (Iyanla), made of a typical Gelede helmet-masked head to which a flat boardlike projection representing a beard has been added. Bearded women are considered to possess extraordinary powers. The length of the beard also implies longevity and commanding status.[46] The nocturnal Great Mother mask inspired reverence and fear because of the destructive and dangerous aspects of womanhood. The dancer, covered in a white cloth, moves in a slow deliberate manner which implies pride, stature, patience and power.

The daytime Gelede masks are divided into male and female categories identifiable by a typical hairstyle or characteristic piece of clothing attributed to men or women. The general form of the face of the Gelede mask rarely varies. However, virtually anything human or animal can be found on top of the helmet-mask. Gelede embodies a force which ultimately controls all of Yoruba society, and as such can stress any aspect of its humanity. Headdresses can represent devotees of various gods, famous warriors or hunters, well-known musicians, minor Yoruba deities, muslim clerics, birds, snakes, porcupines. Gelede masquerades proved to be so essential to Yoruba culture that when Yoruba slaves were brought to Cuba and Brazil in the late 18th century, they continued to carve Gelede masks and hold festivals which were documented as early as 1830 in Salvador in north eastern Brazil.

Contrary to the Gelede, masks among the Dan from Liberia and Ivory Coast have no ancestral connections. According to the research of both Hans Himmelheber and his son Eberhard Fischer who have studied the Dan more or less continuously from 1949 to 1976, these masks are stylized portraits of living Dan women and men. They are considered to be material manifestations of mask spirits which live in a remote area of Dan country.[47] Dan masks are very varied, showing either human or animal features or sometimes a combination of both. Masks are divided into both male and female masks. The male masks are angular, bearded with tubular eyes, while masks with narrow slit eyes and oval faces are female. Another criterion which distinguishes different types of masks spirits is the different types of headdresses attached on top of each dancer's head.

The joking, friendly mask, called *deangle,* with its oval face and slit eyes, is meant to be feminine and beautiful, while the *bagle* mask, the war mask with a bulging forehead, tubular eyes and a powerful mouth filled with large teeth, is meant to be imposing and awe-inspiring. As with the Mende and the Gelede, the Dan ideal of feminine beauty directly inspires the features of the *deangle* mask. According to Dan aesthetic canons, an ideal face should have a strict symmetrical form with a pointed chin, a long slender nose with well-developed nostrils, equal sized upper and lower lips, and pointed white teeth with a small gap between the two upper incisors. The forehead should be framed by a narrow band of hair with the remaining hair drawn in parallel rolls. Ideally, a woman's eyes should be narrow slits and their eyebrows shaved.[48]

Dan artists worked somewhat like Chinese artists. New works of art were considered successful if they were perfect copy of an older model. Dan artists follow stereotypes that they tend to repeat. As Tame, a well-known Dan artist, once said while examining a block of wood about to be carved: 'all the masks which have ever been made by men pass before my mind's eye like something which floats past on the surface of a river.'[49] The practice of copying one's own art is the typical mode of artistic production among the Dan. Only one sculptor, Zra, was considered such a great artist that he was actually called 'god' or 'creator'. He was the only one who was credited with inventing new forms and his reputation was immense. In fact, Zra may have actually created one or more of these elusive prime objects known only by the number of copies they initiated.

The Enjagham people, also called Ekoi, who live in southeastern Nigeria and western Cameroon, have created a unique and stunning art form: human heads covered with gleaming antelop skin. There are two types of skin-covered headdresses: caps and helmet masks.[50] The caps are wooden heads secured on a small basket attached to the dancer's head by a string under his chin. The rest of his body is covered in a cloth costume. Skin-covered helmets on the other hand, cover the entire head of the dancer, resting on his shoulders. Both the caps and the helmet masks are often janus with a male face painted dark brown and the female face light brown. The cap type often shows elaborate coiffures made of large blackened spirals which represent stylish hairstyles in the Cross River region.

These heads, generally very naturalistic, are said to be trophies representing portraits of killed enemies, and were originally covered with human skin. The heads were used in traditional associations of warriors and were danced during the secondary funerals of its members. Just like the Soninke magician-king, Sumaoro Kante possessed an armor and magic drums covered with human skin; by covering wooden masks and heads with human or animal skin and applying a gleaming finish of oil before each dance, the Ejagham were able to attract and master the powerful forces of deceased famous warriors and powerful animals.[51]

5. STATUARY

The study of human statuary in wood brings us back to our introductory remarks on the concept of prime objects and replicas. Among the Tshokwe of northern Angola, one finds that all the statues with a typical ceremonial coiffure and other hunting regalia represent Tshibinda Ilunga, the mythical Luba hunter who founded the Lunda empire of Mwata Yamvo.[52] The prime object which initiated this large corpus of statues does not exist anymore but the amount of copies and replicas of this type of statue demonstrates its importance in Tshokwe culture. This principle of prime object and replicas can be extended to the statuary of other ethnic groups such as the Hemba and the Royal Ndop statues among the Kuba in Zaïre, or the commemorative statues of the Batuffam Chiefdom in Cameroon representing the royal dynasty of kings and most important queens since the founder of the chiefdom. Other examples of prime objects and replicas can be found among the Urhobo in southern Nigeria, with life-size wooden statuary representing real and semi-mythic founding ancestors remembered both as founders of families (hence the maternity figures) and as warriors and soldiers.[53]

The antiquity of the existence of wooden human statuary in Africa needs to be reevaluated. As early as 1460, the Portuguese navigator Pedro de Sintra wrote of wooden statues representing 'idols' in the Bissagos Archipelago. The present-day inhabitants of the archipelago, the direct descendants of the people described by Pedro de Sintra, still worship wooden statues. These statues serve as mediators through which both the spirit of God and those of the ancestors fuse together to communicate with humans.[54]

Wooden statues in the Bidyogo islands belong to large shrines called *baluba*. A *baluba* is composed of an altar on which one finds a vessel filled with a ritual mixture of blood, eggs and palme wine symbolizing Orebuko, one of the high gods. The vessel is surrounded by small wooden planks representing other gods, the children of Orebuko. Different types of wooden statues are placed at the foot of the altar. These statues represent deceased members of the families.[55]

According to recent research, these surrounding wooden statues, called *iran*, represent various types of deities ranging from the most remote representative of God on earth to human gods, deified ancestors and deceased members of each clan. The most abstract of these deities is represented by the vessel on the altar filled with a ritual mixture. Human gods are represented by simple wooden planks, while deified ancestors are mostly three dimensional statues. All of these objects serve as the material supports for a spiritual power called *orebok*, the fusion of both the powers of God and the souls of the dead. Each *iran* is thus an incarnation of the spirit, or divine fluid of God. In effect, each statue is God.[56] Human sacrifices were made to the statues in a fashion similar to the one described for terracotta statues in the Inland Niger Delta. Today, the sacrifice of cattle replaces human sacrifice. The animal's blood is poured on the statue in order to receive the requested favor. Little data has been reported on the function of the Bidyogo statues. Some are used for divination ceremonies, others have judicial as well as protective powers. They can also be used for witchcraft or in warfare. Pregnant women also make sacrifices to them.

The first mention of the existence of wooden statues among the Dogon can be found in Desplagnes's account of 1907. He called the statues by their Dogon name, *dédégue,* and explained that they were wooden representations of Dogon gods.[57] Desplagnes wrote that when a drought or another calamity occured, the wooden statue of the god was exhibited on the roof of the sanctuary, dressed in jewelry, necklaces and clothing. The Dogon would make sacrifices before the statue on the roof of the sanctuary. According to G. Dieterlen, human figurines were created by the Dogon as recipients for the soul *(kikuni say)* and the vital force *(nyama)* of deceased Dogon people. The Dogon carved wooden human figurines resembling dead persons, placing them on the roof of a newly built house along with a small clay vessel, or *bundo,* for libations.[58] The first statue was carved the exact size of the body of the first deceased person. In fact, a whole series of life-size wooden statues may illustrate this practice. Gradually, the Dogon began to make smaller statues which were easier to manipulate, and finally, simple wooden sticks with a notch on the top symbolizing the head of the deceased. These statues became ancestral altars called *waguem.* The composition of any Dogon ancestral altar varied according to the importance of the deceased person and his rank in Dogon society. However, most altars were composed of clay vessels, statuettes, miniature wooden ladders, iron hooks and miniature walking sticks.[59] The altars were situated in a small granary on the terrace or floor of the house. Generally, these altars were established in special houses called *ginna,* the first houses to be built at the foundation of a new village or neighborhood. The sanctuary contained the vessel of the founding ancestor of the clan, as well as those of all of his male descendants.

The altars of ancestors were also venerated for purposes other than relegating the souls of the deceased apart from those of the living. Dieterlen lists, among other uses, the worship of ancestral altars for collective ceremonies to obtain rain, to pray for a good hunt, in cases of disease or epidemics, and in instances of quarrels between members of the same family or clan.[60] The human statuary previously analyzed represents ancestors deified after human life. Other references to the use of wooden statuary among the Dogon relate to cults of Dogon gods instead of human beings.[61] Nommo, one of the Dogon gods, is represented as a standing figure with one or both arms raised. As a temporary conclusion, it can be suggested that statues of standing human figures with raised, out-stretched arms represent Nommo, a Dogon deity, while statues in a kneeling or sitting position refer to various types of ancestors. Rituals involved in the different cults pertaining to wooden statuary are very similar to those practiced for the terracotta statuary in the Delta. First, the Dogon person making the sacrifice pours an offering of white millet porridge on the vessels and the statues. Then, chickens as well as goats and sheep are sacrified above the vessels. After the sacrifice, both male and female statues are brought outside the sanctuary along with the clay vessels. Each object is then immersed in a large jar filled with the sacrificial blood until the blood has totally permeated the statues.[62] Other animals are then sacrificed and ritual beer is offered to the audience. The rest of the sacrificial blood is kept in special vessels in the sanctuary for the spirits of the deceased women to drink.

Among the southern Bamana, centered around the Baninko and Banimounitie region, in an area forming a triangle between Dioila, Bougouni and Sikasso, the seven initiation societies called Jo or Dyo also used human statues for their rituals.[63] Two groups of human figurines were used in these rituals, distinguishable by their size. The wooden statues of the Gwan society called *gwandusu* are very large, up to life size, while the smaller statues called *dyonyeni* measure from 18 to 21 inches in height.

The large *gwandusu* statues of the Gwan society can be classified into several groups. These categories include seated female statues with children, seated or standing females, some of which pregnant, standing women carrying jars on their heads, and men, either standing, seated, or on horseback. Stylistically, these statues are more rounded and naturalistic, showing a wealth of iconographic detail. They contrast with the more severe geometric style of flat planes and sharp angles observed on smaller wooden *dyonnyeni* figurines.

Imperato and Ezra report complementary interpretations of the symbolism of the wooden statues used in these initiation societies. According to Ezra, the statues do not represent specific mythological or historical persons.[64] The statues portray the idealized Bamana woman and are worshipped in ceremonies connected with fertility and child birth. They can also represent two specific ancestors, *gwandusu* and her husband *gwantigi.* South of the Baninko region, these statues seem to represent two supranatural beings or 'divine persons', one female, being called Mousso Koroni or Nyale and one male, called Ndomadyiri.

The Arab traveller Ibn Battuta, during his trip to the court of the Malian empire in 1352, described two alternative rituals for holding court.[65] In the first more islamized ceremony, the emperor receives visitors in an audience hall with a baldachino-type oratory and grillwork covered with silver plaques copied from North African and Spanish Islamic models. In the alternate traditional ritual, the king is seated on a traditional Mande throne, an earthen bench with three steps, under a large tree. Ibn Battuta even cites the Malinke name for this traditional throne, calling it a *bembi* or *bembe.*[66] When the Malian emperor held court on the *bembe,* he dressed in the traditional garb of a Keita hunter. The emperor wore a skull cap of gold with flaps like thin knives tied with a gold strap. He also wore a quiver between his shoulders and a bow. This cap, with thin blade-like flaps tied under the chin, is certainly the *bama da* hat of the Malinke. Ibn Battuta's early eye witness account of the use of this special type of hat demonstrates its importance as a symbol of both sacred kingship and membership in the powerful hunter's association. The presence of this hat on several of the large wooden statues of the Jo and Gwan societies may explain why Ezra reported that some of the large male wooden statues were called *mansa,* meaning 'king' of 'ruler' in Malinke. The statues may have originally represented portraits of important chiefs or kings.

At the end of the initiation of new members to the Gwan society, statues were brought out of their sanctuary, and sacrifices made to them. Sacrificial material was poured on the statues. At the end of the harvest, the statues were brought out again to be ritually rubbed with shea butter and decorated with clothes and beads. They were then carried in a night procession to the house of the *dyo sia,* the head priest of the Gwan society. For a period of seven days, the statues were taken out for daily public ceremonies, open only to those initiated to the Gwan. Statues were also held aloft during the funeral of the *masa,* the senior women of the Gwan society (equivalent to the *dyo sia*).[67]

Smaller statues belong to a large corpus of objects previously called 'fertility figures'.[68] These statues are called *dyonyeni, jonyeleni* or *nyeleni.*[69] They represent standing or seated females with pointed breasts, carved in a geometric manner with flat planes and sharp angles. These *jonyeleni* statues were danced with and displayed during public performances by the initiates of the N'Kenie, N'Tokofa and Duba (called also Numu Jo or N'keribadjo) societies.[70]

Among the Baoule, wooden statues never represent ancestors, rather, they serve as the support for two kinds of spirits, nature spirits or otherworld spouses.[71] Nature spirits would manifest themselves by disrupting a person's life until a shrine is built by that person. The shrine would include a wooden statue whose formal characteristics were dictated by the spirit through dreams or divination. The Baoule believe that each person has a spouse before he or she was born into this world. The statues become the locus for one's other-world spouse. This other-world spouse can be anyone of the opposite sex with the exception of one's own spouse. Once the carving is finished, it is made sacred by an appropriate ritual which informs the other world spouse that he has a new statue. The statue is then cleaned, rubbed with oil, wiped with kaolin or painted in classical way.

Moving east towards the urban civilization of the Yoruba, statues can represent both gods from their pantheon and devotees worshipping these gods. The god Shango was the deified king and founder of the Yoruba kingdom of Oyo whose powers are imaged in thunder and lightning. Shango staffs generally represent the statue of a woman balancing the twin celts or thunderbolts of Shango on her head, symbols of his unpredictability. The woman on the staff may represent the devotee of the cult. The fact that the statues systematically represent women is explained by the fact that many of the Yoruba gods are considered at the same time male and female.[72] Male priests who are possessed by Shango combine male and female valence, wearing partially female dress and a ritual female hair style and are called the wives of Shango.[73] Staffs are held by the priests of the Shango cult as a sculptural sign of their power to invoke lightning. The staff is most expressively used when a priest possessed by the god dances wielding the staff violently to simulate Shango's violence.[74] Other statues of women kneeling and holding a bowl represent devotees of the Shango cult in a gesture of supplication. They are part of a Shango shrine assemblage which would include stone celts, wooden staffs and rattles. Other famous examples of Yoruba sculpture are the *ère ibéjì,* small statuettes representing deceased twins. Twin images are kept on domestic altars but they can also be stored in calabashes wrapped carefully with cloth.[75] The cult probably started in the 18th century with the support of the Alafin, the king of Oyo. Before that, oral tradition indicates that twin births were considered aberrations, with infanticide of twins a common practice.[76]

The *byeri* cult of the Fang group in Gabon honored family ancestral spirits. The word *byeri* means ancestor, that is any family member whose skull was preserved in a bark box attached to the wooden statue or head. The statues represented generic Fang people with precise formal traits balanced against a more conventional Fang type. The reliquaries were kept in a special sanctuary. Once a year, during the initiation cycle of the cult, the statues were taken off their reliquaries and danced as puppets above a palm thatch partition.[77] The controversy over the anteriority of the heads which evolved into busts and then full figures is still not resolved.[78] Both the heads and the full figures styles were already developed when discovered by Western explorers at the end of the 19the century. Since the Fang migrated for several hundred years between the savannah to the north and the equatorial forest to the south, it is probable that they were exposed both to the royal ancestral statues of the grassland chiefdoms in Cameroon and the Kongo statuary which dates back at least six hundred years.

The Fang created one of the few portable ancestral shrines in Black Africa. Like the Pygmy art styles in bark cloth,[79] the Fang created a remarkable variety of styles within a limited canon. What the Pygmies did with two-dimensional art, barkcloth, the Fang did with three dimensional sculpture. Both produced works of art which fuse many different stylistic conventions, jumping from one to another in the same object.

One important feature of Fang heads is the sense of an hypnotic gaze of the statues with eyes usually made of large copper disks. These copper disks were polished regularly by the Fang, creating shining eyes whose flash pierced darkness and whose power of vision was inescapable. The concept of a power vision who could pierce all darkness is also found among the Kongo *n'kondi* statues, sculpted with shining eyes made of glass filled with magical substances. The remarkable formal qualities of Fang art, such as the balance of volumes, the oversized child-like head with well-developed musculature of the body, the serenity of the face and dynamism of the muscles, were meant to symbolize the moral qualities of the Fang person who could always balance his youthful desire for action with the wisdom of experience, in other words a person capable of balancing opposites.

The Kongo is one of the oldest classical civilizations of Black Africa whose roots date back at least one thousand years. When the Portuguese discovered the Kongo kingdom in 1482, it was already an extremely sophisticated culture whose art, literature, hieroglyphic writing, traditional healing and sense of the law were very complex. The so-called nail-fetishes are actually called *n'kondi,* that is oath-taking images covered with blades, wooden and iron nails, each symbolizing the tying or resolution of law suits and arguments. These wooden statues, some nearly life-size, are among the most spectacular in Africa. Other statues in wood and steatite honor important rulers, nobility and glorified ancestors as an everlasting source of power and mystic inspiration.

Finally, among the northern Tabwa, we have a rare first-hand account on the birth of prime objects and a new Tabwa style: when Tabwa chief Tumbwe I wished to thank his ancestors, he asked a Luba artist to carve a pair of statues. He then sent both to his maternal uncle and senior chief Kiubwe, asking him to consecrate them. This was accomplished by giving both statues the names of common ancestors. Chief Kiubwe sent back one of the two statues so that both he and Tumbwe could worship the same ancestral spirits. Tumbwe continued this practice for five more years until both uncle and nephew each kept six statues in their village. These statues representing two men (Kyomba and Kiubwe I) and four women (the eldest and youngest daughters of Kyomba and two of his grand daughters) seem to reflect the lineage structure of the Tumbwe clan in descending importance from the most senior ancestor to the youngest junior lineage.[80]

The photo (right-side photo of page 16) of a group of statues shows a similar pattern among the central Tabwa. The tallest statue, on the extreme left, is Manda, the most famous and powerful chief of the clan. This statue was brought back to Europe in 1884 and is now in the collections of the Musée Royal de l'Afrique Centrale at Tervuren. The next two statues came out of Zaire in 1972 and are said to represent junior Chief Zongwe and Mulilo. The last two statues on the right were also brought back in 1884 and probably represent other chiefs, junior to Manda, and were probably part of the shrine of Manda. More research on human statuary may eventually reveal structural principles governing systems of thought as well as plastic representation in Black Africa.

6. OBJECTS OF THE ENVIRONMENT

The skin has magical connotations in Africa. It is also a living canvas and the primary 'clothing' for the human body and the ultimate expression of beauty. Early explorers of the African continent were immediately struck by the physique of African women and men. As Barbot (1732) wrote:

'The Blacks in this part of Guinea are generally well limbed and proportioned, being neither of the highest nor of the lowest stature; they have good oval faces, sparkling eyes, small ears and their eyebrows, lofty and thick. Their mouth are not too large with curious clean, white and well-ranged teeth, fresh red lips... Their skin (...) is always sleek and smooth. In short they are for the most part well-set, handsome men in outward appearance.''[81]

The human body is not only the main axis of all body decoration, but is also the module of their architecture, furniture and household items. For Africans, the house is the center of the world and each house, and even on a larger scale each village, is modelled on the architecture of the human body, from the Dogon house to the Tabwa village.

The natural sense of design found in African furniture, decoration, jewelry or personal adornment is quite remarkable. Two of the reasons why it has been admired by western audiences have been recently underlined.[82] Firstly, the aesthetic attitude is ubiquitous in African traditional life. An object is not only physical but also enhances the moral value of the person who wears it. Indeed most of the objects considered beautiful have been made by artists who were also good hunters or farmers. The other reason which is more subtle to grasp is the total dominance in Africa of the third dimension, volume, in the sphere of representation. African artists very rarely see objects as painted on a flat surface. An important consequence of this three-dimensionality is the remarkable skill of African artists in the use of contrasts both in sculpture, cosmetics and painting. As D. Zahan noted, traditional sculpture, painting and cosmetics exclude the blending of forms as well as gradual changes from one color to another.[83] There is no tonal blending when colors are combined and very few sinuous transitions in the plastic arts. These general principles are important in understanding why adornment for the body or the house, considered a minor art in Europe, should be admired and considered the aesthetic basis from which other art forms may have been born.

A brief survey of the art of adornment should start with the enhancement of the body with scarifications, cranial deformation, the filing of teeth, piercing and stretching of lips, nose and ears, construction of elaborate coiffures as well as body painting. The human body is also the axis of decor for jewelry and clothing, two art forms in which Africans excelled. By placing jewelry on specific parts of the body, the wearer not only conveys messages about beauty or sexual allure, social status and rank, age or ethnic identification but also about a state of mind or a desire to seek protection from his environment. The materials used for personal adornment are infinite, from beads, shells, feathers and ivory to copper, iron, gold, stone, leather, fibers and seeds. Each material has specific symbolic connotations and religious purposes, and creates the most lavish textural surfaces. Certain materials are generally used alone, such as ivory. Others, like glass beads, thrive in the accumulation and aggregation of various sizes and colors to create surfaces which can be altered both by light and motion. The smooth, luminous and warm patinas of ivory emphasizes the black color of the body it adorns while metal objects not only add a new dimension of sound by the accumulation of bracelets and anklets on the arms and legs, but enhance the prestige of the wearer by affecting his gestures and movements as he is forced to walk in a slower and more solemn way because of the weight of the jewelry.

Such basic utilitarian objects such as hoes to toil the earth or bows to hunt are very often individually owned. Powerful bonds exist between the owner and his tools, which are often included as funerary gifts. At his funeral, a Dogon man's hoe is broken ceremonially by the elders. The Tellem buried broken bows with great hunters.

Headrests, small, portable stool-like objects, show a marvellous variety of forms for a simple use. Although the oldest surviving headrests came from Egypt, it is clear that they have been an essential part of African furniture for many centuries. Beautiful wooden headrests dated to the 11th century were found in a Tellem cave in the Bandiagara Cliff in Mali. They probably had a religious meaning since, among the Dogon, the *hogon,* the divine king-priest of the Dogon, was not supposed to have his head touch the ground.

Stools also played an important role as part of the regalia of kings and chiefs. Some of the most elegant forms of stools carved out of precious materials such as quartzite and dated to between the 12th-15th centuries have been found at Ife. Among the Ashanti, each chief and royal figure had his own stool which became the repository of his soul at his death. After the death of each Ashanti king, his stool was preserved in an ancestral shrine and ritually blackened in order to commemorate the deceased. Stools became much more than utilitarian objects to sit on. They were thrones, powerful symbols of leadership, on which only the king could sit. Caryatid stools demonstrate the political influence of the Luba empire in southeast Zaire. They are found as far west as the Chokwe and the Kanyok, as far east as Tanzania and as far south as Malawi. Their prototype is probably iron stools dated back to the early dispersion of a sophisticated early Bantu culture dated from the seventh to the tenth centuries which has been excavated at their royal site of Sanga.

Containers are generally used for storage, for preparing and serving food, and for eating and drinking. They can be found in an array of materials and an infinite variety of shapes and forms. For instance, bowls can be made from wood, calabash, basketry, pottery or leather. The Kuba are famous for their richly decorated prestige objects in wood: cups for palm wine, small boxes for cosmetics or other small implements, and larger storage boxes. The most preeminent container in Africa however, is made out of calabash. An early traveller (1745) comments:

'The Calabashes grow of different figures and sizes. The bark is thin, not exceeding the breadth of a half Crown, but is very tough. The wood is very smooth, and takes a good polish... Of the shells of this fruit the Negroes make several ustensils. Some of them are large enough to hold above three gallons of liquor."[84]

The calabash is not only a container, but is also used as sounding board for musical instruments, as a water-pipe, snuff-box, medicine case, unguent-pots, masks, drums, rattles. It can be decorated with raffia, cowrie shells, beads, and metal parts. Pyrograved designs are also made by using a sharp metal blade heated until it makes a dark line on the yellow surface of the calabash. With time, the container ages to a beautiful rich red or dark honey patina. As a general observation, Africans choose materials not only for religious reasons but also because of their texture, hardness, brilliance, shape and color, each quality reinforcing the other in order to make an object beautiful to look at.

Bernard de GRUNNE

[1] G. Kubler, *The Shape of Time. Remarks on the History of Things,* Yale University Press, New Haven, 1962, 39-45 and personal communication, May, 5, 1987.

[2] A.F. Roberts, *Heroic Beasts, Beastly Heroes: Principles of Cosmology and Chiefship among the Lakeside Batabwa of Zaire,* Unpub. Ph. D. dissertation, University of Chicago, 1980, 412-413.

[3] D. Zangrie (a.k.a. Luc de Heusch), 'Les Institutions, la religion et l'art des Babuye (groupes Basumba, Manyema, Congo Belge),' in *L'Ethnographie,* 45, 1947-50.

[4] E. Bassani, 'Due grandi sculture Buye gia a Firenze,' *Critica d'Arte,* 1980.

[5] Frank Willet, 'A Missing Millenium? From Nok to Ife and beyond,' in *Arte in Africa,* E. Bassani ed., Edizioni Panini, 1986, p. 98.

[6] Frank Willet, 'On the Funeral Effigies of Owo and Benin and the Interpretation of the life-Size Bronze heads from Ife, Nigeria,' in *Man,* Vol. I, 1:34-46.

[7] J. Gallais, *Le Delta intérieur du Niger,* Mémoires IFAN 79, Dakar, 1967, T. I:12.

[8] B. de Grunne, *Divine Gestures and Earthly God. A study of the Ancient Terracotta Statuary from the Inland Niger Delta in Mali,* Unpub. Ph. D. Dissertation, Yale University, 1987: 71-79.

[9] L. de Heusch, *Sacrifice in Africa. A*

Structuralist Approach, Indiana University Press, Bloomington, 1985: 216.

[10] G. Kubler, 'Preface', in Art of Aztec Mexico, National Gallery, Washington. 1983: 14.

[11] R.F. Thompson, 'Catalogue entry', in For Spirits and Kings African. Art from the Tishman Collection, S. Vogel, ed., New York, 1981: 110.

[12] B. de Grunne, 'Heroic Riders and Divine Horses. An Analysis of Ancient Soninke and Dogon Equestrian Figures from the Inland Niger Delta region in Mali,' in The Minneapolis Institute of Art Bulletin, 1987.

[13] D. Zahan, Antilopes du soleil, Vienne, 1980: 59. The voandzou is called in Bamana tíga-ni-kurú, meaning small round nut. Kurú means round or spherical but also alludes to the word koró or goro which means scarification in the shape of a small bump on the skin. Ka- means a cut, an incision and by extension a scarification. Cfr. M. Delafosse, La Langue Mandingue et ses dialects, Tome I., Paris, Geuthner, 1929: 371 & 612.

[14] E. Leynaud & V. Cissé, Paysans Malinke du Haut Niger, Bamako, Ed. Imprimerie Populaire du Mali, 1978: 25.

[15] Fondation SCOA, Actes du premier colloque international de Bamako, Paris, 1975: 43.

[16] D. Sylla, L'Empire du Ghana. Légende de Wagadou, Paris, Fondation SCOA, 1977: I:54 & III:6.

[17] B. de Grunne, Ancient Terracottas from West Africa, Louvain-La-Neuve, 1980: 49.

[18] Szumowski, 'Pseudotumulus des environs de Bamako (Suite),' Notes Africaines, 1958, 77:1. T. Togola, Inventaire des sites archéologiques du cercle de Bougouni, Mémoire de fin d'étude, E.N.S., Bamako, 1982:31. M. Gilbert, 'Review of Exhibition Excavated Bamana Terracotta', New York Craft Caravan Gallery, African Arts, 1983, 16:74-75.

[19] K. Ezra, 'Early sources for the History of Bamana Art,' Iowa Studies in African Art, The University of Iowa, 1984, Vol. I:157 and K. Ezra, A Human Ideal in African Art Bamana Figurative Sculpture, Washington, National Museum of African Art, 1986: 40.

[20] T. Northern, 'The African Collection at the Museum of Primitive Art,' African Arts, 1971, Vol. V, I:20-27. Ezra, A Human Ideal, p. 44. These dates should be taken with caution. One of the statues yielded two dates: the sample of wood from the center of the statue is dated to 1300-1420 A.D. while and the sample from the periphery is dated 1485-1795 A.D. These problems are discussed in Ezra, Historical Dimensions of Bamana Sculpture, Unpub. Paper, presented at the seventh Triennial Symposium on African Art, April 1986, Los Angeles.

[21] D. Zahan, 'Review of Buffoons, Queens and Wooden Horsemen,' in African Arts, 1984, XVII, 4:91.

[22] G. Preston, Beyond the Thicket of Ghost, ms., n.d., p. 60.

[23] R. Sieber, 'Kwahu Terracottas, Oral Traditions and Ghanaian History,' in African Art and Leadership, D. Fraser & H. Cole, ed., London, 1972: 179.

[24] P. Crane-Coronel, 'Aowin Terracotta Sculptures', in African Arts, XIII, 1, 1979: 30.

[25] G. Preston, op. cit., p. 83.

[26] Idem, p. 79.

[27] Ibidem.

[28] The missionary Godefroy Loyer in B. Holas, 'Sur l'Utilisation rituelle des statuettes funéraires au Royaume de Krinjabo (Côte d'Ivoire)', in Acta Tropica, 8, 1, 1951: 6.

[29] Dr. V. Eban, personal communication, March 1986, A. Kwabena, 'Funerary Effigies from Kwahu,' Ghana Notes and Queries, 1966, 8:12 and R. Sieber, op. cit., p. 179. Preston also briefly speaks of the statues for the priest as being kept in the house of the surrogate who was seized by the deity worshipped by the recently deceased priest. Cfr. G. Preston, op. cit., p. 58. Cfr. V. Grottanelli, 'Asonu worship among the Nzema: a Study in Akan Art and Religion,' Africa, 1961, Vol. XXXI, 1:57 and H. Debrunner, 'Note sur les 'Azongu' de Half-Assini en Gold Coast,' in Notes Africaines, Oct. 1953, 60:111-113.

[30] James Anquandah & Laurent van Ham, Discovering the forgotten 'Civilization' of Komaland, Northern Ghana, Ghames Foundation, Ro-

ckanje, The Netherlands, 1985.

[31] G. Dieterlen, 'Contribution à l'étude des forgerons en Afrique Occidentale,' *Annuaire de l'E.P.H.E.,* V. 73, 1965: 1-28 and Dieterlen, 'Contribution à l'étude des relations protohistoriques entre le Mande et l'actuel Ghana,' *Valmonica Symposium '72 - Actes du Symposium international sur les religions de la préhistoire,* Capo di Ponte, 1975: 367-378.

[32] James O. Bellis, *'The Place of Pots' in Akan Funerary custom,* African Studies Program, Indiana University, 1982: 15.

[33] See essays by J. Bazin, 'Retour aux choses-dieux,' and M. Augé, 'Le Fétiche et le corps pluriel,' in 'Corps des Dieux,' C. Malamoud & J.P. Vernant, in *Le temps de la reflexion,* VII, Gallimard, Paris, 1986.

[34] E.W. Herbert, *Red Gold of Africa. Copper in Precolonial History and Culture,* The University of Wisconsin Press, 1984: 5-11.

[35] *Idem,* p. 7.

[36] F. Willet, 'Nigerian Art: An Overview,' in E. Eyo and F. Willet, *Treasures of Ancient Nigeria,* A. Knopf, New York, 1980: 33.

[37] *Idem,* p. 43.

[38] K. Nicklin, 'The Cross River Bronzes,' in M.-T. Brincard, ed., *The Art of Metal in Africa,* The African-American Institute, New York, 1983: 48.

[39] K. Ezra, *African Ivories,* The Metropolitan Museum of Art, New York,

1984: 5.

[40] *Idem,* p. 7-8.

[41] D. Biebuyck, *Lega Culture,* Berkeley, University of California Press, 1973: 136-137.

[42] S.A. Boone, *Radiance from the Waters. Ideals of Feminine Beauty in Mende Art,* Yale University Press, 1986: 153.

[43] *Idem,* p. 157-161.

[44] *Idem,* p. 35-37.

[45] H.J. & M.T. Drewal, *Gelede Art and Female Power among the Yoruba,* Indiana University Press, 1983: 9.

[46] *Idem,* p. 71.

[47] E. Fischer & H. Himmelheber, *The Arts of the Dan in West Africa,* Museum Rietberg, Zurich, 1984: 8.

[48] *Idem,* p. 182-184.

[49] *Idem,* p. 188.

[50] K. Nicklin, 'Nigerian Skin-Covered Masks,' in *African Arts,* 1974, VII, 3:8-15.

[51] R.F. Thompson, 'Catalogue Entry,' in S. Vogel, ed., *For Spirits and Kings,* New York, 1982: 179.

[52] M.L. Bastin, *Statuettes Tshokwe du héros civilisateur Tshibinda-ilunga,* Suppl. Arts d'Afrique Noire, Arnouville, 1978.

[53] F. Neyt, *La Grande Statutaire Hemba du Zaire,* Louvain-La-Neuve, 1977: 481; J. Cornet, *Art Royal Kuba,* 1984; R. Lecoq, *Les Bamiléké, une civilisation Africaine,* 1953; P. Foss, 'Urhobo Statuary for Spirits and Ancestors,' *African Arts,* 1976, Vol. IX, 9:12-23.

[54] A. Gordts, La Statuaire traditionnelle Bijago, in *Arts d'Afrique Noire,* Summer 1976, 18:7.

[55] D. Gallois Duquette, 'Informations sur les arts plastiques des Bidyogo,' *Arts d'Afrique Noire,* Summer 1976, 18:42-3.

[56] D. Gallois Duquette, 'Catalogue Entry' in J. Fry, ed., *Twenty-Five African Sculptures,* Ottawa, 1978: 95. However, *iran* can also be balls of plants, organic matter or reutilized Western objects. Each *iran* has its own name and circumstances determines which type of *iran* to be used.

[57] L. Desplagnes, *Le Plateau central Nigérien,* Paris, 1907: 295.

[58] G. Dieterlen, *Les Ames des Dogon,* Paris, Institut d'Ethnologie, 1941: 221.

[59] Dieterlen, *op. cit.,* p. 146-7.

[60] *Idem,* p. 165-175.

[61] M. Griaule & G. Dieterlen, *Le Renard pâle,* Travaux et Mémoires de l'Institut d'Ethnologie 72, 1965: 353-355. G. Dieterlen & S. de Ganay, 'Le Génie des eaux chez les Dogon,' in *Miscellanea Africana Lebaudy,* 5 Paris, 1942: 20.

[62] In another ritual to obtain rain, the priest first starts a fire with a plant called *loloryo (Ipomea repens,* Convolvulacées) in front of the statue. Later, the statue is rubbed with a mixture of *sa* oil. The priest drinks a fermented juice made of the pit of the fruit of *sa (Lannea acida).* These two rituals contribute to the smoky, oily patina noted on certain Dogon statues. Cfr. de Ga-

nay & Dieterlen, *Le Génie des eaux,* p. 31-33.

[63] K. Ezra, *A Human Ideal in African Art. Bamana Figurative Sculpture,* Smithsonian Institution Press, 1986 and P.J. Imperato, *Buffoons, Queens and Wooden Horsemen. The Dyo and Gouan Societies of the Bambara of Mali,* New York, 1983.

[64] K. Ezra, *Figure Sculpture of the Bamana of Mali,* Unpub. Ph. D. Dissertation, Northwestern University, 1983: 126, and Ezra, *A Human Ideal,* p. 30-37.

[65] J.E.P. Hopkins & N. Levtzion, *Corpus of Early Arabic Sources for West African History,* Cambridge, 1980: 290-1.

[66] Pâques provide a detailed description of a similar throne still used by the royal family of Bamako, the Niaré in 1953, some six hundred years later. She explains that a python, wrapped in a red cloth, its mouth filled with gold, was buried alive in two upside down terracotta jars. V. Pâques, 'L'Estrade royale des Niaré,' *BIFAN,* 1953: 15.

[67] Imperato, *Buffoons,* p. 41. A. Glaze reported similar findings among the Fodonon group of the Senufo in the nearby northern Ivory Coast. Statues are also carried aloft during the funeral ceremonies held in honor of senior female members of the Poro society. A. Glaze, *Art and Death in a Senufo Village,* Bloomington, 1981: 87.

[68] R. Goldwater, *Bambara Sculpture from the Western Sudan,* New York, 1960, Fig. 77-82.

[69] Imperato, *Buffoons,* p. 38 and Ezra, *A Human Ideal,* p. 17.

[70] Imperato, *Buffoons,* p. 50.

[71] S.M. Vogel, 'Beauty in the Eyes of the Baoule: Aesthetics and Cultural Values,' in *Working Paper in the Traditional Arts,* no. 6, Philadelphia, 1980: 2-5.

[72] W. Fagg, 'On the Art of the Yoruba,' in W. Fagg, J. Pemberton and B. Holcombe, *Yoruba Sculpture of West Africa,* New York, A. Knopf, 1982: 9.

[73] J. Pemberton, 'Catalogue Entry,' in Fagg et alii, *op. cit.,* p. 156.

[74] B. Lawal, 'Catalogue Entry,' in S. Vogel, ed., *For Spirits and Kings. African Art from the Paul and Ruth Tishman Collection,* The Metropolitan Museum of Art, 1981: 92.

[75] R.F. Thompson, *Black Gods and Kings,* Indiana University Press, 1971, chap. 13:2.

[76] J. Pemberton, 'Catalogue Entry,' in Fagg et alii, *op. cit.,* p. 80.

[77] J. Fernandez, 'Principles of Opposition and Vitality in Fang Aesthetics,' in C.F. Jopling, ed., *Art and Aesthetics in Primitive Society,* New York, 1971: 374.

[78] See G. Tessman, *Die Pangwe,* Berlin, 1913, II:118 versus L. Perrois, *Ancestral Art of Gabon,* Barbier-Muller Museum, Geneva, 1986: 143.

[79] R.F. Thompson, *Painting from a Single Heart, Preliminary Remarks on Bark-Cloth Designs on the Mbute Women of Haut-Zaire,* München, 1983: 6.

[80] This account is part of an unfinished manuscript called 'Histoire des Ba-Tabwa' by S. Kaoze, dated Jan. 1950, and is published in Nagant, 1976, Annexe III, p. 39-40.

[81] John Barbot, 'A Description of the Coasts of North- and South-Guinea (...), London, 1732,' in R. Sieber, *African Textiles and Decorative Arts,* The Museum of Modern Art, 1972: 90.

[82] A. Appiah, 'An Aesthetics for the Art of Adornment,' in M.T. Brincard, ed., *Beauty by Design: The Aesthetics of African Adornment,* The African-American Institute, 1984: 17-19.

[83] D. Zahan, 'Ornament and Color in Black Africa,' in M.T. Brincard, *op. cit.,* p. 22.

[84] Astley (1745-47) in R. Sieber, *African Furniture and Household Objects,* Indiana University Press, 1980: 178.

PEOPLE OF THE WORD

The persistence of Yoruba and Kongo art through time and space affirm their philosophic potency and depth. These arts are heroic acts of civilization.

This means civilization in the fullest sense: cultural indelibility, translation of will and moral energy into documents which outlast their makers.

Yoruba and Kongo philosophy have been passed on through art, oral literature, dance, myth, and ideographic writing. Colliding with the slave trade, these signs became trans-Atlantic. They reemerged in the United States, Cuba, Haiti, and Brazil.

The Yoruba evolved a set of signs of divination permutations, written on divination boards *(opon ifá)* which trigger complex parables, moral advice, and legends. The Bakongo miniaturized belief and aspiration in numerous cosmograms. *Ifá,* the art of Yoruba divination, and *bidimbu,* Kongo signs, crossed the Atlantic in the minds of captives.

Jews and their sacred texts were tested in Babylon and survived. Yoruba and Kongo religious precepts also were tested and survived. Their aspirations were remembered in slave-cabins and in the barracoons. Who would have dreamt that by the 20th century their ideals, and the forms associated with them, would be celebrated in the pages of Jorge Amado, in the paintings of two of the most exciting painters of the Caribbean, José Bedia and Manuel Mendive, or that the American poet, Wallace Stevens, would be impressed profoundly by Kongo-American grave decorations seen in Florida. Stevens celebrated those signs, in a famous poem, as a sign of endurance, and a symbol of creative powers of improvisation.

In the year 2000 Houston Conwill, an American artist, plans to complete a monumental earthwork rendering the Kongo diagram, of men and women as 'seconds of the sun'. He will cross one line running from Louisville to New Orleans, with another, running from Memphis to Atlanta. Ed Love, a major American sculptor, has recently signed the earth, before the Washington Monument in the capital of the United States, with another rendering of the Kongo sign of the four moments of the sun, translated into symbolic sculptures and placements of cloth. And very shortly a sculpture representing Shangó, Yoruba deity of lightning and moral vengeance, will be unveiled in a park in Chicago by its maker, Muneer H. Bahauddeen.

These and other signs indicate that Kongo and Yoruba art are abiding world presences. This leads us to the recognition of a black classical tradition. Ideally, in the 21st century, less than fourteen years from this writing, a cultivated woman and a cultivated man will, unselfconsciously, salute the contribution of John Coltrane and Claude Debussy, Michelangelo and the Ifè masters, Martha Graham and the choreographers of Kongo-Angola capoeira, Le Corbusier and the builders of Jenné and Great Zimbabwe.

It is in this ideal ecumenical spirit, of cultural parity and accomplishment, that these pages were signed and written. In the first chapter I shall marshall new evidence on the iconography of the gods of the Yoruba. I shall also probe Yoruba color symbolism as it relates to beaded necklaces of initiation. Similar necklaces reemerge in one of the more Yoruba-centric of the cities of the world, Bahia, in Brazil. The chapter ends with a remarkable translation of Yoruba themes into modern painting, the work of Manuel Mendive.

The focus of the second chapter is Kongo in world art history. We shall consider new data on monuments of Kongo sculpture as well as aspects of the diasporic reach of this major Central African civilization. Objects from the repertory of classical forms will be glossed in terms of spiritual intent and meaning. For the first time it will be suggested that the famous Kongo gestures and flexible dispositions of the limbs, mirrored in the art and life of the ancient kingdom, are in some instances comparable to the Kongo-influenced basic moves of a Brazilian martial art called capoeira. Once again the equation, art = life, is written in Atlantic art history, this time embracing sport.

In some accounts of Kongo art one gets the impression the tradition is extinct. This is not so. The cemeteries of Kongo are a rich source for a renaissance, in this century, for many of the main themes of the classical statuary. Wooden figures with mirrors of clairvoyance embedded in their bellies become huge cement headstones with mirrors embedded in the center. The charms [minkisi] of Kongo are still being made in Kinshasa and Brazzaville. Black America is famous for minkisi, sometimes masked by creole names and styles, and sometimes, as in Haiti and in Cuba, traditional and bearing Kongo names. Recently, an astonishing find of more than seven hundred wire-wrapt objects in Philadelphia were attributed, on grounds of strong stylistic unity, to a single master, The Wire Man. His works were found in one of the oldest continuously black-inhabited sections of Philadelphia. We will argue, provisionally, that they represent an ingenious fusion of two worlds, modern technocratic and traditional Kongo-American.

The second chapter ends with a recent find from a Kongo-influenced barrio in Miami. We conclude with the amazing environmental art of José Bedia, exhibited in the United States in 1986. Bedia's respect for *lo mayombero,* the lore of one of the ancient provinces of Kongo, Mayombé, reinstated in creole fusions among the blacks of Cuba, is profound. Critics may not pinpoint this allegiance but they can sense its potency and pressure.

Chapter Three, on the reafricanizing of 'primitivist modernism' is a logical consequence of the prior chapters. If the Yoruba perennially inspire the Caribbean and Brazil, if Bedia's debt to the *mayomberos* is clear-cut, then surely we have learnt for the last time that Africa's impact on world art did not start or end with Picasso and Brancusi. The persistence of African influence on Western art suggests its abiding relevance. And that, in turn, suggests another way of looking at modern art of the West: the criticism of certain artists, Picasso, Modigliani, Houston Conwill, Betye Saar, Ed Love, Romare Bearden, by African ritual leaders and philosophers.

We cannot fully pursue such research in these few pages. Nevertheless, we can, at least, sample the sorts of insights which emerge when a traditional African philosopher examines Picasso and early cubism and remarks on the spiritual meanings he sees reflected in the glints of Africanizing form. Already in one of his phrasings-*pásula kiini* [shadow-breaking art] — we have at last an African definition of what Westerners call cubism.

I

PEOPLE OF THE WORD: REMARKS ON

YORUBA AND YORUBA-ATLANTIC ART

> Head in luck is crowned with cowries
> Neck in luck is circled with jasper
> Body in luck is appropriately enthroned
> Such was the person who divined for My-Body-Is-Cool
> Who was the wife of Orisha, who initiated her.
> First born of the hill is not disgraced in the
> Eyes of the person who initiates him
> Eji Ogbe is like this.

William Bascom, *Sixteen Cowries*

The Yoruba people number more than eleven million, primarily residing in western Nigeria and eastern Benin. They have created one of the major traditions of Afro-Atlantic art. With their ancient gods and cities, their elegant monarchic traditions and efflorescent arts, the Yoruba felt no awe before Europeans, any more than the Greeks did before the Persians. Like the Japanese, the Yoruba knew they descended from forces which were, ultimately, divine. Thus one of the earliest rulers of the northern Yoruba metropolis of Oyo-lle became the famous thundergod, Shango, whose name resonates in several major Afro-American religions. The ultimate Yoruba, Oduduwa, first king among kings, founder of the ancient holy city, Ife, also was a god.

Against this background of cultural achievement it seems appropriate that the first person in Africa to be honored with the Nobel Prize was a Yoruba, Wole Soyinka.

It seems appropriate to open a chapter on Yoruba art with remarks on Yoruba aesthetics by Wole Soyinka. I had the honor of interviewing him at Yale in the autumn of 1979. In earlier publications I remarked that among the main principles of Yoruba aesthetics three concepts were surely prominent *ashe* [the power to make things happen; spiritual command], *itutu* [composure] and *iwa* [character and custom]. Since then Roland Abiodun has handsomely superceded my exploratory remarks with a wealth of intricately argued exposition on the concept of *ìwà* in Yoruba art and culture. In addition, Babatunde Lawal, another Yoruba art historian, has refined the Yoruba aesthetic lexicon. Thus where I talked about 'mid-point mimesis', inspired by a Yoruba concept of blue being midway between black and red, not too dark and not too bright but cool and bright to see, Lawal gave us the exact gloss in Yoruba, *iwontunwonsi*.

In any event, I asked Wole Soyinka to discuss some of the main principles of Yoruba aesthetics. First he started with the concept of *ashe,* which he defined as 'the ultimate, authoritative word.'

During field trips in rural Yorubaland, I have seen emblazoned over the front of a truck, the following legend: ÌWÀ PELE. This phrase, as Wande Abimbola establishes in an important article, 'Iwapele: The Concept of Good Character in Ifa Literary Corpus, published in the anthology, *Yoruba Oral Traditions* [1975], is central to the understanding of Yoruba art. This was the next concept which Soyinka chose to examine. *Iwa pele,* he said, literally refers to 'cool conduct' to 'coolness or gentleness of conduct'. On that very phrase, he continued, an ideal person's being is constructed. A person who knows how to modulate his character with the insights of patience and deliberation, thoughtfully looking to the needs of his people—all that is condensed in the term, *pele.*

But reflection and patience are not enough. The compensating vitality of ashe assures the Yoruba, wherever it is embodied, that great powers to resist and destroy evil lie ready to be activated by appropriate verbal and physical command. This was the style of the goddess, Nana Bukúu, who defeated the soldiers of the mythical town of Teju-Ade. This was the style of Atandá, who, with one decisive act, set in motion a history of Yoruba music in Cuba.

(Atanda, born in Egbado country in Yorubaland and enslaved in the early 19th century was shocked at the impurity of what passed for Yoruba bata drums in Havana. He made a pure trio of drums to indicate what was real and by that act of assertion planted a dragon seed. Today there are probably a hundred bata drums being played, not only in Cuba but in Puerto Rico and the United States, all stemming ultimately from Atanda's act of determination.)

Henry and Margaret Drewall, in their monograph on the performance arts of Gelede in southwestern Yorubaland, state Yoruba aesthetic issues with admirable economy. Art, they say, is sacrifice. And artistic performance, they continue, discovers in this sacrifice the carrying forward of the sacred power to bring things into existence. (*Gelede,* Indiana University Press, 1983: 6)

Itutu, or composure, to return to Soyinka, is obvious in Yoruba life and art. To pour water symbolically on the ground, consciously to invoke a state of calm and peace, is what he calls 'instant sacrifice'. He goes on to characterize the Yoruba art of praise-singing, the chanting of oriki, as creating ideal coolness around one's surroundings. The word, cool, according to Soyinka is definitely used to praise both faces in sculpture and faces in life. The encomium, *ojú è tútu pùpó* [his face radiates calm, lit. his face is exceedingly cool] is used in contrast to 'his face is hard' *[ojú è ó lè].* Moreover, women in particular can be praised, including sculptural representation, in terms of their 'coolness of body'. Serenity and poise of the body, firm lips, stalwart attitude, radiant calm—all this in bodily deportment and in sculpture is *alara tútù.* It is a quality which immediately communicates, as Soyinka shows, wisdom, authority, and serenity. We find it reflected in Yoruba imagery, as an element of character, where two snakes are symbolically shown in repose, coiled together in a pattern of interlace.

Soyinka's exegesis of the inner coolness communicated by two serpents coiled together sheds light on the Yoruba-related iconography of the Fon of Benin. There coiled serpents not only connote composure but are the very image of Dá, he who helped God build the world, and his female counterpart. According to Soyinka, ephebism, or the imparting of youthfulness to the artistic rendering of an elder, is a form of praise-

poem. *Odo* [ephebism] 'dynamizes the elder with new power'. It is an artistic device, he points out, but it by no means idealizes the youth; this would go against the grain of the age-hierarchic structure of Yoruba society.

By Soyinka's reckoning, ephebism refers to the need of the gods to be forever strengthened. 'And that is why we carve them young.'

Soyinka reminds us that Yoruba sculptors, praise-singers, and dancers, —in fact all who would shape something appreciable in sound or effort—must be aware of the canon of *iwontunwonsi.* This canon broadly means 'balance'. I referred to it, years ago, as 'midpoint mimesis'. Soyinka calls it, in better phrasing, 'a rhythm of proportion, an inner rhythm created by proportion.' Splitting the semantic atom of a standard Yoruba term for balance, *iwontunwonsi,* Soyinka shows how that term literally means a balance shaped, equally by the right hand and the left.

In phrasing a Yoruba mask or statuette, adherence to *iwontunwonsi* means finding proportion through three-dimensional viewing of the object. As the right hand strikes with the adze, the left hand, holding the object must be turning, balancing, collaborating in the discovery of an inner rhythm of proportion.

We come now to a series of remarks on Yoruba symbolism, divided in three parts. First we shall listen to the late Chief Fagbemi Ajanaku, Araba of Lagos, as he spells out some of the connections between color in beaded ornaments for the orisha and their essential character. Secondly, we shall study the transformation of some of these themes among the Yoruba-flavored religious life of the city of Salvador, Bahia, long known locally as the 'Rome of the Africans' because of the intensity and relative purity of its sub-Saharan manifestations. Our interlocutor there will be the late Pai Costa de Oxalá, who was one of the master beadworkers of the city of Salvador and whose understanding of iconography, albeit creolized and sometimes heightened by a strong and assertive personal style, nonetheless traced to the coast of Yorubaland. And then we will return to the Araba's exegesis.

The Yoruba word for deity, *orisha,* according to the Araba of Lagos, compacts the following phrasing: *eniti-orí-sa-da-yato-si-awon-elegbe-re-yoku-ni-ode-isalu-aiye.* This means: 'he whose head has been selected to create in manners different from that of his fellow persons on earth.' There is a theory of accomplishment embedded in this lore. According to Yoruba philosophy, all things are under the control of the Creator *[el-eda]* and the head *[orí].* This is why Sunny Adé, in a song which became world-famous in 1983, asks both the Creator and his head to fight for him *[orí mi jà fún mi].* This is why, as the Araba of Lagos points out, a person who does something so distinguished that he can never be forgotten, has in effect become an *orisha—eniti orí sa da* [a person whose head has singled him out creatively].

What this all means is that the divine potential of ashe exists in every man and woman. The road to the expression of such extraordinary power lies in deliberately distinguishing oneself with God's aid. As the Araba says, distinguished persons rise up because God [His spirit in their head] has created them differently from the rest of us.

This theory of accomplishment, positive differentiation, the spark of potential godhead in human life, is a cultural imperative. It has immediate bearing on strong differences in beaded color symbolism among the deities of the Yoruba.

For instance, the Araba says verses of Yoruba divination tell us why the beads of the Yoruba deity of contingency and surprise, Eshu-Elegba, are black. These jet black beads are called *ere.* Their blackness stands for the condemnation of Eshu, in an elaborate myth. One day a positive deity named Ela descends to earth from heaven. On the following day Ela founds human commerce. The next day Eshu tries to kill Ela out of jealousy. He only succeeds in wounding him. Again, envious of his colleague's prowess in trade, Eshu spoils his career. But the next day Ela has everything back to normal. Finally, God banishes Eshu from earth, together with his son, Paralysis *[egbe]* and Accident *[eshe]* On the final day Ela wins, a day known forever after as the day of immortality.

In sum, the beads of Eshu are black because he suffered exile, condemnation, and shame. We sense that other dimensions of Eshu's character are left out of this account, however, e.g. his loyalty to his friends. For the term, *ere,* also correlates with another myth, positive in nature, when Eshu alone among all deities shed tears of genuine grief when he heard that God had died. The dark color of his beads also summon images of accident and paralysis. I have seen a small black image for Eshu, near Otta in Aworri, showing Eshu as a child with legs curled back, destroyed by polio.

As we leave this recitation on the meaning of the 'blackness' of Eshu let us remind ourselves that the domain of color in Yoruba symbolism is problematic in the extreme and never more so than in the domain of Eshu. No matter what we introduce, when dealing with Eshu-Elegba, we are led into endless contradiction. His is not only the black of shame but also the white of peace. John Pemberton in a recent conversation shares with me his finding that in Ila-Orangun, capital of the Igbomina Yoruba, white sometimes serves as his alternate color.

Duality emerges in the red-and-white beads for the thunder-god. The color opposition is said to bind together 'a hard world with a cool world'. Such beads the Yoruba call *kele.* That word conceals a pun on *le,* to be hard, muscular, tough. It means that one is wearing something hard, something tough. Wearing Shango. Shango, according to one myth, committed suicide, in remorse, when he accidentally killed his wife and children playing with a leaf possessed of the power to bring down lightning. Hence, there is a connexion between *kele* and suicide. It is believed that a person after he has been initiated into the worship of Shango, and receives kele, must put the beads on very, very tight around his neck—otherwise, Shango will make him commit suicide. Clearly to wear kele projects a sense of danger.

The sign of the Yoruba deity of iron and war, Ogún, is an upper-arm bangle *[irin igbunpa].* It mirrors, as it were, the iron in Ogun's bicep. This basic metaphor was magnified heroically by a court sculptor to the kings of Dahomey in the 19th century. I refer to a famous sculpture, part of the exhibition collection of the Musée de L'Homme in Paris where Gu in a loincloth of metal, lifts up his arms threateningly. His muscles flow with myriad pieces of appended iron. His very body becomes a counterpoise of flesh and metallic instruments.

A structural transformation occurs when we come to the perfect white beads of Orishanla, the arch-divinity, the eldest. His hair is white, and this is one reason for the color of his beads. The white beads of Orishanla have their own praise-name, *sheshefun,* 'that which deepens whiteness, that which exalts reputation.'

Finally, Dada-Bayonni, given by some as the elder sister of Shango, given by others as the junior brother of Shango, is, in whatever incarnation, symbolized by strands of cowrie shell money deriving from Aje, deity of money and Olokun, god of the sea. These strands of cowrie wealth—*owó eyo*—are assembled to make a magnificent embroidered crown for Dada-Bayonni. The purity and richness of these emblems attest the belief that Bayonni is one of the gentlest and most perfect of of all the orisha.

Continuing the procession of the gods, with their beaded emblems, given to them by God to distinguish them, one from the other, Orunmila the god of divination, received *otu-tu-opon* [lit. cool-and-hot] a strand alternately green and yellow, or blue and tan. *Pon,* to be yellow, to be tan, to be red, refers in Yoruba to any color that is not black and nor white and nor 'cool' [green, blue, indigo, purple]. That is how the world is: sometimes easy, sometimes hard.

God gave to the goddess of the Niger River, Oya, as her *esho ara* [lit. body ornament] maroon-colored beads, called *mojolo.* What this term ordinarily connotes is something 'long and flexible'. One informant links that quality to the image of the whirlwind, (an avatar of Oya) long, moving, shifting, full flashing maroon glints of laterite, lifted into the sky. But I never heard this version elsewhere.

The goddess of the river which bears her name, Oshun, received brass *[ide]* and chinaware ceramic objects *[omolaganran].* This last item might seem surprising and doubtless dates from trade contacts over the past few centuries. When one goes to a shrine for Oshun one sees, on the altar, ceramic vessels *[tanganran]* and broken pots and white seashells. Old shrines for Oshun illustrate how her presence was symbolized by the use of *omolaganran* [seashells, pottery fragments, and pieces of porcelain] to decorate the walls. It is possible that the porcelain represents a visual loan-translation, as it were, of the more ancient usage of white seashells to chime with associations of water, purity, freshness and wealth. The use of pottery as an emblem goes back for centuries and we may well be looking at Oshun when on the famous Ülm divination tray collected before 1659 we find the image of a woman balancing a clay pot on her head. Today this is one of the standard images of the Olosun [Oshun devotee] in Yoruba art. *Ile,* Earth, about whom so little is known, she who 'founded' *[dasile]* the Ogboni Society in Yoruba culture, an august governing body of elders, received, mysteriously, a special reddish-orange colored cylindrical bead called *okun.*

Obaluaiye, dread earth deity of pestilence and disease, received very strong, hard beads made out of a black seed. These bracelets of black seed disks are called *lagidigba.* The word means to be completely obstinate, to be thoroughly unyielding, i.e. *lagidi* [to be obstinate] + *gba* [completely]. These qualities tie to the arm of the devotee the harsh, unyielding character of the dread deity of smallpox. Enraged by arrogance, by lack of social conscience, he can bring an entire city down in the wake of his epidemics. The switch from beads of glass or stone to seeds is a structural nuance which may well reflect the fact that Obaluaiye is believed to start an epidemic by taking a broom (another one of his primary emblems) and scattering black sesame seeds on the earth. As the wind rises and the dust swirls, these seeds, like signs of fever, the breaking out in spots, take to the air, spreading death everywhere. Olosa, the goddess of the lagoon, received tiny blue beads *[ileke dudu winrinwinrin].* It is possible they pun on the sound of water tinkling over stones or rising and falling upon a beach, *waranwaran.*

The deity of the ocean, Olokun, received large white beads as did another deity, Olojo.

Olojo is a form of Obatala and is very popular in Ile-Ife. It is believed that any time Olojo is worshipped there will be rain. There is a verbal play on rain *[ojo]* and day *[ojo]*. How he received his sobriquet of Master of the Day is explained by this rain-making power. No one can go to market when it rains; one has to recognize him as Master of the Day. His beads are very white.

Erinle, a deity who combines qualities of the river and qualities of the hunt, received an iron metal chain to be worn about the wrist. This emblematic chain is called *sàbà*. It may conceal a reference to hibernation [*sàbà* to hibernate] but this is mysterious and remains to be explained.

Finally, Olokun uses transparent white beads. The type of bead that Olokun uses Oshun Opara also uses, because he is a man. The son of Oshun is Ota [stone, bullet]. He also uses Olokun-type beads. Opara is a tall and lean man. *Opa* refers to a tall and slender wood and *ara* refers to body, hence Opara, tall, svelte person.

ALTO DO CANDOMBLÉ, BAHIA: A REINSTATEMENT OF YORUBA BEAD SYMBOLISM

When the Yoruba religion reestablished itself in the city of Salvador, Brazil, the beads and emblems of the gods reemerged. And when they are awarded to the initiate it is almost as if the servitor were participating in that originating moment when God gave out the emblems, deity by deity, so that they could all be different. In a classic article, 'Borí, First Portion of the Initiation Ceremony into the Worship of the Yoruba Gods in Bahia, Brazil', published in the *Revista do Museu Paulista* in São Paulo in 1955, Pierre Verger shows how the awarding of the beads triggers explanation. As the beads are placed on the neck of the postulate, he is told what they mean, so he will know what he is worshipping.

For example, in the ceremony Verger witnessed, a diviner placed around the neck of the initiate red-and-white beads, plus a chain for Ogún. And then the diviner explained. Each red bead is for Shango, each white for Oshaala. He told from the divination verses a legend in which Shango marries Oshun, daughter of Oshaala. The latter only consented to marry him if Shango agreed to carry her father, Oshaala, on his shoulders, for Oshaala was old and incapable of walking. 'And from that moment on, as a sign of alliance, with Oshaala, whose color is white, the necklace of Shango, originally made only of red beads, was changed to red and white'. Araba Eko calls this an alliance of hard and cool forces which restates Shango and Oshaala marching together. Finally, an echo of this duality, in a famous praise-poem for Shango, 'fire and water at the center of the sky', paints heaven itself in the red and white of the kele beads.

During fieldwork in Bahia in 1983-84, I had the fortune to know Pai Costa de Oxalá [now deceased] who made up beaded necklaces and bracelets for followers of the Yoruba goddesses and gods in the city of Salvador. He was a noted expert in Yoruba bead symbolism. His instructress was a priestess in the Gantois candomblé. She herself had been instructed by an African-born Yoruba. It was fascinating to observe how, at a remove of two generations, creolizing change, and ambiguity, intersected, in his words, with iconographic stability. The point is there is change, there is nuance in the Afro-Bahian usage of the bead symbolism of the Yoruba. But, triumphantly, some colors resonate with meanings close to the testimony of the Araba. Let us attend to Pai Costa's definitions, in the order in which he shared them with me.

Oya, as in Nigeria, is identified by maroon beads. Pai Costa had lost the vernacular original term, mojolo. But he had a clear sense of this fiery woman among women. Maroon, he said, is a color of blood, what she wants. She likes terrifying things, gore, horns, storms. Maroon is her love of all that. She finds no felicity in love. She exists, in order to be alone.

Oshumare, the rainbow-serpent cognate with Dá in the classical religion of the western neighbors of the Yoruba, the Fon of the People's Republic of Benin, calls for green beads striped with yellow. Pai Costa said that green was the 'cobra aspect' of the deity and yellow reflective of his rainbow propensities.

Ogún, who is identified by the biceps ornament of iron in Yorubaland and in parts of old Dahomey, in Bahia receives deep blue beads. Pai Costa, availing himself of creole argument, said Ogún carries the color of a sword-bearer. By that he meant the navy blue of a military officer, fighting at the front.

Waves of change were implied in further readings of beads for other orisha. There were strands of alternating red and white beads which he said were for 'Shango from Angola' [i.e. for patrons at the Bate Folha candomblé where Yoruba, Fon, and Kongo themes famously are interwined.] Then he showed me a strand of maroon-and-white alternating beads which he said were for a proper form of Shango, Shango de Ketu. He said the red was 'Shango's fire' and the white was 'peace'. We sense a phantom understanding of the relationship of Shango and Obatala [Oshaala].

Next came beads for Omo-Olu, in two avatars, the younger,

correlated with athletic São Roque and the older, correlated with São Lazaro. Both took beads striped black and white. These necklaces had protective 'firmas' [large signature beads placed on the strand and worn, at the back of the neck, as a guard against what one cannot see behind]. The understanding of this emblem had undergone a sea-change. In fact the material, glass beads, departed from the black seed *lagidigba* which more traditionally symbolize this dread deity of pestilence. To Pai Costa the black element was 'sadness', he's sad because he came to an end, all ruined by leprosy'. The white, on the other hand, was 'victory', invincible young Omo-Olu. When he was a strong young man, he did what he wanted *[quando era moço muito forte, fazía tudo o que quería]*. One could sense the intervention of Roman Catholic lithographs of Omo-Olu/São Roque and Omo-Olu/São Lázaro. The white beads recalled Omo-Olu's youth, he added, when he was sovereign in love and war. But then he suffered, was severely tested, and reduced to public charity. All this *tristeza* we see in his color, black.

A white-haired elder's wisdom lies exalted in the beads of Oshaala. Pai Costa insisted that Oshaala beads are white throughout the different African nations in Bahia—*Oshaala um só* [only one Oshaala]—despite the many avatars, Oshagiyan, Oshaala, Ogunte, Oshaala Beji, Obalufon, Oshalufon.

Warming to the theme of love, he picked up a strand of transparent golden beads for Oshun, deity of the streams. The transparency in itself, he said, marked a shift, from solid land to a substance through which we see—water.

Ancient Yoruba associations, linking this powerful woman with brass, passed through a creole alembic. Brass turned to yellow beads of glass. Pai Costa was speaking very enthusiastically now: 'she is gold and her beads are yellow. She is absolutely rich. She has a gun made of gold, she wears clothing made of gold, and the yellow beaches, the sands, the corals, belong to her.'

Pai Costa interrupted this revery. He picked up another strand of beads, large spherical glass beads of pure white, punctuated by a single 'firma' [signature], a dark blue *segi* bead, cylindrical in shape. A white necklace so nuanced was for Oshagiyon, but also appropriate to Jesus, whose purity he shares. He regarded the transparent beads for a hunter deity, Logun Ede. Three clear light blue beads alternated with three clear light golden beads, like a fusion of Oshoosi and Oshun. What he said was this: 'the gold is wealth, the blue is heaven.' Logun Ede lives sometimes in the water, and sometimes on land'. At the back of this opulently rendered necklace, with multiple strands, were three enormous firmas, two light blue cylindrical beads [segi] framing a central bead, also cylindrical, slightly darker blue. The three beads marked the three evils Logun Ede encountered in his life—hunger, harsh people, and poverty. 'Is there anything worse than that', he asked, with a lean and studied smile.

Finally, he showed me bright red transparent beads for Yewa, a river goddess, a river which flows by the important Yoruba town of Oke-Odan in western Nigeria. Her beads are becoming very difficult to find in Bahia, he complained. They must be red, he stated, because they represent the blood of Christ. She loves red. She was born in the blood of combat. Doubtless fearsome avatars of what the Yoruba in Nigeria would euphemistically refer to as the 'work of the mothers' are being signalized here, mysteriously mixed with Christian references. We have barely tapped the surface of Yewa symbolism in Brazil.

Naná Bukúu, mother of the intimidating Obaluaiye, takes white beads ['earth', 'Nana loves to dance on the white ground'] striped with blue ['water and the sky.']. A strand may be guarded at the back with two firmas, a large blue bead for Naná, a large white bead for 'Abaluaiye', her son.

Finally, he ended his seminar with remarks on beads for Eshu. Note this strand, he said, strung in multiples of three black beads, followed by three red beads, and so on, to form a circle. The governing number was a form of praise: 'he is three-three, he is three roads coming into one, he is one road branching into three. The red is blood, the black, darkness. Also red is the devil.' We have come some distance from the straightforward allusion to the tears of shame on the day Ela expelled Eshu from the human community. Satanic colors filter in. They reflect a Christian misreading of Eshu probing, with provocation and surprise, the depths of our moral being. Christian and Yoruba symbolism are strongly mixed now in Brazil, particularly in the Umbanda fusion faith, centered in the south. Here Exu [Eshu] appears with a pitchfork, tail and horns. But his original imagery rests intact in certain religious centers noted for their purity, especially the one governed by Balbino de Paula, in Lauro de Freita.

What I hope I have shown thus far in this chapter is that there are several universes of Yoruba art in existence in the modern world. A classical religion, served in Nigeria and Benin, and a creole religion, served in the black New World.

Now let us return to the compound of the late Araba of Lagos, one of the great sources of the lore of Yoruba divination poetry in this century, and listen to what turned out to be a final testimony on the meaning of the iconography of some of the major deities.

Araba refreshes our sense of art for Eshu, wearer of the long tailed headdress, as a sculpture of provocation.

When Eshu arrived upon the earth, he arrived as a child. He collected some pebbles inside his calabash. He was carrying the calabash to the homes of the privileged and the rich. He asked all the rich, to bring what they could share, and carry it to the cross-roads. There less fortunate people could get something to eat. The haughty, who refused to share—Eshu threw stones at their compounds. Immediately these houses were consumed by a strange heat and burst into flames.

So people started bringing all that they had and soon everybody was eating from these gifts. Dogs were eating. Pigs were eating. Chickens were eating. Aje Shaluga, god of money, appeared and brought out a wealth of cowries and everyone was glaring at him [out of jealousy]. Some people started exchanging surplus food for cowries. And Eshu got some of these cowries and made a garment out of them. That is why to this day we say that Eshu is Master-of-Money. Ifá also says that the money-strands, worn about the trickster's shoulders, are called *ogbara owó eyo,* 'a pelting rain of money, a torrent of money, like the torrents which flow after a heavy rain'.

This myth nuances our understanding of Eshu. His cowrie emblems associate him with the birth of marketing. He saved the world from its first problem, lack of capital. Eshu, emerging as a child, relates to various images of diminutive size in his program of sculpture.

Such is the complexity of this problematic deity that we can enter, at almost any point and discover nuances. Another myth, which Araba shared, explained the mound of laterite into which is adfixed a wooden representation of Eshu's phallus in a state of sexual excitement.

It is told Eshu fled into a lateritic mound, when once he and Obaluaiye were fighting. There was a mighty dance in the house of Obatala. Obaluaiye was dancing, joyous and celebrating., but one leg was lame. Eshu laughed at his infirmity. Enraged, Obaluaiye swore to destroy him. They began to fight. Eshu did not win. On the contrary, Obaluaiye pierced and wounded his body.

At first it seemed Eshu was the victor. He succeeded in driving Obaluaiye out of the city. Obaluaiye escaped [to the house of] Ogún. He went on to Bariba country, north of Yorubaland, and met Inako, his mother and married a Bariba citizen. There he learned the dread medicines that cause disease, or as they say, make earth-heat-up. After he was made knowledgeable in all this he returned to try his skill on his enemy, Eshu. He inflicted him with smallpox. Flies swarmed about the sores of Eshu. That is why Eshu fled into the mound of laterite, the *yangi,* to hide his pock-marked body. That is why he appears in raffia, as Ejiwa, in Lagos to hide what happened to his body when Obaluaiye's earth-inflaming medicines took effect.

In Eshu-in-the-laterite, we see other qualities. He loves women to excess. And thus we praise him, as we insert his wooden phallus, as 'erection of all erections'.

At that moment in our conversation [3 January 1983] we were interrupted by a servitor bearing a tray of beads. Araba began to talk about their color and their meanings. I took this down too, knowing that a fieldworker who cannot handle interruptions, in the vibrant bustle of an African compound, had best go into some other profession. In any event, he began to talk about beads, like a flash-forward to what I learned a year later in Bahia. He was repeating prior themes we had discussed. Again, a taste for repetition is best acquired in African iconology, for the second or third or fourth time a story is repeated may be the time that the vital missing element of explanation finally emerges.

Red and white beads are *kele,* sign of Shango, sign of hard world/cool world, the unities of our father. The pure white beads for Orishaala are a sign of harmony [recall the Afro-Bahian vision of peace symbolized by their color]. Orishaanla is an elder among orisha. White-haired, we call him father and make his beads pure white. They stand both for the whiteness of his hair and the peace and understanding which only he can effect. *Sesefun* symbolize Orishaanla, creating harmony among all orisha, as arch-divinity.

In contrast, the maroon beads of Oya, tempetuous wife of Shango and orisha of the whirlwind and the river Niger, symbolize 'hard things among married couples, themselves hard people' [cf. Pai Costa's remark that Oya liked maroon because she was fond of dangerous things and liked to live alone] Dejo Afolayan, a Yoruba linguist, in glossing the Araba on this point points out a hidden paradox. One of the components of the word, *jolo,* means 'softness', or 'smoothness', as in an amiable relationship. So the harshness in the beads, he says, is only apparent. We wear 'hard beads' to advocate, by contrast, and by inner pun, peace and harmonious living in a state of marriage. But Araba said *mojolo* were for 'hard people' who were angry all the time and enjoyed it.

We sipped some lager and returned to the discussion. He led the argument to the nature of the goddess of sweet water, Oshun. First, he made clear that the splendor of her nobility is symbolized by mighty staffs of brass encircled with jingling bracelets made of the same yellowish metal. This we call, he said, *opá osun pèlú ide owo.* When Oshun married the god of divination, he explained, she did so many fabulous things for him that he praised her as 'Ore Yeye O!'. The god of divination loved her so much he said she should have a staff of power just as he had one, and that she should walk about with this privileged symbol. And it was done.

Araba discussed Oshun's famous shrine in the city of Oshogbo. He used Pierre Verger's photograph of two servitors seated in front of the main altar as the basis of his discussion. He noted the placement of striped cloth upon the wall behind the altar. House decoration in ancient times, he said, consisted of putting rich cloth on the walls when, as he put it, 'the house was not as glamorous as in heaven' [nigbati ara ilé kò dán bi ti ode orun.] You see an image of a leopard in the middle of the wall. This stands for the Male Leopard, Ifá, with the Female Leopard, Oshun, his wife.

Suddenly, he was talking about initiation into the Yoruba religion. The special relation of Oshun to the image of the leopard explained the intensity of the dotting (the spots of the feline) on sculpture rendered in her honor both in Oshogbo and in Bahia. 'White dots on a person or a statue are a sign of the time when Orunmila [deity of divination] turned into a leopard. This applies to all orisha for they are children of the leopard. The source of this is odu ifa, Ofinran Ekun. It's the one that says this, that this is known'.

The vertical or horizontal marks put on images of the orisha or their followers, when they are initiated, also relate to leopards. Some of these lines, he added, are cat-whiskers. (One thinks at once of that motif on the famous Olokun Walode terracotta head from remote Yoruba antiquity in Ile-Ife. Doubtless the association linking gods to servitors to felines is very, very old. It stems from the deepest rendering of Yoruba iconography).

The feline motif came with the Yoruba to Cuba and New York. In his study of the Yoruba religion in New York City, George Edward Brandon, [*The Dead Sell Memories: An Anthropological Study of Santería In New York City,* Ann Arbor, University Microfilms, 1983: pp. 398-9] ran full tilt into this aspect of Yoruba symbolism. At the moment of initiation a person is ritually marked, in a rite called *finfin okan* [lining or spotting]. This is a continuity of the belief Araba Eko was describing. As these marks and spots are applied to the ini-

tiate, singing explains what the action means: 'spotting changes one into a leopard / mother changes into a leopard / father changes into a leopard / leopard signs, cut or dotted one by one / Elegua becomes a leopard today.' In other words, *finfin,* the sacred spotting, 'makes the [initiate], his godparents, and Elegua all kings', for the leopard is a sovereign.

The feline icon is easy to overlook in a photograph of an altar for Yemoja, goddess of the water, in Ibadan. A central image towers above the others and wears a rich swath of cloth 'because Yemoja has many cloths as a sign of Gelede', the dance society studied by the Drewalls. Cloth cascades down from the head of another image because 'it's Yemoja who gave birth to Efe-Gelede and to Tetede', i.e. various personifications of that clothloving ritual.

Right in the middle of the altar stands a china image of a cat. Here, according to Araba Eko, feline imagery is scaled down to a domestic level. He said that the cat [*ologbo*] is an animal that Yemoja used to keep her house in order. Cat would bring her bush-rat, to fill out all her stews. Toby Jugs were also on the altar. Araba did not see these images as Western inspite of their provenance. 'Yemoja gave birth to many children and she celebrated them by daubing them with white powder or with camwood and that's why these images look like white people but they aren't really. Children usually surround her, that's the point'.

We were interrupted by a mother with a sick child, brought in for treatment. The iconologist became a doctor. I watched in amazement as he administered a strong traditional medicine. This drove a long and dangerous-looking worm out of the body of the child. He calmly wound this horror around an implement, administered Western antiseptic, and dismissed the relieved-looking child and parent. He resumed our conversation. (Parenthetically, I might add, that in these last years of his life the Araba had suffered a stroke. But this did not stop the flow or brilliance of his mind. He simply wrote, in Yoruba, directly into my notebooks whatever he wished to say. Our conversation was a mixture of my words, spoken, and his, written.)

Curing the child got him thinking about medicine and disease. He wanted me to take down further commentary from Ifá on the deity of pestilence and disease, Obaluaiye. He drew an *ajere shoponnon,* an inverted half-sphere of terracotta punctured with myriad small holes, like a fugitive from a strange sprinkler system. This is the example, he said. This is the example of a person breaking out in spots. This is a symbol of the disease that Obaluaiye throws on the body of a person. Obaluaiye works his dread medicine. The medicine has its own name, Earth-Heats-Up. He takes this medicine and throws it on the ground or on the verandah. [The main ingredient: black *imu* seeds]. He sweeps the seeds and they are gathered by the wind and become Earth-Heats-Up. No one in the whole world knows the basis of this medicine and that's why they call him Lord, Master of the World [obaluaiye].

We talked about other matters on the last day I saw him, 5 January 1983. I have recorded the following: let me leave you this, he said. I know you will take it where people are interested in learning about our religion and so let them know. I want to talk about the chameleon, a very powerful example in our relation with the orisha.

The chameleon holds *ashe* in the power of transformation. He holds *ashe* in the power to change color, just as the Gaboon viper and the other serpents, who yearly change their skins, surpass other spirits in power. When he uses his unusual eye to see, when he uses his inner heart to think [when he meditates] when he thinks of something, he will change his color to match the perception.

Chameleon is the son of Orishaanla. He was there at the beginning, when the god of the sea and the other orisha were fighting for supremacy. And he survived. Because he was wise enough to appease all dangerous forces. He went to a diviner and he learned the sacrifices used to appease orisha. And this is what we learn from him—that the sacrifices used to cool the orisha are what the orisha use to uplift mankind. Blessings become truth.

Manuel Mendive is a black Cuban painter who was born on the 15th of December 1944 in Luyano. This was the same Havana barrio, Gerardo Mosquera tells us, in his *Explorations In Cuban Visual Tradition,* 1983, where Wifredo Lam lived for a few months in 1942. But unlike the world-famous Cuban modernist, Mendive's art is a direct transcription of the visual traditions of the Yoruba. He knows the secrets of the chameleon. Operating in the medium of Western painting he spends a certain portion of his life serving the orisha with what might be termed sacrificial paintings. And they in turn, in meaning-drenched forms and colors, uplift mankind.

Mosquera identifies two main periods to his style. The first period, dating from c. 1962 to 1968, is characterized by painting on wooden boards. Mendive also appliqued small wooden silhouettes and figures to these boards.

This was his most Yorubaizing period, sometimes lightened with amazing touches of humor.

Then came the trauma of an accident, in 1968. A bus ran over his foot, maiming him for life. Mosquera remarks, from this point on, a gradual thematic shift towards themes taken from ordinary life and history. But love of things Yoruba remains in place. In November 1986 I saw him at the opening of an exhibition of art at the IInd Biennial in Havana. Onlookers stared mystified at an empty plot of earth, taking this entry, perhaps, for a severely minimalist earthwork. Suddenly Yoruba bata drums sounded outside the museum. Mendive's *séquito* of followers marched into the exhibition. Their faces were painted in the style of his paintings. And a live tortoise, sacred to certain orisha, was released in the framed square of earth, animating the space with its careful motion.

Some persons assume 'modernist primitivism' occurred only once. That would mean that, for example, Picasso visiting the Trocadéro, Henry Moore visiting the British Museum, and what they learned before the powerful objects in those places, was now a closed issue. In fact, the chapter is eternally open. Manuel Mendive occupies an important position in that history. In the early 'sixties, when his style was forming, Mendive visited the library of the Institute of Ethnology and Folklore of the Academy of Sciences in Havana. He wanted to steep himself in Afro-Cuban lore. One of the first indications of how much he had learned, how effortlessly he was able to condense these lessons, was a painting from the early 'sixties called *The Birth of Oshun.*

The *Birth of Oshun* is put together with a logic which indicates knowledge of Yoruba carved doors and / or knowledge of Yoruba-influenced bricolage among the santero altars of Havana. The sides of the composition are framed with strong zig-zags, spotted as if they were leopards and lightning at the same time. He is clearly praising the association of Oshun with love, for one of the horizontal bands which compose this work is devoted to an alternation of male and female sexual signs. In the largest panel, a boat bears the arch-divinity, Obatalá, clearly identified by cascading hair of the purest white. Obatala discovers Oshun in the water.

In a work dating from 1967/68, he returns to the theme of Oshun. This time he focuses on a *camino* or avatar known as Oshun kole. Oshun kole flies to heaven with her vulture to ask God to save the world by bringing rain. Below all humanity patiently kneels, praying. The seriousness of their condition is underlined by the unprecedented dotting of the landscape with black. This is negative *finfin,* frightening in its departure from the white dotting of initiation. Black dotting says the world is dying. And yet, modulating the ancient symbolisms to his own purposes, he dots and spots the supplicants with specks of gold.

Above, golden rain already is falling. God has been appeased. Oshun is believed to be so beautiful that she has no need of further argument, as Lydia Cabrera memorably described her in a book published in 1948, *Porqué.* She reappears in another painting by Mendive called *Endokos.* Multiple copulations is what this means, in creole Yoruba. This painting makes explicit what is implied in the *Birth of Oshun.* Now even butterflies take part in a massive copulation. At summit we find Shango and Oshun, seated. Coquettishly, Oshun crosses her arms before her body, saying no—at this point—to the advances of the thundergod. His body is a spot-

ted feline and his red trousers bear the same motif. She of course is dressed entirely in gold. And the whole world responds to her call to the pleasures of sexual passion. In the process, an elephant makes love to a woman, a man seduces a butterfly, a bird mounts a human. And, at the bottom of the composition, the god of thunder and the goddess of love finally combine in pleasure.

Mendive seems embarked on a chameleon-like odyssey of transformation. If Osanyin, deity of herbalism, has the power to communicate with insect life, hearing, with his tiny ear, the noise of an ant walking and the brushing together of the wings of a butterfly [*El Monte,* Lydia Cabrera. 1954: 70-71] it is not that much a challenge to be able to make love to such a delicate creature.

Two last examples bring the orisha to life in extraordinary compositions. *Eri wole,* creole Yoruba for 'my head is upside-down' is Mendive's philosophical document of the accident he suffered under the wheels of a guagua, the Afro-Caribbean word for bus.

The top of the composition is guarded by ghosts—*égun*—and the image of Eshu—one face smokes a pipe in contentment and the other face, evil, devours the head of a rat. Black women and black men stare forward. From the colors of their dress we know that they are gods. Another copulation between beasts and mankind takes place, but it no longer looks charming, no longer looks metaphysical. At this precise moment Mendive's foot is destroyed by the guagua. And he illustrates himself upside-down. He was cast, by contingency, into the domain of Eleguá, the street. And yet, arms stiffly out, signalling distress, he contemplates the moon. And the moon at that moment, as he was later to tell a Cuban critic, Nancy Morejón, seemed the only witness in his favor.

Time goes on. The style of Mendive is changing. Now he uses floral patterning, as a softer form of filling space and indicating elegance. A recent composition shows the Malecón, the famous walk from which the magnificent view of the open sea spreads out before Havana. Lovers haunt the Malecón. He shows them. But Eshu is also there, on the curb, as in Rio de

Janeiro. And rising from the sea, unseen, undreamt of, by the lovers, are the watchful eyes of the dead, the Egúngún. They are emerging from the sea which brought the Yoruba to Cuba more than a hundred years ago. They are dressed in rising cones of cloth decorated with floral print. By whatever means, readings in the library of the Academy of Sciences or tapping some other source he had made an acute observation. In other words, he knows that cloth symbolizes the wind of the spirits, in Havana, as in Nigeria.

CODA: HONEY IS THE KNIFE
THE ANSWERING YORUBA VISION
OF CHARLES ABRAMSON

Mendive has a kindred spirit, a leading Afro-American artist in New York, Charles Abramson. I consider the work of Abramson at this point because it follows so logically, and so closely, the charm and intensity of Mendive.

Charles Abramson was born in New York City 11 June 1945. In 1975 he was introduced to New York's Yoruba religious life by Stephanie Weaver, priestess of Obatalá, and also an artist. She played orisha-oriented music by Justi Barreto, a black Cuban composer, while she painted. 'She brought me into all this', he says.

Three years later, in 1978, Abramson was exhibiting an image of Eleguá Laroye, at Fifth Avenue and 14th Street 'in all that commerce, in all that people, a perfect setting for him'. In later exhibitions he has fused biography and the imperatives of the Yoruba religion. Thus in one installation of the early eighties, meant to combat the multiple witchcrafts of racism, he refracted his own image photographically over and over again. This recalls modern-traditional photography among Yoruba in Nigeria. A Yoruba will call upon a photographer to take multiple shots of himself and then later decorate a wall with these very multiple images. [Marilyn Houlberg, personal communication, 1981].

Abramson in the spring of 1987 was working on an altar for Oshun. 'My road of Oshun', he told me 'is Kole. She moves where the vulture moves' [cf. Mendive's image of her]. 'In this *camino* she destroys what needs destroying. She sweetens and illumines the world with honey. Honey is the knife; she cuts with sweetness, she cuts with love'.

Abramson works in spiritual affinity with Manuel Mendive. As Abramson brings a pot of honey and places it on an altar for Oshun in Brooklyn, he knows he is adding, to her image, the necessary wildness, the necessary aliveness which activates and safeguards her mercy.

II

THE PATH OF THE SECOND SUN:

KONGO ATLANTIC ART AND

PHILOSOPHY

Man ...conjures up for himself, in play, the perfection which he misses; he builds in miniature a world in which the cosmic laws appear before him... self-contained and in this respect perfect.

Gottfried Semper, *Der Stil*
[translation, Michael Podro,
The Critical Historians of Art, 1982:7]

When the Portuguese arrived in Kongo in 1482 they were greatly impressed with what they found: 'a vast and complex kingdom, a well-organized land receiving the imprint of a single, strong civilization. There were six main provinces, each presided over by a governor and centered on a royal capital, Mbanza Kongo. By 1556 Camoens was lauding Kongo, in his verse, as 'the greatest of the kingdoms on the shores of Central Africa'.

[Thompson and Cornet,
The Four Moments of the Sun, 1981]

Art historians have equally been impressed, at least, by the wealth and historical depth of Kongo visual art. It is possible to trace four centuries of continuous achievement in the history of Kongo art. From the cinquecento, for example, there are two Kongo masterworks of carved ivory collected by Cosimo de Medici, now in the Pitti Palace in Florence. Kongo raffia textiles, emblazoned with intricate designs, number among the 17th century holdings of the museums of Copenhagen and the Vatican.

As the historian Jan Vansina has pointed out, there are at least one hundred dated objects of Kongo art since 1520. The number becomes infinitely richer after 1830.

A good deal of this art was linked to the honor and the memory of the dead. In an earlier volume, co-authored with Frère Cornet, I tried to show how the tomb sculpture of Kongo, in painted wood and steatite, recreated ideal noble personages from the ancient capital, Mbanza Kongo. Such is the glory of the ancestors, deep source of power and mystic inspiration in Kongo, that the towns of the living are sometimes drab in comparison with the beauty of the cemeteries. The latter glow with painted sculpture in concrete, with handsome structures sometimes entirely sheathed in ceramic tile. Such tombs constitute, as John Janzen pointed out many years ago, perhaps the major Kongo art form of the 20th century.

The art of Kongo was disseminated in Central Africa, through the influence and commercial prowess of the twin capitals, Mbanza Kongo in what is now northern Angola, and Loango, on the coast of what is now the People's Republic of Congo. From this widespread area of artistic and cultural happening, one of the great art traditions of Africa, stems a major source for African-influenced art in the Black Americas. More slaves seem to have come from the coast of Kongo and Angola than other parts of tropical Africa. Professor Joseph C. Miller, in an article published in Martin Kilson and Robert Rotberg's *The African Diaspora: Interpretive Essays,* 1976:75, finds that 'approximately 40 per cent of the 10 million or so African slaves landed in the New World between 1500 and 1870 began the dreaded Middle Passage at the ports of the Congo and Angola coast.' In addition, speaking of the United States, James A. Rawley, in his *The Trans-Atlantic Slave Trade* [p. 335] reports that 'scrutiny of the African origins of American slaves in general reveals that about one-quarter of the whole came from Angola'.

In prior publications I have dealt with problems of Kongo iconography, especially the blade images [*zinkondi*] used to record legal agreements and settle problems of a mystical nature. I have also stressed Kongo as a major root in Afro-American visual tradition. In this book I will continue the argument, with new evidence about the importance of gesture in Kongo and Kongo-Atlantic art, plus remarks about making 'the medicines of God' [*minkisi*] on both sides of the Atlantic. Then I will end the chapter with a brief look at some of the works of a rising star in Afro-Caribbean art, José Bedia, whose drawings and environments are sometimes endebted to the formal vocabulary and spirit of Kongo-Cuban art.

Kongo art, above all, is illumined by an indelible cosmology; Fukiau Bunseki was the first person to make this plain, in an important publication, *N'kongo Ye Nzá Yakun'zungídila,* 1969. The title of this work, *The Person in Kongo And The World Which Circles Around Him,* of itself states the essence of Kongo ritual belief:

The N'Kongo thought of the earth as a mountain over a body of water that is the land of the dead called Mpemba. In Mpemba the sun rises and sets just as it does in the land of the living. Between these two parts, the lands of the dead and the living, the water is both a passage and a great barrier. The world, in Kongo thought, is like two mountains opposed at their bases and separated by the ocean.

At the rising and setting of the sun the living and the dead exchange day and night.

The setting of the sun signifies man's death and its rising his rebirth, or the continuity of his life. Bakongo believe and hold it true that man's life had no end, that it constitutes a cycle and death is merely a transition in the process of change. [cited and translated in John M. Janzen and Wyatt MacGaffey, *An Anthology of Kongo Religion,* 1974:34]

The four moments of the sun—rising, ascending, fading, and returning, in the dawn,—enliven Kongo myths and rituals. In other words, they believe that the circle of the sun and the circle of the soul are one. Put another way, for the Bakongo, *woman as such, and man as such, are second suns.* The concept of the soul as a travelling miniature of the sun goes a long way towards explaining why images for the dead on tombs in Kongo were daubed with white clay, the color of which was associated with the arrival of dawn's light from the world of the dead, as far away as the Luba among the cultures of Central Africa. It also explains, I suggest, the perennial fascination with the flash of light in quartz in Kongo, as an essence of spirit, and the fascination of the religiously inspired in Kongo-mediated areas of the Americas with tinfoil and chrome and glass and other objects which capture spirit in brilliance.

We get a sense of the controlling power and precision of Kongo cosmology even when we look at a painting attributed to the Dutch school of the 1660's, *View of Mbanza Kongo,* exhibited at the Fondation Dapper in Paris in 1986. The painting shows some of the principal buildings of the famous capital of Kongo in the 17th century, the Roman Catholic church, reflecting the early conversion of the kings of Kongo to the Christian faith, the palace of the king or *luumbu* [lit. enclosure], a 'citadel', and another church. But when I showed a reproduction of this painting to Bakongo they were not interested in the traces of European influence. They were interested in the siting of the city on a hill: 'we built our ancient capital at a position of perfection, the level of prayer. In all areas in Kongo today where you have a hill or mountain, the chief goes there to make prayers for the community'. In Dutch eyes, a landscape, and the profile of a city on a hill. In Kongo eyes, a cosmogram, a mountain as a charm for elevation of the spirit and enhancement of the ruling forces in the city. The king in deliberation was himself placed upon a dais, furthering his ideal proximity to the second moment of the sun, noon, where all is radiance and efflorescence.

BIMPÁNGULA: RITUAL GESTURES IN KONGO AND THE AMERICAS

The sign of the four moments of the sun was not the only ideograph enacted in Kongo life and culture. Bakongo, like the Ejagham in Cameroon and eastern Nigeria, and the Bamana in Mali, have richly elaborated a body of ideographic signs by which vital matters of initiation and rebirth are encoded and preserved. They call these signs *bidimbu.* They may be written in chalk on the ground, or carved as messages on staffs and pot-lids and other objects. Bidimbu may also be rendered materially, by placing objects on a grave which are 'signs for the family', a pipe standing for the passage of the soul in a tunnel to the other world, a stone for perdurance, or a shell in which time and immortality were spatialized by nature in a

shape and color which traditional Bakongo read metaphysically as another rendering of their cosmogram. European documents, of Kongo ability to notate in traditional material signs important issues, go back nearly five hundred years. Thus on 6 June 1491 the Portuguese recorded a meeting with the queen of Kongo, receiving missionaries to her court: 'she received them with honor, and posed many questions about the [Roman Catholic] faith. And while a Father gave her explanations, she placed on the dais upon which she was seated small stones, saying they would help her the better to retain her lessons'. [Mgr. J. Cuvelier, *l'Ancien Royaume de Congo*, 1946:82] The queen was using one of the writing systems of the Bakongo. In this case she was 'tying the affair' [*koma mambu*], using stones of different shapes and colors to record important points, just as lawyers in the traditional trials of the Bakongo used coded stones to take down each count of an indictment. There was no way for the Portuguese to know the full ramifications of what they were witnessing on that day in June 1491. But they must have been impressed because they recorded it.

Gestures [bimpángula] are an extension of the Kongo ideographic writing system. A cultivated woman or man in Kongo civilization had to use and know many of them. Alexander Delcommune, who lived in Kongo between 1874-1893 [*Twenty Years of Life in Africa*, Brussels, 1922 vol. 1:52] recorded gestures among certain rulers of Kongo. From his text, recording an encounter with a dignitary in Boma: 'I saw him arrive, around noon, preceded by two gong-players and followed by about twenty armed riflemen. He was dressed in a large cloth in loud colors, bare-chested, with a red scarf tied around his neck, the points of which were turned back. He had two long feathers of a rooster inserted in his hair just above the ears'. The symbolically folded cloth, the feathers, symbolizing plenitude, —all of this was material writing. Then Delcommune continues: '[men saluted this leader] by placing one knee on the ground and placing the right hand on the top of the head, each of these signs finished with a clap of the hands. The response of [the leader] to this salute took this

form: he brought his hands together, palm of right hand over back of left, while agitating the fingers of the right hand'. Later Delcommune saw the same Boma leader greet a person of ordinary rank: the leader simply 'lifted his right hand to the height of his chest and lightly agitated the fingers'.

I remember a gesture a Kongo leader used, when communicating with his ancestors. On 3 June 1980 in the village of Kiyaki, in the hills above the territory where Delcommune worked one hundred years ago, I watched the local chief in a cemetery at dawn invoking his ancestors and asking their blessing. He knelt before their graves, and made his oration, and clapped his hands twice, three times. Kongo, like ancient India, is clearly a land where important matters are 'sealed' by gestures of the hands and body. Another example: near Matadi in June 1980 I saw a Mu-Kongo receive a present. He extended both hands forward, palms cupped and open, as he received the *matondo* [gratuity]. It was a way of receiving a gift with thanks, while reminding his colleague [with a proverb rendered many times in Kongo ideographic writing] that life depends on generosity [*kiyaala mooko, kufwa ko*].

When we review the history of Kongo art we frequently find the arms akimbo gesture. This gesture is called *pakalala*. It is a verb of attitude. It means, to stand with hands upon the hips. It is a very aggressive gesture and not to be rendered lightly, for pakalala puns on *paaka* which means 'to cut meat into pieces'. Where we see blade images standing, hands upon their hips, we know they are also proclaiming ability to *paaka mambu*, to cite the issue completely.

Pakalala is a challenge-pose in Kongo traditional wrestling. Again, in the corpus of figured *minkisi* it means the charm will defend a righteous person and throw his adversary, mystically speaking, to the ground, like a wrestler. Or, he will deal with him, like a butcher before a slice of beef. It should not come as a surprise, then, that most representative collections of figured charms from Kongo, particularly those studded with important issues rendered in pegs and thorns or blades, will show one or more images in this position. Take for example, Adolf Bastian's *Die Deutsche Expedition an der*

Loango-Küste [Jena:1875]. A plate at the end of this volume illustrates a series of figurated minkisi, many in the pakalala pose.

Pakalala with its panoply of proud meanings came to the Americas. In his *Dictionary of Bahamian English* [Cold Spring, New York: 1982:10] John A. Holm gives the following entry: 'to stand akimbo' to rest one's hands on the hips, keeping the elbows square, and sticking out from the body; an insolent, bullying attitude'. He gives, in addition, a special nuancing of the gesture 'standing *bakimba,* motionless posture as opposed to *winding bakimba,* with an especially insulting gyration of the hip toward the object of scorn'. For those who doubt the connexions between this feisty gesture and the fighting charms of Kongo, I suggest the following experiment. Adopt the pose before Americans of European descent and take down what happens. Nothing, I predict. Now take this pose before black people. There should be comment. Because in the Black Americas to stand akimbo carries a charge of cultural electricity. As one Afro-American woman told me at a seminar at Brooklyn College in the fall of 1986, 'if you were a child in a black household, I don't care where, New York or Georgia, and you stood in that pose before your parents, *you'd lost your case'.* The gesture, in short, continues to communicate valences of arrogance and a fighting attitude among black people in the Americas. John Szwed suggests that linguists have yet to examine the African-sounding implications of the word Anglophone Americans use to signify this pose, *akimbo.*

Télama lwimbanganga is another important Kongo gesture. It cuts through life and art. *Télama lwinbanganga* means: to stand with left hand on hip (tying down evil) and right hand up or forward, sometimes brandishing a cane or sceptre of authority (releasing power, stopping or starting an important matter).

So strongly associated is this pose with its homeland, in Haiti, that it is known there as 'La pose Congo'. It surfaces among Kongo dancers of Panama, the Mayomberos of Cuba and among black people of the United States.

There are a number of *zinkondi* standing in this pose in the museum of Figueira da Foz in central Portugal. When I showed photographs of nkondi to Fu-Kiau he said they were 'standing against power'. In other words the nkondi gesture, left hand on hip, right hand with weapon, means that while the priest and his nkondi are engaged in the search for a solution to the client's problem, that nkondi, standing superbly, has 'built a wall between the client and his enemy. It means your enemy no longer has access to you'.

Some memory of this assertion, and what it means, travelled to the Americas, Télama turns up in athletic contests. This applies to battles of dance, an especially Afro form of self-assertion and competition. It also appears today very frequently where young black men are performing the rhythmized rhymes known as rap. In the winter of 1985 I watched a black New Yorker named G.L.O.B.E. punctuate his rendering of the rap song, *Celebrate* (Tommy Boy LP 1006) with a constant usage of this gesture. The telling of black folktales and the jazz dance are full of this sign.

Yángalala is another Kongo pose in the Americas. This gesture symbolizes happiness *(kyese)* in the lifting of both hands above the head, with the fingers wide apart. There is a variant, where the hands are held before the body, fingers again wide apart. So frequent does the latter gesture occur in Afro-American dancing that some choreographers call the variant 'jazz hands'.

Mention of the jazz dance involves us in another relation with the impact of the Bakongo on the New World. When, in 1896, Toulouse Lautrec illustrated *'Chocolat Dansant',* moving elegantly, left hand on hip and right hand forward, through a bistro in Paris, he was, without realizing it, announcing the coming of a wave of black choreographic influences. Many of these trends, like the beat of the tango (cf. *ntangu,* Ki-Kongo, 'sun; time') came from the Americas but can ultimately be traced to Kongo.

This was certainly the case where black dancers used the

hands, not to make gestures, but to strike percussion, intricately rendered, across the arms and chest, and thighs.

Michael Kaya, a Mu-Bembe from the Bouentza area of the People's Republic of Congo, took pains to emphasize in my presence, in the summer of 1986, how very deeply such traditions are embedded in the country of his culture. 'We Bakongo use the body as percussion instrument' [*sadila nitu bonso sikulu,* lit. strike the body as a drum]. When, for whatever reason, there was a lack of instrumentation, then one danced *kamba* [cf. *hambone,* the name for the same dance among Black North-Americans, almost assuredly an Anglicization of the original Ki-Kongo term]

'As you dance kamba', Kaya informed me, 'you chant to those around that *you* are the one who will sound your arms, *you* are the one who will sound your thighs [*na wu simba koko, na wu simba kulu*]. You strike these and other portions of your body with your palms'. The whole body can be resonated in this dance. To dance kamba means striking not only the forearms and the thighs but the biceps [*mpindi-mpindi*], chest [*tulu*], mouth [*nwa*] and cheeks [*mabundi*].

Kamba rebuilds the body with signs of excitement and energy, applied like a fiery acoustical salve to trunk and limbs and other parts. Fu-Kiau says that there is an association between kamba and the notion of medicated massage [*ziola*]. Beating of the body in the dance therefore signifies not only joy but bringing the frame alive with special inner strengthening.

Given the impact of Kongo on North America it was not long before kamba, creolized to hambone, appeared among the blacks of the United States. American writers of the 19th century, Lafcadio Hearn and Mark Twain, notice this Kongo move. Hearn closely observed black roustabouts, rivermen, in Cincinnati in the last quarter of the 19th century. And when these river workers came to the most Africanizing portion of their tunes, the call-and-response part, then, unsurprisingly, this special Kongo body-drumming came alive: 'the chorus is frequently accompanied with that wonderfully rapid slapping of thighs and hips known as 'patting Juba' (Hearn, 1949, 223-4).

Dena Epstein, in the fullest documentation of this choreography in 19th century America [*Sinful Tunes and Spirituals,* 1977:pp. 141-144] gives us copious attestations: Mississippi in 1851; Louisiana in the 1850's; near Granada, Mississippi in 1858; New Bern, North Carolina in 1862; and Craney Island, Virginia, near Norfolk, in 1863.

Epstein discovered a fascinating attestation, written by one Solomon Northup. (He was a black citizen of New York who was kidnapped in 1841, forced into slavery near the Red River in Louisiana, then escaped in 1853). Northup reported: 'striking the hands on the knees, then striking the hands together, then striking the right shoulder with one hand, the left with the other—all the while keeping time with the feet, and singing'. Whites were amazed by all this, just as they would be amazed by the inserting of moral energy into the body of the *zinkondi* images. A musician tried to notate hambone/kamba as best he could in 1880, noting it should be performed 'allegro vivace'. Hambone was a way of driving energy and determination into the body, even as Bakongo across the sea were driving signs of justice into the zinkondi images.

Assertion and defense, coded in gesture, links the classical statuary of Kongo to living gestures in the Americas another way, in the field of sports. One of the amazing things about Kongo sculpture, is the variety of poses and formulations of the limbs. Such poses sometimes communicate inherent flexibility and a sense of athletic limberness.

Consider a single example, a funerary image in steatite, illustrating a figure bending his arm across his chest and holding his left knee. Demonstrating great flexibility, the figure folds one leg horizontally behind an upraised vertical leg. With this pose the image powerfully locked himself into silence and mystical defense (Thompson and Cornet, *Four Moments,* Fig. 98). Complex renderings like this in Kongo sculpture are distillations from a larger universe of defensive gestures. For example, there is a Kongo gesture, where one leg is bent inside, and the other leg extended forward *(kulu kumosi kafutuma ye kwankaka kwalambuka).* This happens to be one of the core elements of the Kongo-derived martial art of the blacks of Brazil, 'capoeira de Angola'. In Brazil, bending one leg inside, with the other extended, is called *negativa*. It is a classical move of self-defense. The athlete drops into this pose, one leg bent, the other flat and parallel against the ground. An Austrian painter captured this move in an important document dating from the early 19th century in Bahia (Bira Almeida, *Capoeira,* San Francisco, 1986, frontispiece): Moreover its earliest manifestations in Brazil, *negativa angola* (defense in Angola style) explicitly were related by blacks to the coast of Kongo and Angola.

The gesture lives on among Bakongo youths and children. Thus Fu-Kiau: 'in our villages in northern Kongo, when the moon is full, you will see sometimes children playing this move'.

In Kongo, the gesture of one-leg-bent, the other straight-and-parallel-to-the-earth, is associated with a game called 'drawing the horizon'. In this game, the inner leg, bent, marks the center of an imaginary circle and the extended leg, while the player spins, marks its circumference. This is also interesting because that pose in the black martial arts of Brazil is frequently followed by a circling of the legs called *role.* The *role* gesture is used to return the athlete to the vertical position.

I am suggesting a relationship, binding the sculpture of Kongo to the New World, in a new and unexpected way. Further niceties of gesture and flexibility in the use of the body in Kongo art were also present in games and other assertions of the self. In this regard, there is another gesture, in Kongo sculpture, departing dramatically from the symmetry of sub-saharan statuary. I refer to the fact that kicks are sometimes represented in Kongo art. In the *Four Moments of the Sun* I illustrated (fig. 59), a terracotta funerary jar [*diboonao*] the program of decorations of which included the representation of a hunter with gun, seated on the ground, lifting up his right foot, kicking forward. It was said that, in this context, the gesture meant 'kill by kicking, kill by rifle, kill by all means possible [*luvonda mu nzila zazo*]. Since 1981, and the publication of that text, I have discovered both in Kongo and in a European museum further examples of the kick-motif. Thus the current [1987] exhibition collection of Kongo statuary in the Society of Geography Museum in Lisbon includes a relevant piece of wooden funerary sculpture. A square of wood is hollowed out in the center with an empty circle, symbolizing death. Surmounting this symbol are various figures. One places hand on chin, a classic mourning [*kyaadi*] pose. Another kneels, perhaps in prayer on behalf of the dead. But the third is extraordinary: a figure, stands and kicks, forward, with the flat of the right foot. I can suggest what it means—a gesture of defiance against the sorts of person who cause, through jealous action, misfortune to fall upon their brothers. Certainly we already know something about the motif of the kick in Kongo life. As Fu-Kiau told me in the summer of 1986, 'if your enemy behaves as an animal, why should you use your hands—use your feet, they touch earth, they tread filth, kick him with all that implied'. He says that in athletic contests it is, like arms akimbo, a kind of challenging insult, to beat a person with something 'lower', instead of using the hands, 'which give you life'. In a sense, then, the kick in Kongo art [*wanda kinsi*] is the reverse of the sculptural gesture of giving life with a double prestation of the hands. We have known this for some time. Thus MacGaffey, in his *Custom and Government in the Lower Congo* [1970:216] documents a ritual called 'nail the oath' [*koma nloko*] where a person who wished to arouse, for ritual reasons of protection, the anger of a chief would wipe his foot [*dyata va mbulu*] across the forehead of the latter. This was an outrage. Bittremieux has a chief muttering *'A zal ik mij zoo laten vertreden door een voet die drek vertreedt!?'*) In any event, there are myriad ways in the Kongo-derived martial arts of black Brazil of delivering a kick, including standing with the flat of the foot brought directly forward, as in the Lisbon statuette, or, delivered with the body down upon the ground, as in the case of the *dibondo* motif. The latter gesture is, in fact, called 'delivering a blessing, Angola-style' [*benção angola*]. Undoubtedly further research will reveal other continuities linking the gestures of the blacks in Brazil, to gestures in Kongo art.

We turn now to important manifestations of the art of Kongo legalistic sculpture, *zinkondi a mábika,* fashioned with raffia ties and knotted cloth. We shall also consider more ordinary forms of *zinkondi,* with inserted blades and nails of metal. In both cases we shall see that these important forms of Kongo art reappear, in creolized form, in those portions of the Americas strongly influenced by Kongo culture.

The class of oath-taking images in Kongo art called *zinkondi a mábika* [zinkondi of contract] have not to my knowledge fully been explicated. It is a variant of the blade charm, of which a fine example, recently illustrated in the 1984 modernist primitivism catalog, exists in the Berlin Museum. The example I am referring to shows the figure of a dog [*mbwa*], a classic medium-animal in the Kongo imagination. The dog is wrapt with a multitude of raffia ties. Small cloth bags, some dyed indigo black, are also appended to the animal.

Unlike the blades and screws and wedges of the classic nkondi, the symbolic knots [*makolo*] which enliven this image are made by the clients, instead of the ritual expert. Thus, for example, if a couple is experiencing marital difficulties, they may go to the owner of such a charm. He listens to their problem. He may make both swear to cease certain actions which were endangering their union. He will give them raffia [*mpusu*] and ask them to formalize the agreements. The husband ties a knot. The woman ties a knot. So doing, they are tying invocations [*nsiba*] destined for the watchful canine object. They may tie several knots, several dependent clauses, as it were, of the final legal agreement. But whatever the man ties must be mirrored by a corresponding tie belonging to the woman. The priest will then make an invocation and tie their vows and agreements onto the dog. The case is closed. They dare not break these vows for *nkisi nkondi a mábika,* with the superior scent of his species, will find them and destroy them. Zinkondi a mábika were specialised zinkondi. Their realm covered family problems, marital conflict, dissent about payments having to do with marriage, the problem of infertility, and so forth. (Parenthetically, it was suggested to me that tying with *makolo,* i.e. tying with knots, was suppos-

ed to have been the oldest form of the nkondi, predating the period of efflorescent blade usage. One informant said it is even older than the use of thorns, fish-bones, animal-bones, ('arrows of wood, arrows of bone', he called them).

There is one other trait to the Berlin nkondi a mábika which merits discussion. Near the haunches of the animal appear small bags of cloth, dyed dark indigo. They represent sensitive issues [*mambu mampinda*] like murder or manslaughter. The phrase used to designate them is simple and straightforward. They are called 'knots tied in dark cloth' [*vo makolo makangwa mu kaaza*].

In the New World, raffia ties, in charm-making were sometimes creolized into *wire,* or elegant ribbons of *silk.* On the Kongo side of vodun, the people's religion in Haiti, one finds various charms where vows or wishes are tightly bound to a central object with various encircling lengths of wire. Remaining to be decoded is an extraordinary bottle in the collection of the Museum of Ethnography in Port-au-Prince. This image appends, to spirit-attracting glass, two spoons, to form a cross, and a pair of scissors, wired forever open [to prevent mystic cutting?]. The shaping of the sign of the cross with metallic spoons meant that the object was used as a guard against the horrific powers of the deity of death, Baron Samedi when invoking his powers at the cemetery. In Cuba there are charms which resemble *zinkondi a mábika* but entirely fashioned with store-bought twine or cord.

As we close this miniature essay on the *nkisi a mábika* and evident redistillations of its binding impetus in the Kongo-influenced new world we should take a look at an astonishing body of objects, numbering over seven hundred, recently found in one of the oldest, continuously inhabited black neighborhoods of Philadelphia. The person who made these enigmatic objects has been called 'The Philadelphia Wire Man'. He characteristically ensnares the detritus of the modern Western city, a fragment of a beer mug, a folded matchbook, a tiny bottle of brilliant cobalt blue glass, all in what Ann Jarmusch, writing in *Art News* in the summer of 1986, calls a 'tornado of shiny wire'. It is assumed the maker was male, of great muscular strength, because traces of plier marks, on the wire which shapes his compositions, are virtually non-existent.

It is too soon to come to conclusions about these incredible objects. Yet it is clear that their maker was imbued with the power of master diarist and the insight of a messianic mind. Diarist, because he seems to be writing, in wire, a journal of contacts with the material world. He 'wired' objects that impressed him, objects that light, bale, speak, let enter, bring luck, illumine, wrap, shine, and close. In the iconicity of all this, the fascination of binding and capturing brilliance, texts, and gestures, there seems a whiff of Kongo.

The problem is establishing *how* the assumed influence was mediated. Was the mediation self-conscious and literary (like Manuel Mendive, entering the Academy of Sciences). Or were the sources urban but traditional? Or did they stem from rural traditional sources, cognate with earlier expressions in Kongo-influenced South Carolina where a number of remarkable ceramic objects were made, with surfaces into which, *nkondi*-like, were embedded screws, ladles, shells and so forth. We do not know.

The Philadelphia Wire Man, where he covers wire structures with transparent wrap, works in spiritual affinity with a leading Afro-American sculptor, Ed Love. Love wraps whole series of mannikins in transparent plastic. Moreover, Wire Man and Love both like to capture luminosity with deliberately selected industrial materials, chrome in the case of Love, all kinds of glass in the case of the Wire Man. (cf: R.F. Thompson, *Soundings,* Washington, D.C, 1986).

Sometimes the Wire Man breaks the plane of his work, as it were, with a protruding nail or automobile antenna. But most of his works are just as Ann Jarmusch describes them, a tornado of wire. The level of accomplishment here is comparable to the work of black artists who append chrome objects, in strongly indented repetitions, to the body of their automobiles. One thinks of the 'flash car' of C. Black of Houston, Texas, c. 1972, of which a famous postcard has been printed. One also thinks of informal street bands in Black America, 'Spasm-

band' noted for combinations of wire and bright metallic objects used as percussive instruments. And one also thinks of the incredible motorcycle of Charles Chisolm of Baltimore, shining with more than a thousand pieces of chrome-plated light. At the very least, the time when The Wire Man could be trivialized by categorization ('naive', 'primitive') has passed. He moves where flash moves, he moves where quartz and bottles and other luminosities suggest the arrest of the sun's own passage. And he is not alone. He was binding something with his wire just as intensely and meaningfully as Bakongo bound their vows with ties of raffia. A message repeated seven hundred times is a serious mambu.

An earlier literature gave the impression that Kongo charms and medicines, minkisi, were swept away by the winds of change. They were not. They continue to exist, under myriad masks and guises. And this should not surprise us. Thousands of Roman Catholics wear St. Christopher medals about their neck. Some Jewish homes are guarded with mazuzahs, just outside the door. For every major religion has its popular expressions that help build confidence.

Hence there is nothing exotic about the flourishing of minkisi of love in modern Zaïre and Congo. MacGaffey [1970:223] talks about one lad in modern Zaire who styled himself '*kiwaya*' [knows the 'language of the wire], meaning a man skilled in wiring to his person young and attractive women. Another modern mu-Kongo calls himself 'métro d'amour' which puns on his knowledge of love, the tunnel of pleasure, and, vaunts that he is master of this art [maître d'amour].

Although figured wood minkisi of the type gracing the museums of Europe and North America are rarely made today in Kongo, other manifestations of the charm-making tradition are thriving. Lydia Cabrera (1954) illustrates one kind of Kongo charm—*masango*—used in black Cuba to give an advantage in sport or love. The logic of this charm, the intensity and focus of its mystic binding are immediately comparable to the modern love charms of Kinshasa, especially the celebrated *muselebende.* This charm is so famous and so widespread that it has even been documented in the history of Brazzaville/Kinshasa dance music, now increasingly heard in New York and Paris.

In his masterpiece of music history, *50 Ans de Musique de Congo-Zaïre,* [Présence Africaine, 1984:76] Sylvain Bemba mentions the famous nkisi d'amour, *muselebende.* A veritable war of love philtres was waged in the 'forties and 'fifties on both sides of the River Kongo. We catch a whiff of the atmosphere in the following vernacular lyrics: *kisi nini osali ngai/okomona kisi na yo/eko kweya na mayi.* This means: what charm have you cast?/you'll see that love-charm in the water.

CODA: MINKISI IN CUBA AND MIAMI

It is said that nothing invites war more than weakness. The opposite is deterrence. Bakongo tradition translated this basic assumption of realpolitik into memorable works of art.

I can think of no stronger example of metaphysical deterrence than an nkisi nkondi which Visser collected on the coast of Kongo and which was accessioned by the Leipzig Museum in 1903. This nkisi is now in the African collection of the Fine Arts Museums of San Francisco.

To begin with, the chest of this nkisi displays a feather, put on the body, as nganga would put it on the body of a sick person, already an ominous sign. But the clincher is the presence of a tiny little bell *(ngunga)* strapped onto the chest of the figure. In traditional times, this bell announced the coming of a leper. In other words, vows made upon this nkisi were backed by a terrifying possibility: leprosy and the status of a pariah lurked for those who broke whatever vows were nailed into the chest of this nkondi. The bell of leprosy, the medicated feather, a special strap, with medicated bag—all these and other qualities identified a potential source of moral vengeance.

Other horrific charms in Kongo functioned like the electric chair in America—rarely used but impressively intimidating. And thus when they made their powerful grand charms called *mpungu,* priests warned the neophytes that mpungu was not

a game. 'Enter it', they added pointedly, 'and you will see the truth which it embodies' *(wakota yo si wamonia kimansuna kia yau)*

Minkisi mpungu are often made within an iron kettle. The ritual expert places within the mpungu kettle all sorts of ideographic messages—earths to capture spirit, coded knives and blades, pebbles for mystic hurling, or for longevity, or to assure the positive presence of the marvelous simbi spirits, and many other things. This virtual broth of medicines was covered over with the skin of the civet cat. The latter skin was very thin and was smeared with camwood impasto, deepening the association, of the civet with mediation of power across worlds, with the very color of mediation, red.

Traditional Bakongo believed that properly enacted invocations said before mpungu would cause its cat-skin to buzz ominously, to vibrate like a drum. Beneath its sounding surface was hidden an extension of the nkondi paradigm. In other words, blades and nails and wedges were inserted in mpungu, tying vows or other matters just as they did when driven into zinkondi. We listen with a pointed interest to Fu-Kiau explaining the nuances of mpungu nails and blades, then, for such evidence will help us decode those exceptional cases where the blades and nails of standing images have been 'symbolically modified'. Thus a nail that was placed within an mpungu that was bent [*fúmbika*] 'increases the pain of the felon, the pain is activated by the bending of it']. If one straightens out the nail [*súngika*] this gives the enemy a little repose. But the most horrible thing to do was to break the nail or wedge or blade off, or to cut a blade in two [*tábula ntumbu*]. This told the charm 'let him go to death'. Indeed there is an instance where a Western person on the coast of Kongo in the late 19th century, learning the language of the zinkondi, caused nails to be driven all the way in to emphasize the seriousness of what he was saying. He was not ignored.

The very securing of a nail or blade is a message. Delcommune (1922, Vol. I: 97) was an early source on this matter: '[nganga] forced into the body of the nkisi a nail with a small hammer. This meant the nkisi was invoked. If the nail did not fall out, the nkisi was thought to accede to the demands of justice addressed to it. If the nail fell out within a few minutes or did not lodge firmly and permanently into the trunk of the image, nkisi nkondi had rejected the demand... if one removed the nail, the effect on the nkisi was rendered nil'. In other words, just as the tying on of raffia accoutrements to the waist of the most elaborate kinds of zinkondi symbolized the priest accepted the mambu of the clients, so bristling nails are signs of acceptance.

It may seem a long distance from zinkondi in Kongo to Miami, Florida. But Miami includes thousands of Cubans. Among its Spanish-speaking population are *mayomberos,* men and women versed in the charms of the Kongo-Cubans even though in some instances they themselves are of Spanish blood. The moral deterrence, the spiritualized militancy which so strongly characterize of the traditional religion of Kongo passed through Cuba to Miami and New York.

Recently an mpungu charm was found in Miami. David Brown, a scholar of the Kongo and Yoruba religion practiced in the United States, kindly shared a photograph of this mpungu with me. It was originally placed in an iron kettle, as in Kongo. But apparently the tradition of covering the opening with the skin of a civet cat was lost. No trace of such a pelt accompanied the mpungu. However, inside the vessel were many messages, instantly comprehensible to ritual experts in Kongo, who were astonished that much of their ritual language was alive in the United States today.

They read the ingredients fluently. The finding of an iron bow crossed with three iron arrows [showing also the influence of the rival faith, the Yoruba religion, where Oshoosi, deity of the hunt, has a similar emblem, but with a single arrow] caused this comment: *'imvita!* war! the charm was at war with the other side, the enemies of the owner'.

Nails found in the charm expressed an obvious continuity of the nkondi paradigm. They were 'tied matters' [*makolo,* lit. tied knots]. They were also interpreted as 'tightly written messages', designed to communicate determination to block [*kakídila*] or destroy [*bunga*] some unseen enemy. Without question, the nkondi process is alive in Miami, representing, as in Kongo, life and death issues.

Creole additions brought smiles. But Bakongo informants caught the gist of what was being communicated with modern objects. The horseshoes in the Miami mpungu 'have to do with hooves'. 'They mean motion'. In other words, for an enemy 'any motion possibility is tied up'. Positively, the owner takes flight, moves out.

The blade of a lawnmower in the Miami mpungu was to them just another nkondi *baaku,* a blade, calling on the spirit in the charm to *baka,* destroy. When they were told this blade cut grass, the said, 'yes, to cut him *down,* like any *baaku*'. Finding a large round stone in the *bilongo,* among the coded ingredients, elicited this remark: 'the war in this charm is not being fought alone by the owner. *Bisimbi* [the highest class of the dead, powerful spirits associated with stones, quartz, waterfalls, and the ocean] are with him. They will hurl their stone, like a bullet *[nkúmbula],* in the direction of the enemies of the owner of this charm'. Undoubtedly many more *minkisi mpungu,* in Miami and New York, will become available for study as time goes on.

JOSÉ BEDIA:
MASTER OF THE KNIVES AND METEORS

José Bedia was born in Havana in 1959. He works as a restorer at the National Museum of Art in Havana. But rarely has a biographic notice had less to do with the vision of a person. Working within a style of deceptive simplicity, this remarkable young man is an artist of the 20th century moved, to striking consequence, by Kongo or creole Kongo art.

This is not to say that he is only a 'Kongo-izing artist'. He also has enormous sympathy for the culture and visual traditions of the Dakota Sioux. For example, at the Second Biennial in Havana, in November 1986, his environmental entry had little to do with Afro-Cuban art. Instead, a Sioux ghost, phallic, towering, rose out of the floor and moved across the wall in search of a curved lunar feminine element.

Every element of this composition was spiritually nuanced, however. The formal language was partly private and inventive, and partly reflective of his own residence among the Dakota Sioux of the Rosebud Reservation. There Bedia lived with a shaman and was given amuletic objects.

Significantly, red amuletic objects were tied, at rhythmic intervals, across a deliberately blurred photo-mural of a Native American galloping on a horse in the direction of the woman. Planting in the ground an actual staff of a dead Sioux elder, marking his grave with a small mound of actual stones, then drawing his released ghost on the wall, one could understand how Bedia could be moved by Kongo, too.

Numerous of his compositions of the 'eighties directly reflect the inspiration of the rites and lore of the *mayomberos* of Cuba. (Parenthetically, I should point out that a distinction is drawn on the island between serious and genuine priests of the Kongo religion, who call themselves *mayomberos,* and *paleros,* who merely collect branches, ferns, and herbs for Kongo rites. Outsiders confuse these terms).

The museum of the town of Guanabacoa, across the harbor from Havana, included in its exhibition collection of November 1986 a fascinating Bedia drawing of a Kongo-derived charm concealed in the roots of a tree. In a conversation before this object, Bedia explained that the drawing refers to a famous mayombero song about a wondrous *nkisi* that lives beneath a tree and guards its people there.

Bedia is close to the language of the mayomberos as well as their material culture. He titles an arresting drawing of a 'pig', a work of the early 'eighties, by its creole Kongo name, *ngulo* (classical Ki-Kongo; *ngulu;* 'pig). From the same period comes a wonderful sketch of a deer mysteriously thinking of itself *(venado pensándose)*. The latter is rendered in a kind of pictorial code (a tiny image of a deer within the deer's own head) that has more in common with Native American pictography than the bidimbu of Kongo.

There is a climactic example of Bedia's handling of mayombero style, an environment which he set up in a corner of an exhibition of art at the State University of New York at Pur-chase, New York in 1986, (*Art in America,* April 1956, 28). Bedia made a simulated altar on the floor and set it apart from the rest of the room with a boundary. He filled this space with myriad vertical knives, bristling with nkondi logic.

He took further bricks, these coded alternate red and white, like heroic *kele,* and made another enclosure, and filled it with straw and a tiny image. With these two mysterious gestures he was honoring two of the most famous of the creole minkisi of Cuba—*Sarabanda* and *Siete Rayos.*

Lydia Cabrera, in her *Kongo Vocabulary: the Ki-Kongo Spoken in Cuba* (Miami; 1984: 129) identifies Sarabanda as the first charm which an initiate into the mayombero faith receives. Sarabanda's medicines are deliberately intimidating and radiate Kongo notions of crossing boundaries and mediating worlds: 'earth from seven churches, from seven graves; sand from the sea, the river, from seven penitentiaries, from three jails, seven metals, 21 branches of wood from the forest, earth from an antheap, three stones for Oshun, three for Yemayá, three stones for Shangó, iron dust, pepper, a litre of whisky, three black roosters, an iron bow and arrow for Oshoosi (Yoruba deity of the hunt) a bullet, and three railroad nails, of the heavy duty sort used to lay down railroad tracks.

Bedia knows why railroad nails are part of the panoply of Sarabanda—like John Henry, the spirit was once a black man, working on the railroad.

Mayomberos keep their *prendas* (iron kettles) for Sarabanda in the corner of a room or in the corner of a closet. In both cases they separate the powerful medicine from the ordinary world by a *luumbu* (enclosure) made of red bricks. This is exactly how Bedia honors Sarabanda in his installation.

He has given us a very powerful abbreviation, concentrating on the knives that Sarabanda worked with, and omitting the rest.

Bedia draws outlines of knives, in black, on the wall beside the altar, mirroring and extending the knives on the floor.

In the midst of these drawn knives appears a single spectral axe, drawn in red. This is Siete Rayos, the fusion spirit that combines valences of Shango and valences of Kongo thunder medicine. His altar is marked in bricks, with the Thunder-god's own colors, red and white. The bricks enclose a figure in straw, potential match in potential tinder.

Bedia brings together objects which, in Kongo terms, vibrate life itself. *Sarabanda y Siete Rayos* orchestrate, as one, bullets and meteors, workers and saints.

His sympathy of vision goes deeper than Picasso, because he restored the actual metaphors of belief. Iron vibrates earth. Red axe/meteor brings down moral certainty. In the end, the multiple insertions, the *diambu* hidden in the standing knives, form the deepest incursion yet documented of Kongo *nkondi* influence on modern art.

III

BREAK-SHADOW ART [PASULA KIINI]: TOWARDS AN AFRICAN READING OF 'MODERNIST PRIMITIVISM'

Insofar as art is a concrete index to the spiritual accomplishments of civilizations, the affinity of the tribal and the modern should give us pause.

William Rubin, *'Primitivism' In 20th Century Art,* Vol. I, 1984.

William Rubin, in the richest account yet written of Modernist Primitivism, succinctly defines the phenomenon as 'the interest of modern artists in tribal art and culture'. But the time has now come to complement this essentially modernist perspective with an African reading of modern art.

Such a reading, conducted by African experts on art and theology, and necessarily spiritually based, will help us build a fully appropriate characterization of African impact on modern art.

If African art inspired certain formal innovations at the turn of the century then it seems logical to believe that African leaders in art and aesthetics should also be consulted as we shape the fullest possible accounting of that influence. Thus far their opinions have been ignored because, at least in terms of one leading modernist art historian, they are believed to be irrelevant to the Western tradition until approximately the time of World War II. Only then, he argues, is there the kind of cultural exchange, involving artists and others related to the artistic milieu, that would make an indigenous reading of modern art germane.

However, as I suggest the importance and the logic of such research, in a wholly exploratory chapter, I am *not* asking Africans to comment on the *Western* context, nor the *Western* influences brought to bear on modernist primitivism. That, as William Rubin has pointed out to me, would be a daunting enough task even for those who lived at the heart of the scene at the turn of the century. No, the meanings that would concern *African* critics of *Africanizing* works of modern art are, naturally, *those Africanizing meanings caught within the objects themselves.* African traditionalist critics are not interested in the relationship between Picasso and Cézanne. Nor are they interested in the problem of departure from one-point perspective. We simply listen, for example, to what they are inspired to say before the *Ngi*-like elongation of the nose, the *Ngi*-like shaping of the face, in the finest pieces of Modigliani's sculpture. We would also study their remarks on the subsaharan indentation of form and line which enlivens Brancusi's *Adam and Eve,* and so forth.

In all this be it clear what we are *not* attempting to do. It is not being implied, that African traditionalist experts played a role in what Picasso and his colleagues did in Europe at the start of the century. Western artists were ignorant of such concerns. They clearly could not be changed by an unknown criticism. But Picasso *et al were* changed by available *forms* of African art, by the *intensity* of black sculpture which they owned or studied in museums. They were changed by these forms because they found them appropriate to their self-appointed role as rediscoverers of a lost vision. And African philosophers can certainly recognize and discuss the intensity and rhythms of their own art where they resonate in modern art. That firepower was honed in a world of cultural pluralism. Cosmopolitanism characterizes life in the ancient cities of Mali, Nigeria, and Kongo. Far from being condemned to a single formulation, the urban Africans of Mali, Yorubaland, and Kongo have long been conversant with styles from beyond their boundaries—open frontiers, René Bravmann, an art historian, calls the phenomenon—and their internal aesthetics can combine different styles as well.

Fine, the modernist primitivists might say, but however cosmopolitan these civilizations were, they did not, in fact, abut Picasso; they are not relevant, repeat, not relevant.

Perhaps the best way of anticipating this misapprehension is to make an analogy with what is going on today in the strongly mixed Afro-Brazilian iconography of the religion of Um-banda. This intensely Kongo- and Yoruba-izing faith takes as one of its primary emblems, the seal of Solomon. This ancient Jewish symbol has been incorporated as a positive calligraph. In ritual settings, it is written on the earth in sacred chalk, to center power, from Kongo, and other ancient sources, including Jerusalem.

I have watched Jewish scholars thumb through my papers and photographs and stop at this emblem. It is theirs. The fact that the emblem is being used a different way, blended into a context far removed, by no means indicates they will not notice it, be fascinated by its novel setting, and add their insights as to how it enobles an altar built with ecumenical intent. Most Umbandaists would welcome their insights. Some would weave them into their rituals.

Picasso himself, that marvelous seeker of fresh vision, had he lived to hear it, would probably have been charmed to hear African critics nuance what they saw (or heard) within the forms he left behind. It is almost certain he would have been intrigued by *their* definitions of his revolutionary handling of shadow, bodily disjunction, and intensity.

Traditional experts in tropical Africa have the analytic means to talk about Picasso, Modigliani, and Brancusi. They are heirs of a long tradition of exegetical richness and explication. If this were not so, the gestural types of ancient Kongo or ancient Mali, the color-coded beads for the gods of the Yoruba—all these traditions would have long since dissolved for want of conscious exposition and classification. And even if for a moment we were to entertain the argument that traditionalist Africans would not be capable of assessing their influence on the art of the modern West, because of the strangeness of the mix, other evidence exists with which to resume the argument.

For instance, Africans in Haiti were challenged by an alien iconography, that of the Roman Catholic Church. Yet, swiftly and fluently they evolved a system of correspondences between two formal worlds. Working by visual puns on key attributes for example, they linked their own iron god to Saint James the Elder because the latter is shown brandishing a metal weapon.

To sum up, if the classical arts of the Yoruba and the Bakongo were powerful enough to sustain the Middle Passage to an alien land, their strongly developed traditions of philosophy and criticism ought to be considered as an alternative source of enlightenment in the study of modernist primitivism.

Eventually I hope to write an entire volume in which I will attempt to redefine Gauguin's 'primitivism' in terms of Western and Marquesan criticism, sound the formal innovations of Modigliani in terms of not only Western art history but also voices heard among the priests and priestesses among traditional Fang and Baoulé.

What I should like to do in this chapter is simply look at a few of the monuments of early modernist primitivism and invite one of the richest minds in traditionalist Kongo, Fu-Kiau Bunseki Lumanisa, to comment. Fu-Kiau is the director and founder of the Kongo Academy in Kumba in Bas-Zaïre. He is used to metaphysical argument and disputation and he entered into the problems of Picasso fluidly, as if he had always known him and his work. Indeed, given the depth of Picasso's debt to Africa, Fu-Kiau's immediacy of argument is not that strange.

To begin with, Fu-Kiau says, art is spirit. Art brings vitality from the forest to the village. *(Kwa Bakongo, Kinkete i mooyo wau kibeni. Vanga kinkete i nata mfinda mu vata evo kanda.)* Prime matter *(ma)* captures vitality in shells and kaolin and stones and clays and ochres. If we embed a shell within a statuette we have added to its realism metaphysical dimensions of spatialized time and spirit. If we daub an icon with white clay we have drenched it with the purified realm of the dead, beneath the river or the sea.

And thus the ancient citizens of the urban civilization in Central Africa known as Kongo were as interested in artistic rawness and freshness, in addition to urban elegance, as was Picasso. Their spiritualization of the object by recourse to the inherent force within a stone or clay or feather runs parallel to modernist concerns. In fact the modernist attempt to recapture vitality, materially, in the broadest perspective becomes absorbed in the deeper and wider and older 'primitivism'.

Picasso and his colleagues invoked 'primitive' strengths of color and texture as means towards a stylistic revolution. Bakongo add camwood or kaolin impasto to a mask or figurine to complete a revolution in a deeper sense, to wheel icons of the community back into the energies of the dead, where real authority lies forever accumulated.

Visual formulae, spiritualizing expression, have shaped the arts of key Black African civilizations for centuries. Let us examine three major cases.

[1] *Mande.* Thanks to the researches of the MacIntoshes and other scholars we know that the peoples of the nuclear Mande area in what is now modern Mali have been urban for almost as long as the ancient Greeks. Jenne-Jeno, ancient city of the inner Niger delta, was flourishing around A.D. 200. Formal polish and self-confidence, such as we have come to associate with long-seated traditions of urbanism, immediately characterize a terracotta figure attributed to the proto Bamana by Bernard de Grunne. This terracotta figure depicts a servitor, portraying composure and collectedness of mind. Kneeling, she carefully presents open palms upon her knees, suggesting openness and giving. We sense a dialog with an unseen deity or elder, accomplished in utter purity and calm.

A sense of classicizing grace here is not unlike certain of Picasso's figures inspired by antique art of the Mediterranean, figures which stand and gesture like fugitives from the Parthenon frieze. Yet Picasso was capable of abrupt shifts into horror and darkness, from well-weighted compositions à la grecque to rythmically indented bodies and intense colors à la africaine. But so were the artists of Mali. Thus, in sharp contrast to the lucid flow of the body of the supplicant from a proto-Bamana workshop stands another Bamana work. I refer to a *boli* figure, spiritualized not only in terms of powerful accretions of blood, clay, poisons, and other 'heavy' substances, but also in terms of the mystery of its silhouette, the absorption of known bodily coördinates, and familiar outlines, in dark humps of clay and blood and medicine.

Boli stem from the imagination and from religious inspiration as opposed to academic canon. *Boli* function on a plane fusing the concrete and the surreal. And the point is this: *boli,* so different from the inherently elegant and gesture-rich terracotta statuary of medieval Mali, represent a kind of internalized 'primitive art' within the classicizing arts of Mali. Terror and decorum. Control of a double optic. The sheer presence of the contrast tells us volumes about the range and sophistication of the civilization.

[2] *Yoruba.* We document again a continuum running from elegance to spontaneity, from what is clear and open to what is deliberately mysterious and dark, in the art history of this well-known Nigerian civilization. Brass heads from the ancient city of Ife, dated roughly 960-1160 A.D. radiate ideal moral watchfulness deepened by composure and self-discipline. World art history reveres these images because they sense their civilizing power and the elegance of their originating context.

But elegance is not enough to rule a city. Evil must be confronted and expunged. And for this a different kind of art emerged. Clays and bones and accretions of sacrifical blood crown the head of certain lords of the dead, *àwon ere egúngún,* which are brought back by special priests and priestesses to judge the members of the community. This is an art of moral intimidation. We can exemplify the genre by study of an image on the altar of the goddess of the whirlwind, Oya, in the compound of Balbino de Paula in Lauro de Freitas, Brazil, one of the purest and strongest Yoruba influenced shrines of all Brazil today. The altar image is made of human bones and coins embedded in a mass of clays and sacrificial materials. It was rendered very purely in the style of Yoruba ancestral arts of moral intimidation. It compares strongly with the skulls and gritty textures, of blood and medicine, characterizing the famous *Alateorun* ancestral headdress in the weavers' town of Iseyin in Oyo Yoruba territory in Nigeria.

[3] *Kongo.* The Kongo penchant for legalistic color-coding, black for serious matters, red for a matter of transition, white pertaining to the ancestors, and so forth should be born in mind. It is one of the sources for Fu-Kiau's strong and original reading of cubism.

We should not be surprised that a Kongo theoretician can effortlessly make the leap from analyzing traditional Kongo sculpture to analyzing paintings in Paris that embody traces of generically African formal power (to say nothing of other 'primitivizing' impulses). Kongo art itself intricately can embody and combine the visual potency of forces associated with the forest and the great beyond plus the stately and noble gestures of courtly life within the ancient capital of Kongo. In other words, if subtleties and nuances of spirit itself, [*kimooyo*] can be analyzed and detected in classical Kongo statuary then it is not an overpowering challenge for a Mu-Kongo to assess analogous insertions of formal brusqueness, and vitality embedded in the paintings of Picasso.

Let us illustrate Kongo subtlety of symbolism with a well-known example of classical statuary. I refer to a figurated medicine published in William Fagg's *Tribes and Forms in African Art* in 1965 (Plate 82). It is an *nkisi mbeevo* [lit. Medicine-Icon-For-A-Fevered-Person], identified by the combination, of the stance, and medicine, appended to the head.] *Nkisi mbeevo* kneels on one leg, a gesture called *fúkama.* In this context the fukama gesture means that the person so depicted kneels to receive the medicines which crown his head. Here we find a kind of medicated cap which in real life would have been composed of cloth, medicated with clay and two herbal decoctions. One of these herbal medicines would have come from a plant native to the river, the other from a plant collected in the forest. The total medicine is called *bumfundi*—medicated clay-and-cloth bundle. In sum, *nkisi mbeevo,* outwardly an elegant mirror of courtly etiquette and bodily deportment, inwardly conceals the liminal, healing energies of the forest and the river to seal the fevered brow of an important person with a sign of his personal salvation.

The search for nuance in this civilization, famed for its arts of sculpture, textiles, and litigation, sometimes attains almost algebraic levels of condensation and fluency. Bakongo in their visual and verbal arts can move in and out of canon and spontaneity. They can leaven *kinzonzi,* the arts of oratory, with yodel-punctuated bursts of the freest of sounds. Yodelling in a law-suit, sounding dadaist to a Westerner, is in Kongo a matter-of-fact way of mitigating a rise in tension with a move towards neutrality, sound without text.

Bakongo elders therefore have no difficulty whatsoever in comprehending or discussing Picasso's modification of Maillol-like elements in the *Demoiselles d'Avignon*. Maillol elegance of gesture, hands behind heads, is suddenly cut short with abrupt recourse to vitalizing striation and brusqueness of hue and corporeal realization, a 'break' in the composition. Hardly challenging to the civilization which most probably invented the 'break' in dancing and the 'break' in the playing of the drums as well as breaks in raffia velours patterning.

At the risk of overarguing the point, the perception of Kongo spiritualizing art *[kimooyo]* richly imbues traditional connoisseurs and leads them to talk about the very imperatives of life-spontaneity, surprise, initiative—where and when they lift art to a higher or deeper level of exposition.

For example, suspension of expected patterning in textile design and the dance is more than a well-known trait of subsaharan art. It is the very road to spirit possession. In the history of Kongo art we can date this trait, call it suspended visual accentuation, at least as far back as three hundred years ago. In the 1600's a piece of Kongo raffia velours was received in Rome. It was marked with a strong and deliberate passage of off-beat phrasing. The example to which I refer is in the Museo Preistorico Etnografico Luigi Pigorini in Rome and was last exhibited, in Paris, in 1986, at the Fondation Dapper.

In the decoration of this old textile we find upper register vertical bars staggered in relation to repetitions of the same vertical strokes below.

Bakongo associate such spontaneity with the potency of the other world. Thus Fu-Kiau: 'every time there is a break in pattern, that is the rebirth of [ancestral] power in you'. We know quite well that 'breaks' [suspension in phrasing] in drumming cause the servitors of the traditional Kongo religion to become possessed by a spirit. Suspension of drum patterning, *cassé,* produce the same result in Haitian vodun. Thus break-patterning suggests spirit-possession. Break-drumming di-

rectly occasions it. This is a very spiritualizing form of aesthetic stratagem indeed. And it is ancient. Its abiding presence in Kongo aesthetics provides a fluent ground for a vernacular reasoning of Picasso's own love of spontaneously staggered and reassembled accents. And it is relevant. Kongo influence is the strongest on U.S. black Atlantic art tradition. Ragtime syncopes and the stylish moves and poses of 'Chocolat', the dancer immortalized by Toulouse Lautrec, were in Paris *before* the *Demoiselles*.

There is another reason why traditional African elders have always been ready, at least in the major urban civilizations, for the challenge of out-of-field criticism of cubism and other subsaharan-tinged modes of modern Western art. And that is the fact that Mande, Yoruba, and Kongo peoples since time immemorial have been confronted with foreign styles in juxtaposition with the indigenous vernacular. For instance, the ancient ruler Sundiata, founder of the Mali Empire in the middle of the 13th century, is described as moving, in terms of dress alone, across two different worlds. On certain occasions he donned the rich formal robes of the black Islamic city; but one gathers from the text of his saga that this heroic figure felt more at home in the simple unadorned smock of the Mande hunter. And so he dressed himself on ordinary occasions.

To this day in Mali, there is a continuing dialog between the visual parlance of Islam and the parlance of the traditional religions. Not only that, but the great cities of the inland Delta were by no means locked into a single style of art or performance. Citizens of the cities of the Sudan took for granted exposure to the different arts and styles of decoration of the Fulani, the Songhai, and other cultures in addition to the arts of the Mande proper.

The same cosmopolitan situation applies to certain areas of Yorubaland. During residence in Ijebu Yoruba country, I found the inhabitants of the cities and the towns of that important Yoruba group able to talk about art from three entirely different traditions, all three of which sometimes were present in their compounds. They could praise Yoruba twin sculpture, Benin-related omo bells, and Ijo-derived Agbo masks. In addition, during brief field study of Dan art in northeastern Liberia, I took down positive reactions to a mask type whose textiles were Mande, and imported, and the sculpture locally Dan. Finally, among the Ejagham and their neighbors in the upper Cross River in 1972, I remember a marvelous woman, a critic, Nnimm priestess, and master dancer who considered skin-covered headdresses from a bewildering mixture of workshops and ethnic settings. She made comments, sifting bad from good, effective from indifferent, across all 'tribal' boundaries without any difficulty. I had the impression that the Ejagham and their neighbors the Banyang and the Efik have been criticizing and buying art across ethnic boundaries for some time. Vili traders, among the Bakongo, in their peregrinations up and down the coast of Kongo and northern Angola must have built up a similar level of experience and expertise at least.

Surely one of the reasons the West has received a skewed and parochially 'tribalist' impression of the arts of the great cosmopolitan civilizations of Africa is precisely because we received such a filtered sample. As René Bravmann recently remarked to me in conversation, if we had the total visual situation of each major African civilization, the diversity and range of styles 'would probably shock us in every instance'. Even with a restricted sampling we can establish that numerous African civilizations enlivened figural sculpture and other elegant art by inserting or mixing elements partaking directly of forest vitalities and spontaneities of expression. We are dealing, after all, with a zone of spirit-possession religions. Here artists may invent forms in a state of ritual ecstacy—visual glossolalia, of which there are many Kongo instances—and where images or combinations of forms and colors seen in dreams are sometimes put together the next morning by artists. Western surrealists absolutely have no copyright on such procedures. Nor can they claim to have invented techniques of spontaneity.

What this all means is this: traditional urban African civilizations were elaborating forest/urban fusions of elegance and brusqueness, terror and decorum, centuries before the *Demoiselles d'Avignon.* So thoroughly rooted is this process—shall we call it intra-African 'primitivism' or better, sylvanization?—in the art history of the Mande, the Yoruba, and the Bakongo (to say nothing of other major subsaharan civilizations) that modernist primitivism, inspite of the fact that works like the *Demoiselles* tap various Western sources, may one day be seen as a sub-chapter in a wider chronicle.

No doubt this very depth of expertise, orchestrating impulses taken from observation and from dreams, from release and arrest, from pattern and syncopation, has given the arts of traditional Africa an edge over their modernist admirers. Surely this is one of the reasons why African objects—except the finest works of the best artists, such as Modigliani, Picasso, and Brancusi—outshine modernist works.

If African artists can do that, upstage the richest minds of early 20th century art, then the time has surely come to seek out their discourse and disputation. The time has come to listen in all humility to what they have to say about the merits and implications of the embedding of their pulsations, their vitalizing face-painting, and so forth in the work of Picasso and his peers. Otherwise, we are telling Christian critics to stay out of the mozarabic experiments in Spanish architecture, Japanese to stay out of early Buddhism because it took place in India and not in Japan, and so forth.

So let us listen at last to Fu-Kiau Bunseki on Picasso. I focus on Picasso for the same reason William Rubin focussed on him, for in the latter's phrasing, 'in no other artist's career has "primitivism" played so pivotal and historically a consequential role'. Fu-Kiau is chosen because his readings of Kongo statuary are profound and unfailingly proved reliable when tested across northern Kongo country in the field. Moreover, major scholars in Central African ethnography laud his pioneering role as the first person to identify and explain Kongo cosmology.

Now let us listen to what he has to say. Fu-Kiau carefully considered a color reproduction of Picasso's *Woman's Head* of 1908 (p. 291, Volume I, the MOMA catalog edited by William

Rubin, *'Primitivism' in 20th Century Art*). After a few minutes, he made these remarks: 'one eye is light, the other is dark. The images sees as much in terms of shadow as in terms of light'. And then he explained what he meant by this: nothing was opaque to the vision of the maker of this image. The maker had forcefully displayed his power to pass, conceptually, through all kinds of worlds. Fu-Kiau had put his finger on an element of style announcing Picasso's intention to revise nothing less than Western vision. To my knowledge no art historian writing on Picasso and the roots of cubism has focussed on the fact that Picasso, (for whatever stylistic reason) blacking out one eye and leaving the other open, in several compositions, especially the famous right-hand *Demoiselle*, was, unconsciously or consciously, signalling the beginning of an optical revolution, a revision of vision, a new art history. Almost certainly Picasso's intent, however revolutionary, was secular and private to his creative restlessness. But Fu-Kiau insists upon a spiritualizing interpretation of the way he paints a face with deliberately Africanizing intensity. The shadow-accented parts of the *Woman's Head* of 1908 betray a deep side. The shadows announce a reflecting or thinking image [*mpeve yayindama*, lit. thinking brandished like a banner, a spirit imbued with thought]. The brusque darks and lights which Picasso has caused to play across her face represent, to Fu-Kiau, an attempt to key an opening to her mind. He would say no more about this image.

I found particularly fascinating what happened when I showed him page 270 of the Rubin catalog where there were comparisons of a Kota reliquary figure with Picasso's *Head* of 1907, now in the Collection of Claude Picasso in Paris and Picasso's *Nude With Raised Arms* of 1907 from the Thyssen-Bornemisza Collection, in Lugano, Switzerland.

First he launched into a series of remarks on the meaning of the use of the medium, copper, in the making of the Kota reliquary figures. Copper [*nsongo*] is a symbol of longevity and power. Anything made in copper in north Kongo and among their neighbors to the north was clearly made to be kept for a long time. The medium, he continued, probably related to initiatory teaching, because the head shines in copper to symbolize that 'which is beyond the image'. Copper also means: the concepts, of veneration of the dead, and the invoking of their superior insights, will continue to remain.

For some time scholars wondered: if Fang and Kota reliquary figures shared similar functions why were they shaped in such contrastive modes of figuration, the Fang muscular, fleshy, corporeal, the Kota schematic and essentially two-dimensional. The reason I would submit is obvious—Kota proximity to Kongo cosmology. Therefore I listened with fascination as Fu-Kiau launched into a Kongo interpretation of this famous form.

He had no hesitation in identifying the crescent which floats atop the illustrated images as a symbol of heaven. The lozenge in openwork was simply a way of saying that since the person(s) honored is dead, his world is empty and void. His spirit, revolving as a second sun, has gone elsewhere. And yet because of the importance of the role the man played in human society he is honored in copper to show his spirit still remains. The image flashes in polished copper, in fact, as an incarnation of his mind. Finally, the strong sectioning of the face, in quadrants, implied that 'one of us is dead, our world is split in two'. 'We are left hanging in the middle'. 'We come before this image in rituals to reunite the two'.

Fu-Kiau was not altogether persuaded that Picasso was directly influenced by the Kota reliquary. Assuming that Picasso was indeed influenced by such art, he said, he was veiling it with strange new colors. It seems to me, he said, that Picasso was not trying to help people understand the [kota] image but was trying to *mystify* it with complications of colors and darkness. [*Weti fuka kedika kia banza dia nza diswemi ku nim'a zizi*]. If Picasso was influenced by the Kota image he misread the nimbus of allusion to the sky as hands, for such a position of the hands does not exist in the reliquary figure. He said flatly that Picasso was misled by lack of understanding of African cosmology [*weti kipupika mu kondwa kwandi kwa mpisulu mu nz'Afelika*]. 'We see entire worlds in such forms; he did not.'

But Fu-Kiau was by no means reducing the talent of Picasso by pedantically 'one-upping' the painter for not knowing what he could not have possibly known at that time about Central African cosmologies. On the contrary, he said, 'what was cosmology he took to be anatomy'. And he found that utterly fascinating, Picasso's independent transformation of cosmology into anatomy.

There was an implied note of admiration in that fascination and this became more and more explicit as it became clear to him how sustained, how continuously searching, Picasso's work became as he worked his way towards what Westerners call cubism.

Contemplation of Picasso's Standing *Nude Seen from the Back* of 1908 (MOMA catalog, p. 297) drew this astonishing comment: 'he's trying to express the dynamic of the cosmos and compare it to the dynamic of the body.' And he said that there were no such images in Kongo art. Cubism, to him, as to us, remained unique to Picasso and his followers. But the more he perused the reproduction of the painting, and he contemplated it for a very long while, the more he began to think of analogies to its fusion of body and analogic to his own history of art. He made me turn back to an *nkisi* we had looked at, illustrated at page 66 of Vol I of the MOMA catalog. The particular charm is a Kongo *nkisi nkondi a mábika* [lit. an oath-taking charm of contract]. It is a legalistic nkisi. The multiple rattan ties and small dark bags combined with the image of a dog-medium identify its function. From Fu-Kiau's exegesis: 'when plaintiff and defendant agree to the decision of the priest/owner of this charm, the priest [nganga] ties a knot in raffia upon the dog to seal forever upon the image that person's vow'. What might simply be characterized as 'mixed media' in overgeneralizing art historical idiom is in fact quite something else. The ties are material vows and invocations. They symbolize also agreements. *Zinkondi a mábika* had to do with domestic *mambu,* arguments about marriage, divorce, maternity, and so forth. In the case of the illustrated example, from the Museum für Völkerkunde in Berlin, serious matters of martial discord seem coded in the rattan ties and

loops which surround the mediumistic dog image.

Particularly fascinating are the knots rendered in cloth dyed indigo black which appear at the haunches of the animal. These dark elements indicate sensitive matters like murder. The color-coding here and elsewhere in the corpus of Kongo art informed what Fu-Kiau remarked in the *Standing Nude Seen From the Back* of 1908.

He mentioned again for emphasis the impressive pulling together of what he took to be 'the dynamic of the cosmos and the dynamic of the body' [*tuntatunta dia nzá ye tuntatunta dia nitu*]. This was his initial phrasing for the phenomenon of cubistic handling of lights and darks: 'Thinking', he continued, 'is connected with darkness. Whoever thinks, passes through the shadowed forest.' To him, at another level of analysis, cubism was figuration laden with signs of thought, 'using different shadows he expresses the many forces fighting in our body.' He concluded, 'this image represents a struggle in society, as reflected in a single body.' He had a phrase for the technique employed—'shadow-rending [*pásula kini*]'. We see a revolutionary play of illumined facets. *He* sees shadows, torn like black silk, and pasted on a human body to indicate a struggle in society. His point is eerie. For from the perspective of a traditionalist philosopher in Kongo Picasso's cubistic figure was well-nigh sensing, like a seismograph, the approaching roar and reverberation of World War I.

Cubism, translated into Kongo traditionalist terms, is break-shadow art, the debating of form with shadowed facets.

The full implications of what Fu-Kiau meant by defining early cubism as shadow-rending or shadow-tearing or shadow-breaking art became more clear when he addressed further development of the style in Picasso's *Portrait of Daniel-Henry Kahnweiler* of 1910. Fu-Kiau: 'the artist is moving from detail to unification—the more he understands moving through color and shadow, the more the image disappears. Like the Kongo proverb—first we see the forest, then we see the wood, then we see the log, then we see the drum, and then the drum disappears, in sounds which surround us with their pulse—sound and color emerging, that's what we love, not the drum itself. Hence another proverb, drum is nothing but the summation of its sounds [*ka ngoma ko kansi n'ningu yi kumu kia ngoma bieti dikitisa mooyo,* lit. it is not the drum-log itself but the sounds which spill out of the drum which vibrate life].

Thus Picasso cuts through shadows which are worlds. He hammers in facts with torn or broken shadows to remake a social picture. Just as a forest disappears in a drum which in turn disappears into an acoustical surround, so what remains here, in his terms, after breaking down the shadows, is the music. And the music in this instance is the richness of what Picasso meant.

In Fu-Kiau's translation of cubism (shadow-breaking art) the shadows on the human forms are the heaviest matters (e.g., murder, war). If we can't break the shadows, if we can't tear apart the shadow-fabric, we can't pass through them to comprehend the problems which they indicate. Beyond torn shadows lies the understanding which is unifying.

In other words, by this traditionalist reckoning, while Picasso was rebelling against the canon of an exhausted Western realism, he was also inserting intuited social problems into his forms.

Another example: when the Kongo philosopher looked at Picasso's *Head of A Man* of 1908, formerly in the Douglas Cooper collection, he resumed his dialog with shadowed planes. This image, he said, tells us where Picasso stands in terms of an African-looking countenance. By emphasizing shadow over the eyes, it seemed to Fu-Kiau that he was once again focussing on a new concept of vision, a dark focus. I give his concluding remark—*'kini biángolo va mezo, kieti siámisa banza dia mbweno, ku nim'a kiau mu bambanza ma Picasso'*. This means: 'strong shadows on the eyes express a concept of vision-beyond-vision in Picasso's mind'.

Again and again, Fu-Kiau dealt with Picasso's debate with the human form. His reading is no less brilliant than Rubin's. In terms of characterizing metaphysical affinities and differences, he can hold his own, insight for insight, with an art historian.

In dissolving a rhetoric intent upon proclaiming the genius of Picasso in favor of a communally based idiom of social and spiritual vision, he has added a corrective to the secular bias of modernist scholarship. Art historians, although gravitating towards issues of instinct and feeling which Braque and Picasso and others claimed they found in tribal objects, do not normally discuss such influences in spiritual terms. They have their own agenda.

But the Kongo reading also returns us to grounds of discipline and problem-orientation, not 'feeling' nor 'instinct' alone. The spiritually based rhythmic dislocations that influenced Picasso are being semantically read back into cubism by Fu-Kiau in spite of all the distances and changes.

Surely the fact that Western summations analyze light, and the African shadow, suggest that in the future a combination of both art historical and traditionalist readings will unlock a richer determination of cubism and other forms of modernist primitivism.

That history, re-ethnologized by traditionalists from South of the Sahara, will redound to the benefit of us all, just as the fusion of musics, African and European, gave this century perhaps its most distinguished classical music, jazz.

Robert FARRIS THOMPSON

DEDICATION

For John Szwed, Lydia Cabrera, Gerardo Mosquera, Gustavo Echevarría, Ed Love, M.M. de Belo Horizonte, Roger Abrahams, Dejo Afolayan, Dan Dawson, John Mason, Jelon Vieira, Boneco, and most especially, Fu-Kiau Bunseki, founder of the Kongo Academy, Kumba, Zaire, always my master.

I dedicate this book to the memory of the late Araba of Lagos and the late Pai Costa de Oxala, Alto do Candomblé, Bahia. Their last interviews make up much of Chapter I.

Finally, for Alicia, Ian, Caitlin, Ann, and Clark.

ACKNOWLEDGEMENTS

I heartily salute colleagues who listened to or read portions of this manuscript: John Szwed, James Ponet, William Rubin, Eugenia Herbert, and John Pemberton. All shared, with customary generousness, insights and criticism. Junellen Sullivan, Rich Krevolin, Kim Duncan, and my son, Clark, immeasurably helped me through the mazeways leading from computer to typewriter to computer to print-out to manuscript. Finally, I thank Gerald Berjonneau and Jean-Louis Sonnery for their patience, their colleagueship, and their hospitality in Paris.

R.F.T.
Paris
St Patrick's Day, 1987

INDEX

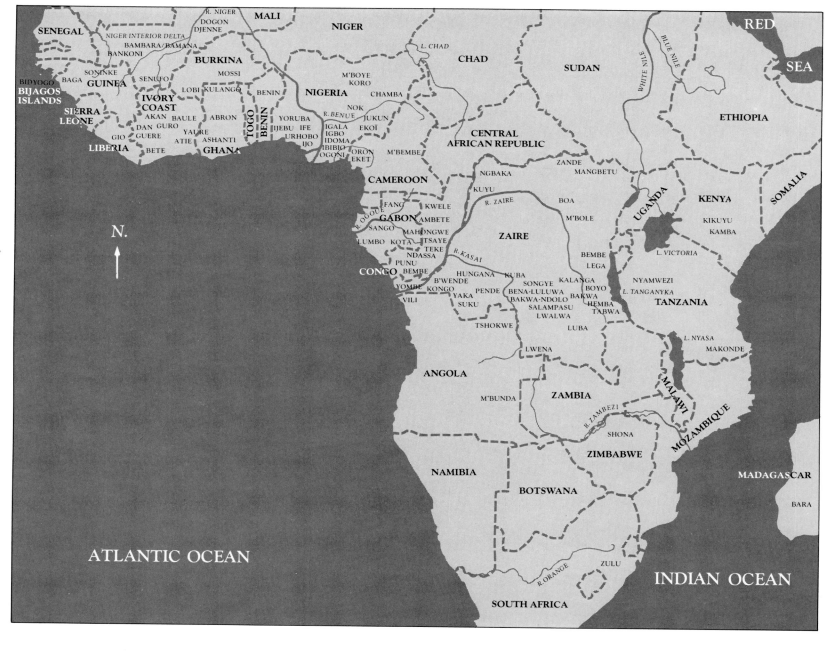

ATLANTIC OCEAN

INDIAN OCEAN

N.

SENEGAL
NIGER INTERIOR DELTA
BAMBARA/BAMANA
BANKONI
BIDYOGO
BAGA
SONINKE
GUINEA
SENUFO
BIJAGOS
ISLANDS
SIERRA
LEONE
AKAN
BAULE
ABRON
DAN GURO
GIO
GUERE
YAURE
BETE
ATIE
ASHANTI
LIBERIA
GHANA
IVORY
COAST
LOBI KULANGO
MOSSI
BURKINA
BENIN
R. NIGER
DOGON
DJENNE
MALI
NIGER
M'BOYE
KORO
CHAMBA
NOK
R. BENUE
JUKUN
YORUBA
IJEBU IFE
URHOBO
IJO
IGALA IGBO
IDOMA
IBIBIO
OGONI
ORON
EKET
EKOÏ
M'BEMBE
NIGERIA
TOGO
BENIN
CAMEROON
L. CHAD
CHAD
SUDAN
CENTRAL
AFRICAN REPUBLIC
NGBAKA
ZANDE
MANGBETU
KUYU
R. ZAIRE
BOA
M'BOLE
FANG
KWELE
R. OGOUE
GABON
AMBETE
SANGO
MAHONGWE
LUMBO KOTA
TSAYE
NDASSA
TEKE
PUNU
BEMBE
CONGO
YOMBE
KONGO
B'WENDE
YAKA
VILI
SUKU
HUNGANA
PENDE
R. KASAI
KUBA
SONGYE
BENA-LULUWA
BAKWA-NDOLO
SALAMPASU
LWALWA
KALANGA
BOYO
BAKWA
HEMBA
TABWA
BEMBE
LEGA
ZAIRE
TSHOKWE
LUBA
LWENA
ANGOLA
M'BUNDA
ZAMBIA
R. ZAMBEZI
SHONA
ZIMBABWE
NAMIBIA
BOTSWANA
R. ORANGE
ZULU
SOUTH AFRICA
WHITE NILE
BLUE NILE
RED
SEA
ETHIOPIA
SOMALIA
UGANDA
KENYA
KIKUYU
KAMBA
L. VICTORIA
NYAMWEZI
L. TANGANYKA
TANZANIA
L. NYASA
MAKONDE
MALAWI
MOZAMBIQUE
MADAGASCAR
BARA

TERRA COTTA
TERRAKOTTA

4a, 4b

BENIN
H. 24 cm.

5

ASHANTI
H. 30 cm.

8

MALI
H. 20 cm.

9

BANKONI
H. 52 cm.

10

MALI
H. 36 cm.

11

MALI
H. 48 cm.

12

MALI
H. 39 cm.

14

BANKONI
H. 50 cm.

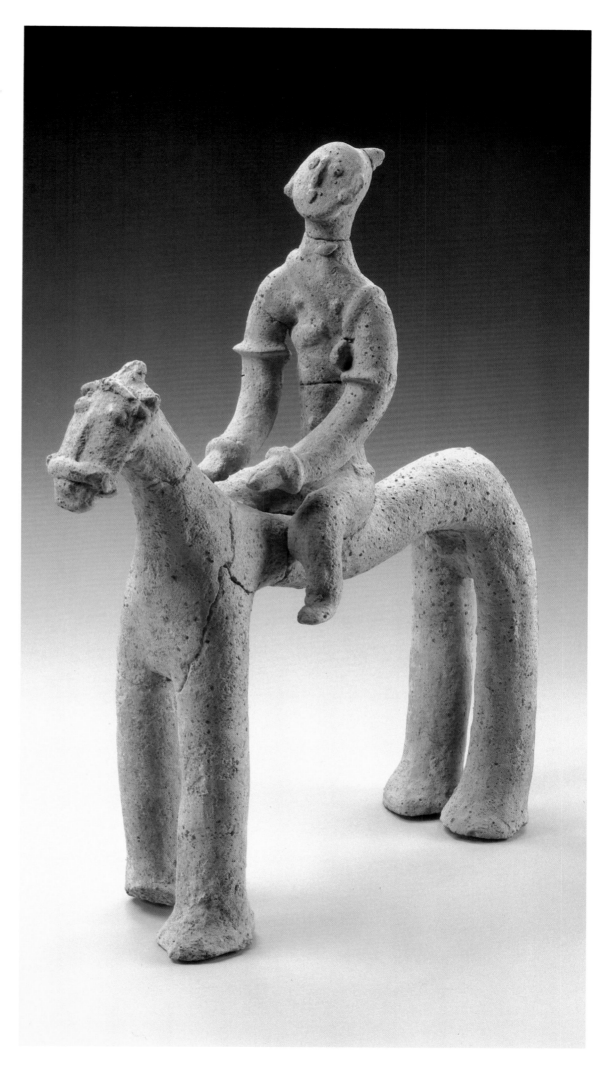

15

MALI
H. 38 cm.

16

BANKONI
H. 48 cm.

17

MALI
H. 55 cm.

METAL
METALL

MALI
H. 22,5 cm.

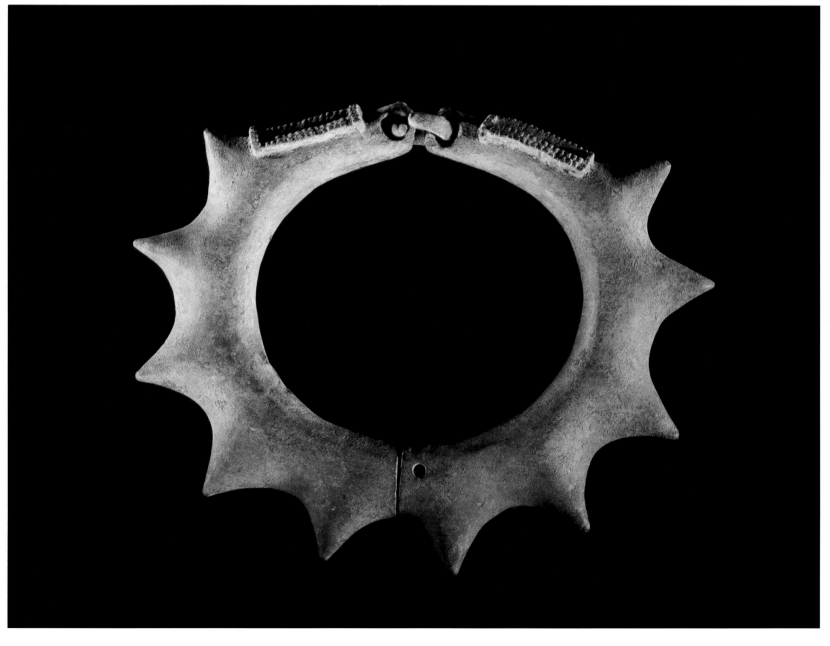

31

BENIN
H. 45,7 cm.

32

BENIN
H. 23 cm.

33
SENUFO
H. 9,8 cm.

34
KULANGO
H. 8 cm.

35
SENUFO
H. 28 cm.

39

BENIN
H. 9,3 cm.

40

NIGERIA
H. 18 cm.

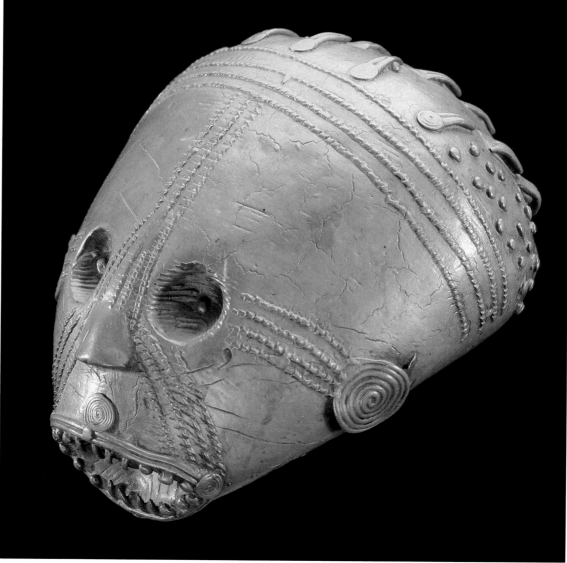

41/44

DOGON
H. 4,9 - 6,8 cm.

45

SENUFO
H. 5,2 cm.

46

AKAN
H. 7 cm.

47

ASHANTI
H. 8 cm.

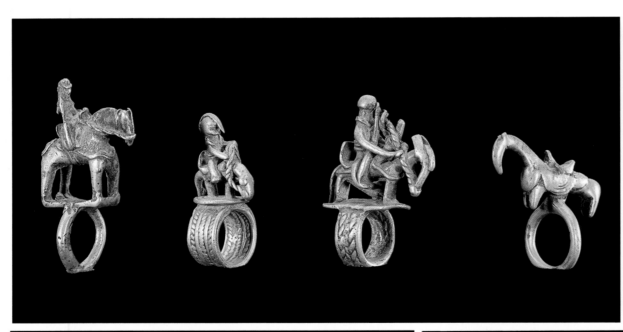

BAULE
H. 6,2 - 5,4 - 3,6 cm.

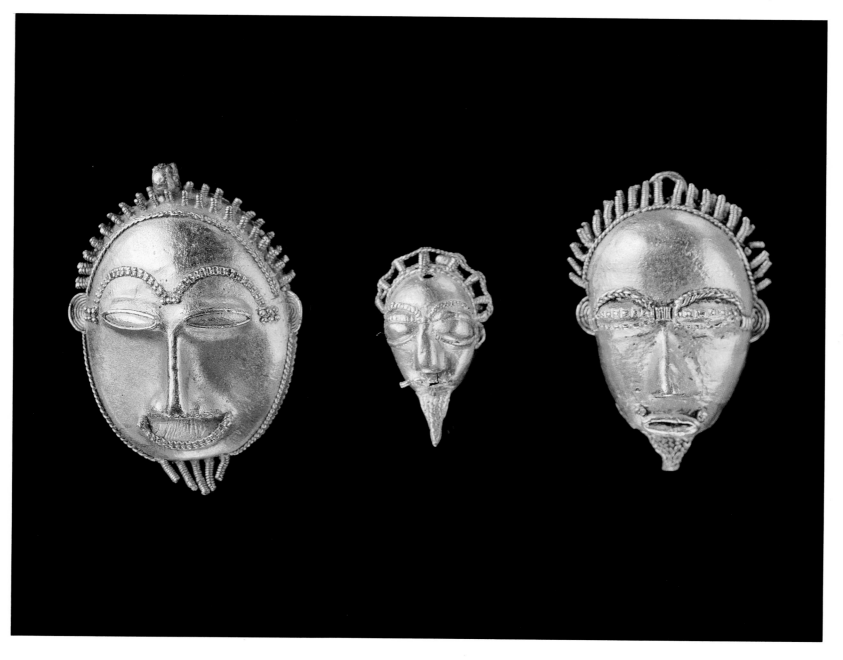

MALI
H. 12,5 cm.

AKAN
H. 8 cm.

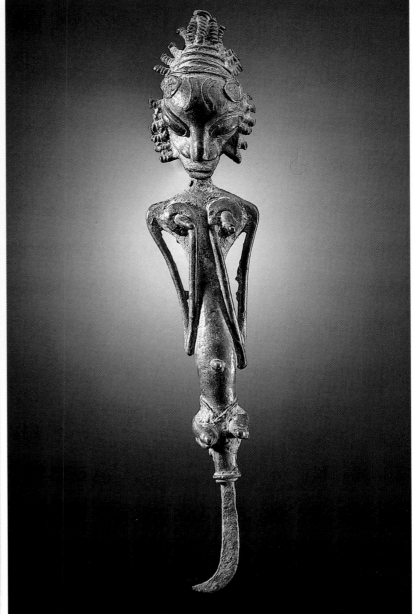

114

IVORIES
ELFENBEIN

61

LEGA
H. 10 cm.

62

LEGA
H. 15 cm.

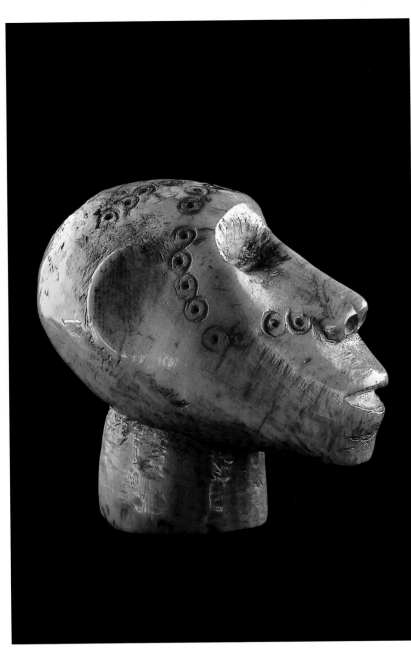

LEGA
H. 30 cm.

64

YAKA
H. 18,5 cm.

65

LUBA - TABWA
H. 7,2 cm.

66

PENDE
H. 11,5 cm.

67

LEGA
H. 8,5 cm.

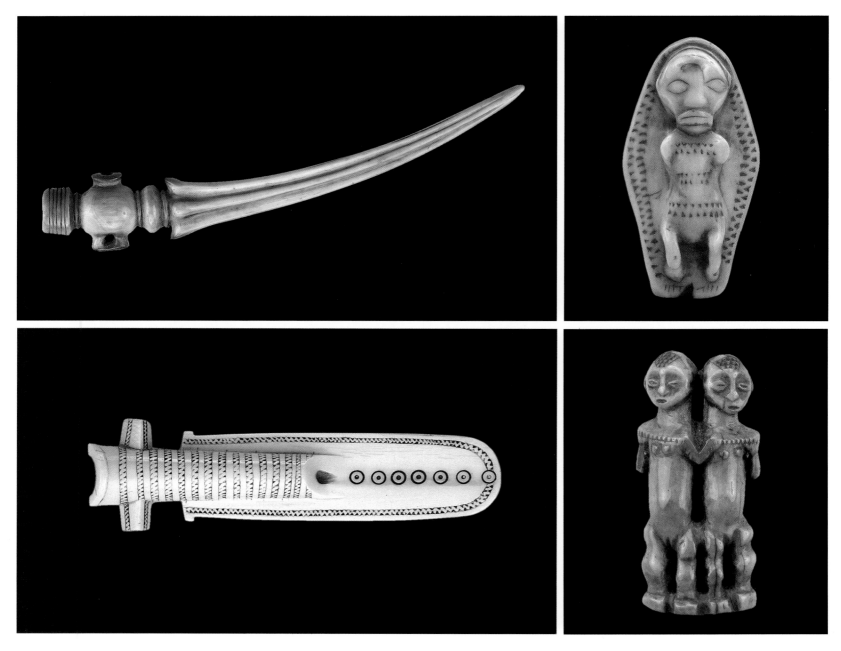

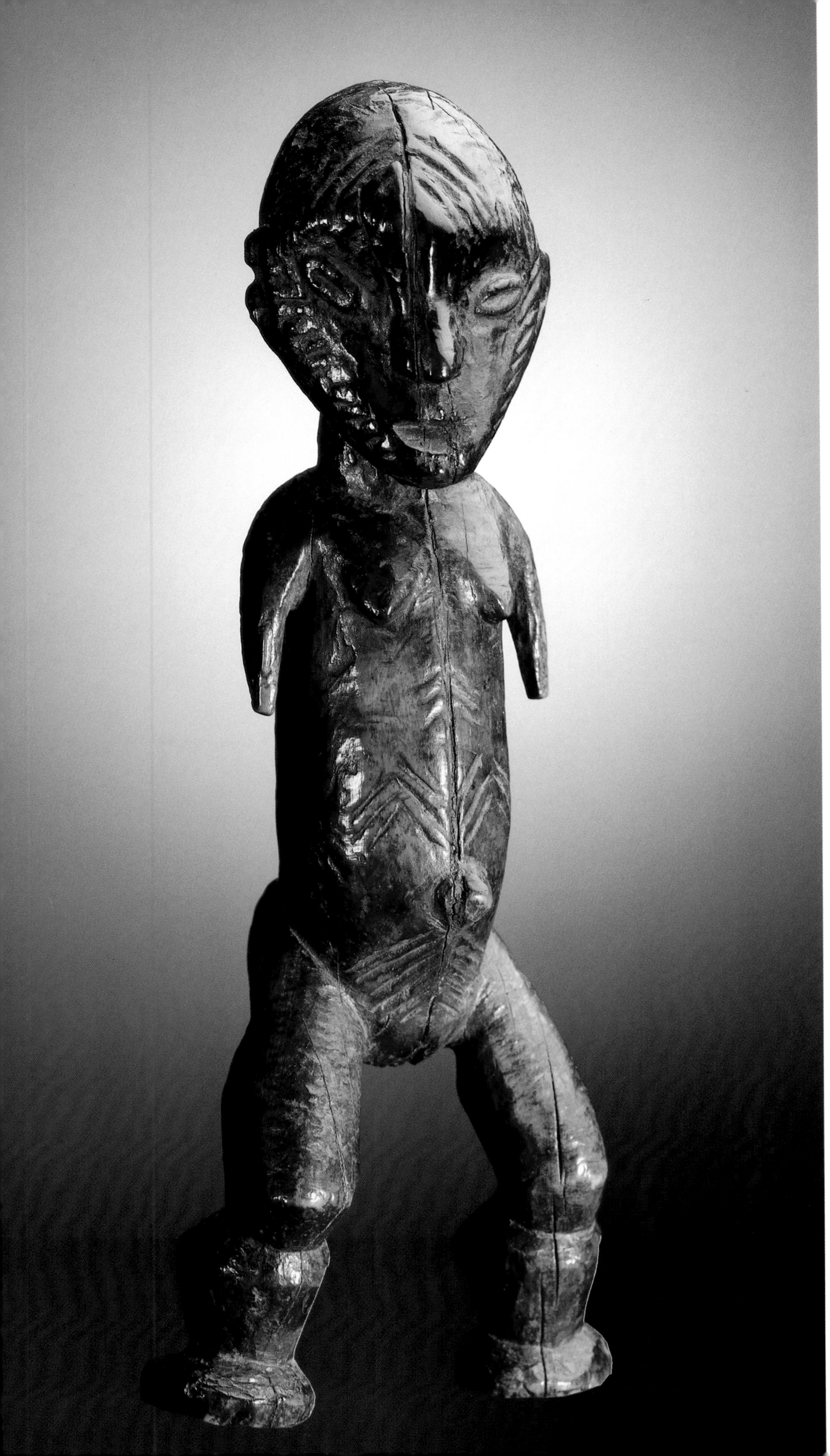

70

LEGA
H. 24,5 cm.

73

LEGA
H. 18,6 cm.

74

ZANDE
H. 19 cm.

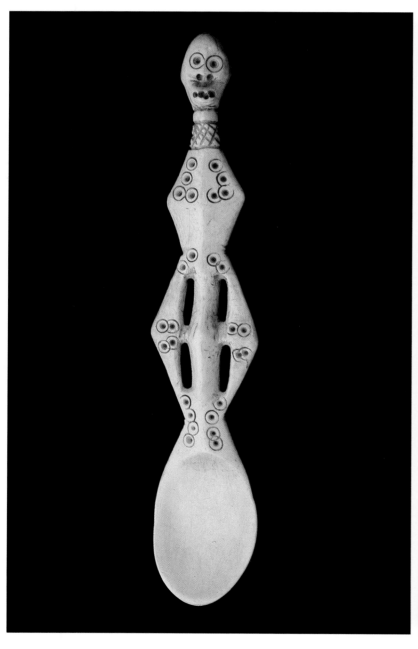

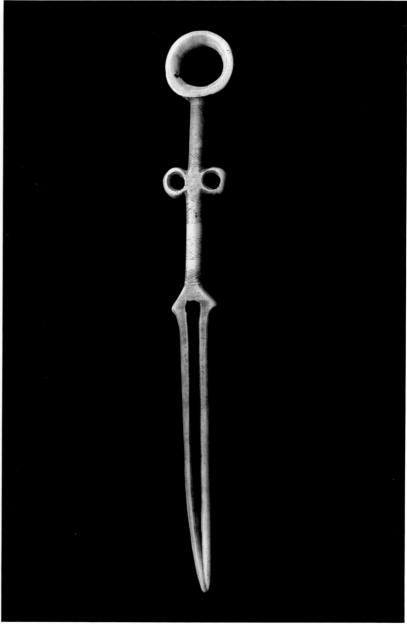

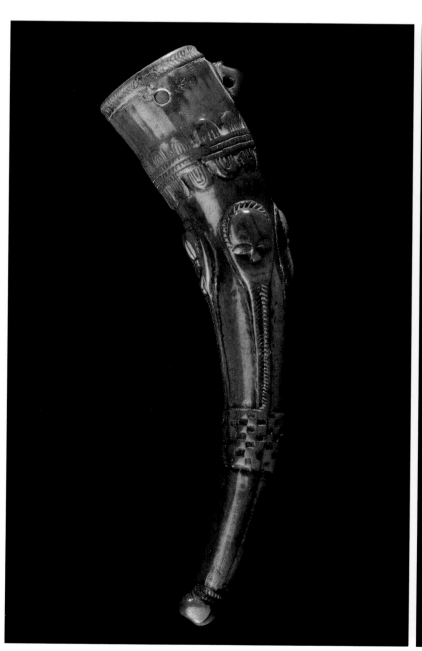

MASKS
MASKEN

KULANGO
H. 29 cm.

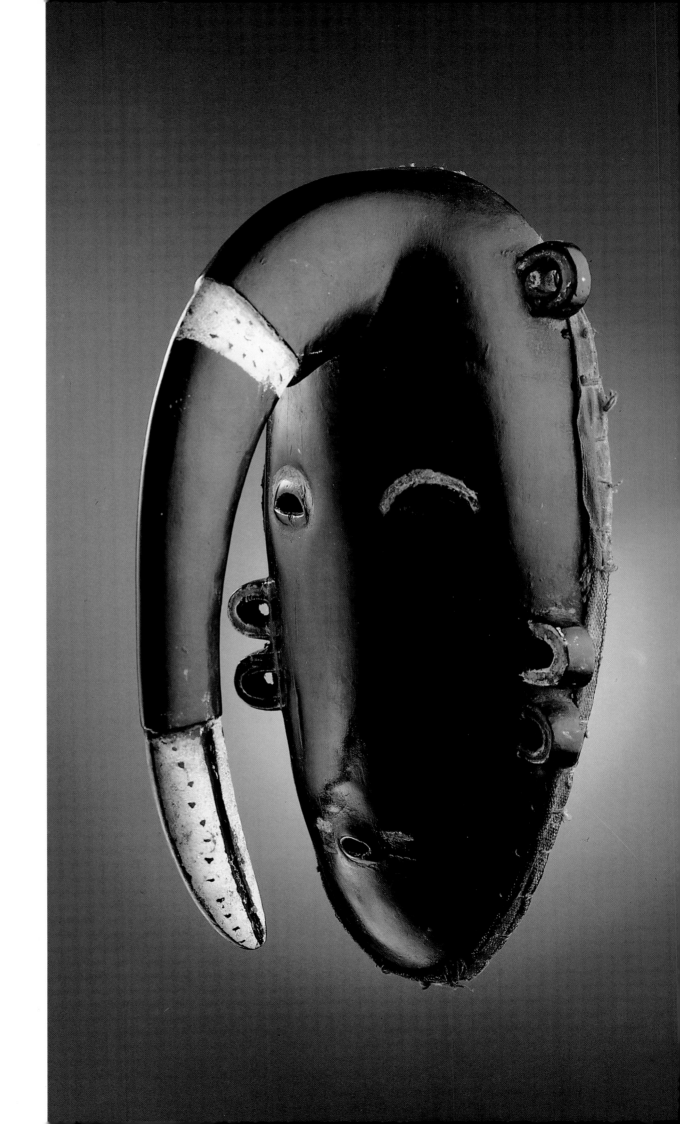

86

BAMBARA/BAMANA
H. 39 cm.

87

BAMBARA/BAMANA
H. 45 cm.

88/89

BAMBARA/BAMANA
H. 87 - 66 cm.

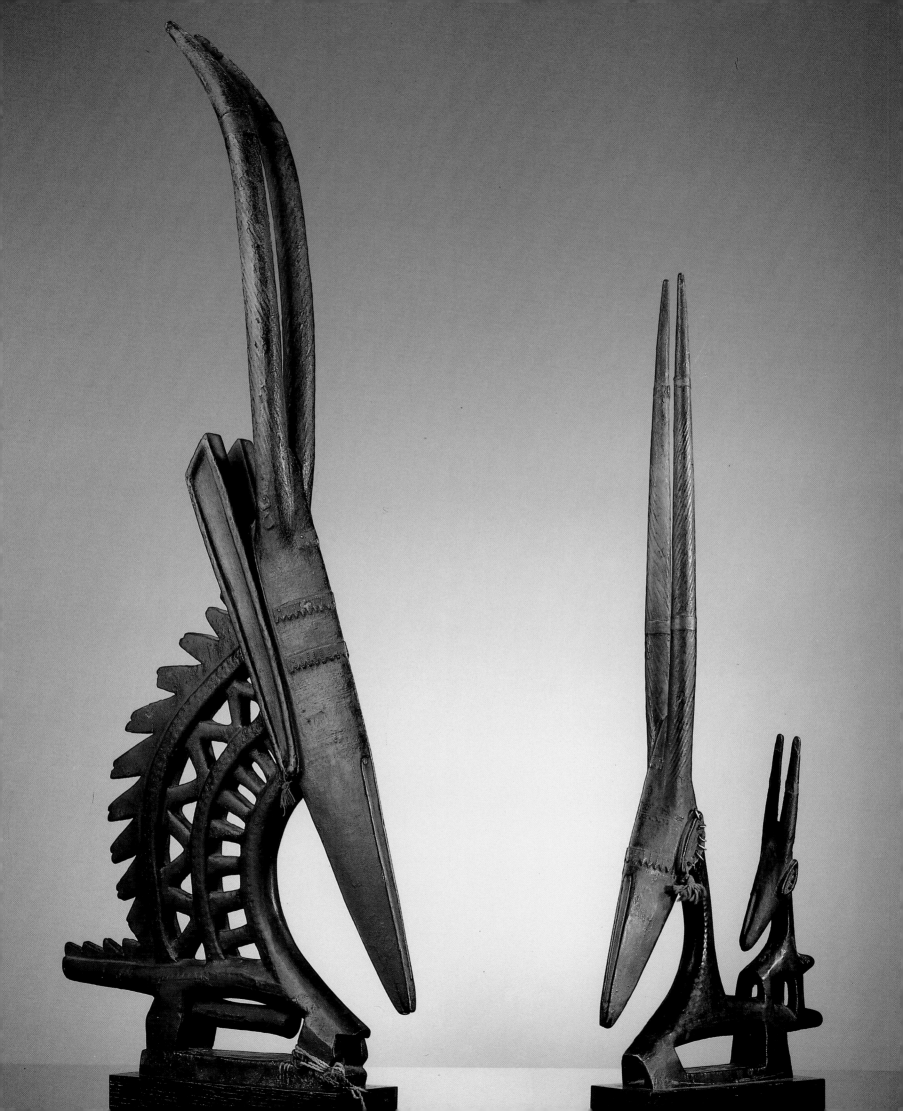

BAGA
H. 134 cm.

BIDYOGO
H. 66 cm.

GUERE
H. 32 cm.

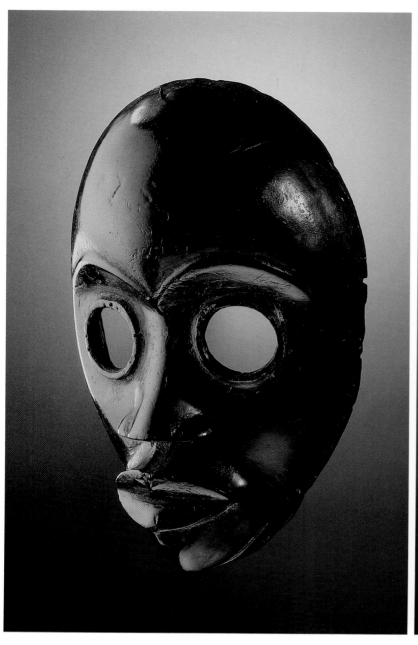

101

BAULE
H. 25 cm.

102

BAULE
H. 32 cm.

103

YAURE
H. 44 cm.

104

BAULE
H. 39 cm.

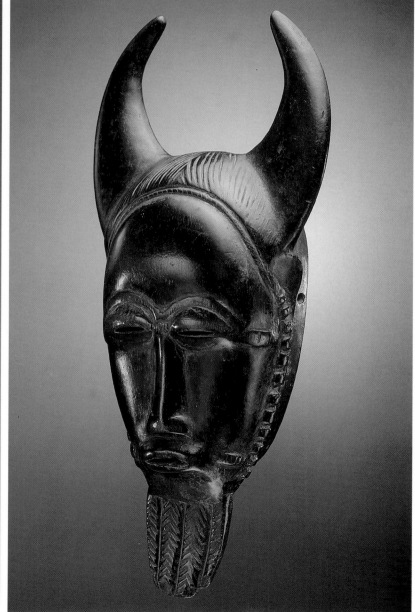

105
IBIBIO
H. 27,5 cm.

106
OGONI
H. 21,5 cm.

107
YORUBA
H. 36 cm.

108a, 108b

IGBO
H. 43 cm.

109

IGBO
H. 56 cm.

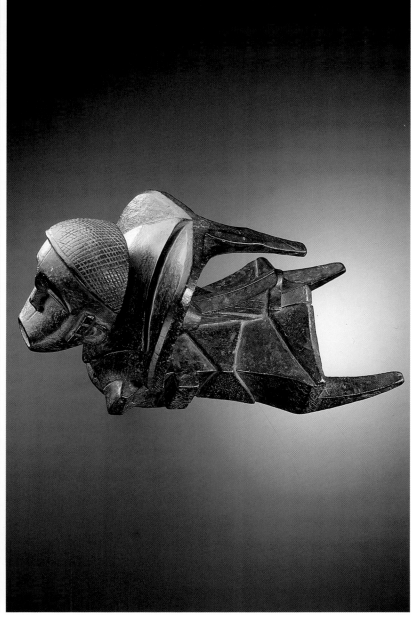

110

IDOMA
H. 23 cm.

111

IDOMA
H. 22,5 cm.

112

IDOMA
H. 36 cm.

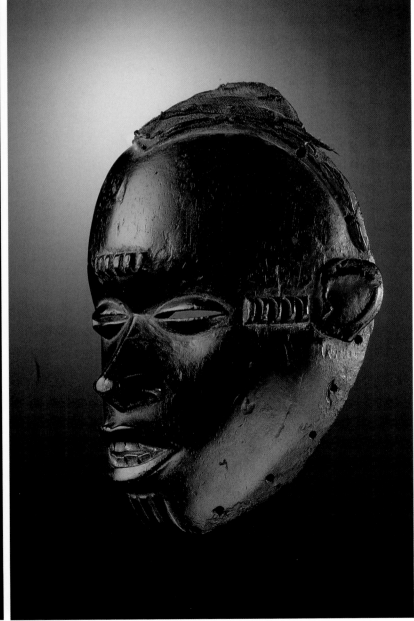

113

IGBO
H. 54 cm.

114

IGBO
H. 57 cm.

115

IDOMA
H. 29,5 cm.

116

EKET
H. 65 cm.

117

EKET
H. 61,5 cm.

118

EKET
H. 27 cm.

119

EKET
H. 32,5 cm.

120

EKET
H. 34 cm.

121

IGALA
H. 30 cm.

122

IGALA
H. 31 cm.

123

EKOI
H. 29 cm.

EKOI
H. 36,5 cm.

IGBO
H. 75 cm.

126

EKOI
H. 40 cm.

127

EKOI
H. 54 cm.

128
IJEBU
H. 54 cm.

129
OGONI
H. 38,5 cm.

IJO
H. 54 cm.

131

PUNU
H. 28 cm.

132

PUNU
H. 30,5 cm.

133

PUNU
H. 31,5 cm.

134
KONGO
H. 30 cm.

135
KONGO
H. 23 cm.

136
TSAYE
H. 30 cm.

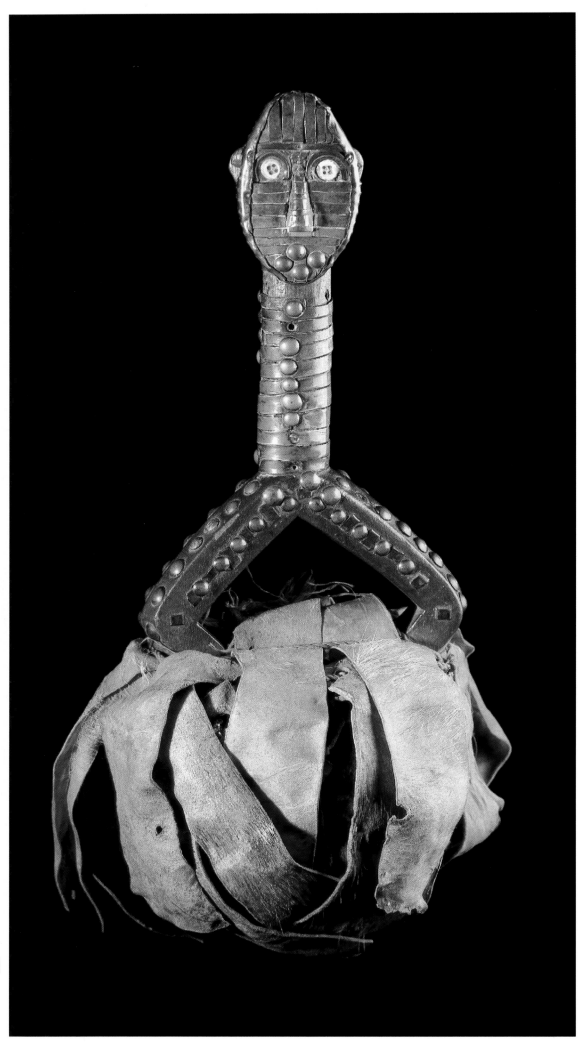

137

SANGO
H. 45 cm.

138

MAHONGWE
H. 55,8 cm.

139

KWELE
H. 38 cm.

140

KWELE
H. 24 cm.

141

KWELE
H. 37 cm.

142

MAHONGWE
H. 40 cm.

143

KOTA
H. 23,4 cm.

144

KOTA
H. 57 cm.

145
LWALWA
H. 31 cm.

146
LWALWA
H. 32 cm.

147
SALAMPASU
H. 35 cm.

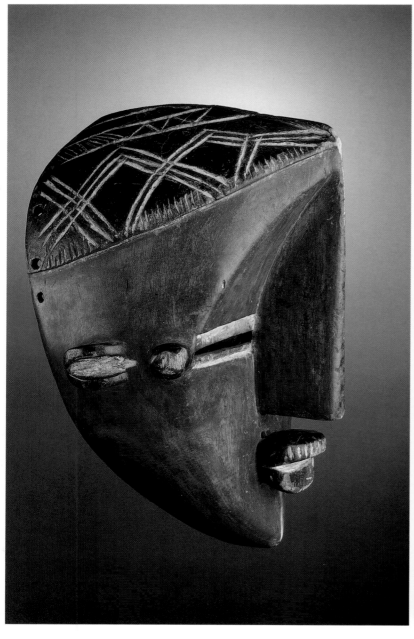

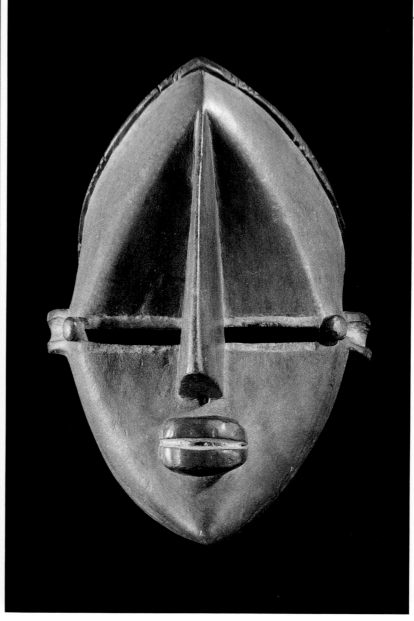

148

BENA LULUWA
H. 21,5 cm.

149

BENA LULUWA
H. 31 cm.

150

KUBA
H. 41 cm.

151

SONGYE
H. 37 cm.

152

SONGYE
H. 38 cm.

153

TSHOKWE
H. 24 cm.

154

TSHOKWE
H. 22 cm.

155

LUBA
H. 41 cm.

156

LEGA
H. 22 cm.

157

LEGA
H. 32 cm.

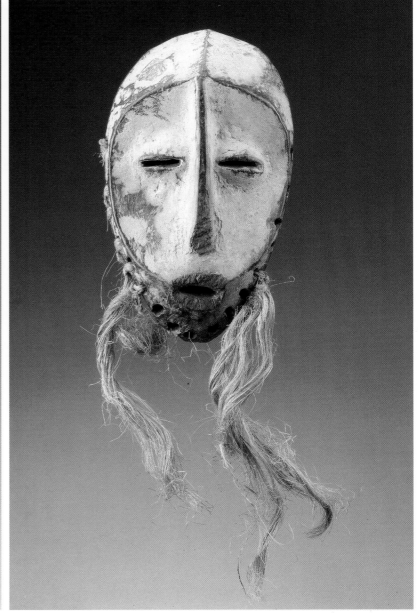

158

BOA
H. 36 cm.

159

NGBAKA
H. 36 cm.

STATUARY
STATUEN

160

SONINKE
H. 69,8 cm.

161

DJENNE
H. 65 cm.

162

SONINKE
H. 29 cm.

163

DOGON
H. 21 cm.

164

DOGON
H. 58 cm.

165

DOGON
H. 46 cm.

BAMBARA/BAMANA
H. 66 cm.

BAMBARA/BAMANA
H. 61 cm.

MOSSI
H. 47 cm.

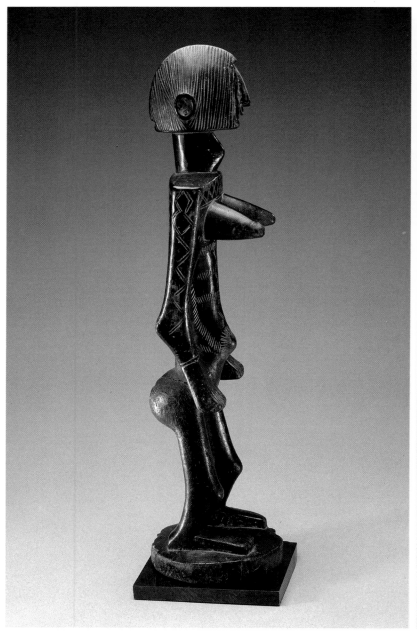

171

SENUFO
H. 34,2 cm.

172

SENUFO
H. 57 cm.

173

SENUFO
H. 108 cm.

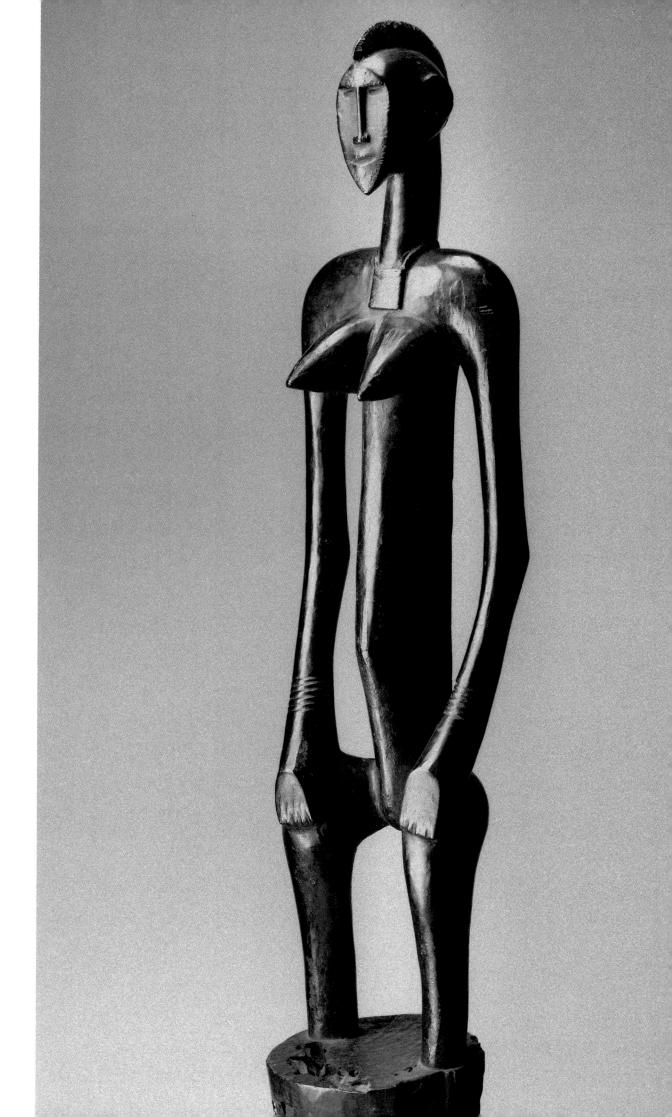

176

BAULE
H. 37 cm.

177

BAULE
H. 47 cm.

178

BAULE
H. 28,5 cm.

179

ABRON
H. 36,5 cm.

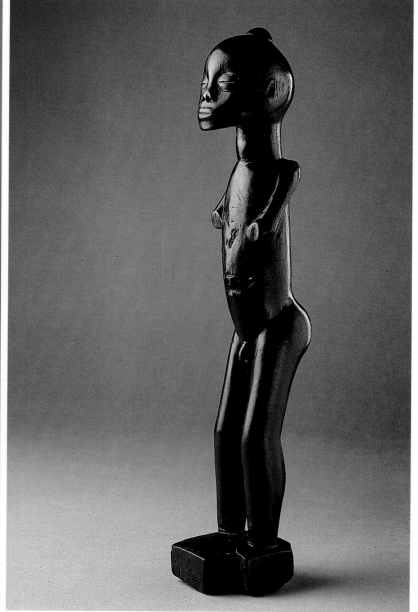

180

BAULE
H. 41 cm.

181

BAULE
H. 45 cm.

182

BAULE
H. 45 cm.

183a, 183b

ASHANTI
H. 30,5 cm.

184

BIDYOGO
H. 37 cm.

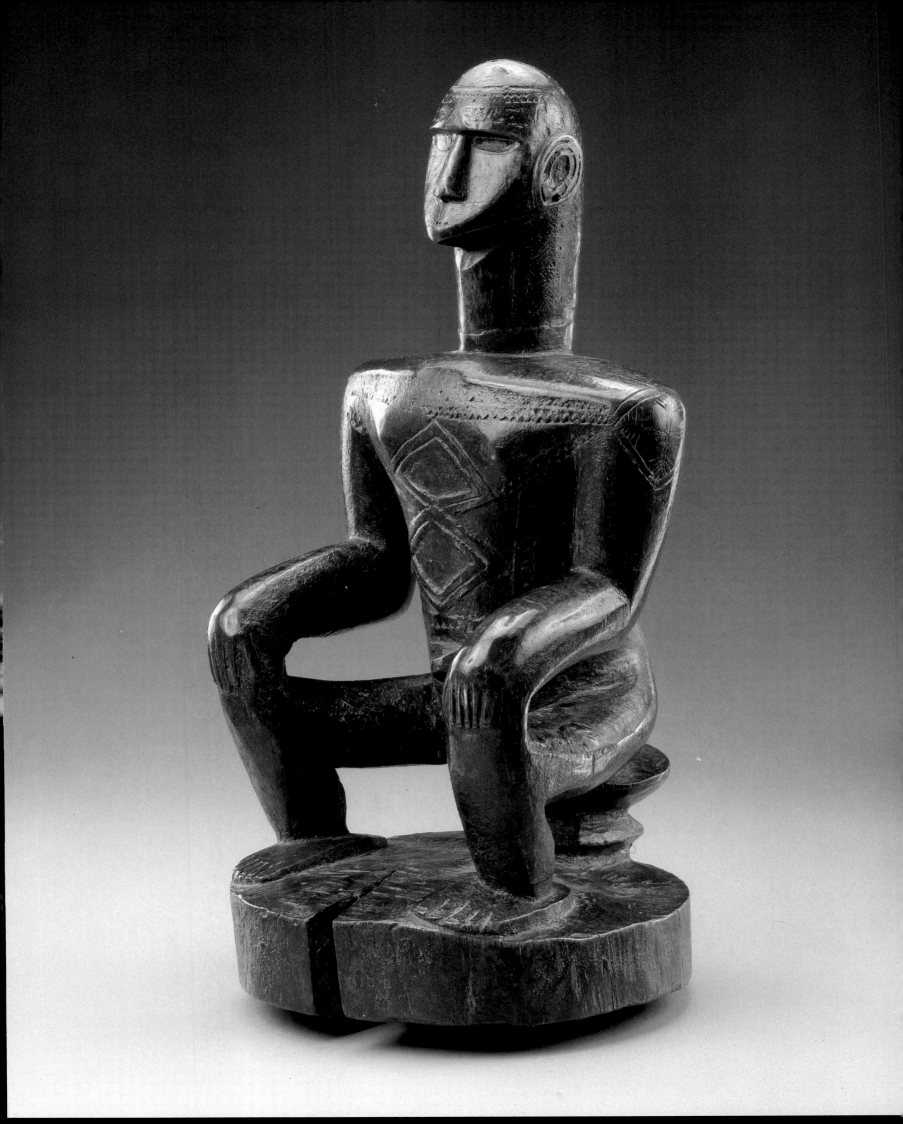

185

YORUBA
H. 49 cm.

186

YORUBA
H. 50 cm.

187

YORUBA
H. 49 cm.

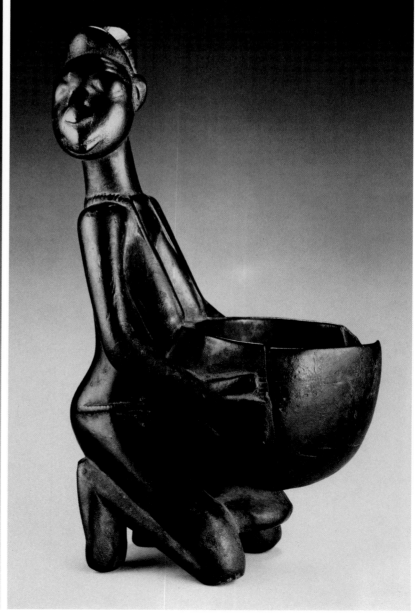

188

YORUBA
H. 56,5 cm.

189

YORUBA
H. 57,5 cm.

190

YORUBA
H. 47 cm.

191
URHOBO
H. 124,5 cm.

192
IGBO
H. 108 cm.

195

M'BEMBE
H. 94 cm.

196

M'BOYE
H. 108 cm.

197

JUKUN
H. 82 cm.

198

CHAMBA
H. 47 cm.

199

CHAMBA
H. 61 cm.

200

FANG
H. 41,5 cm.

201

FANG
H. 23 cm.

202

FANG
H. 21,5 cm.

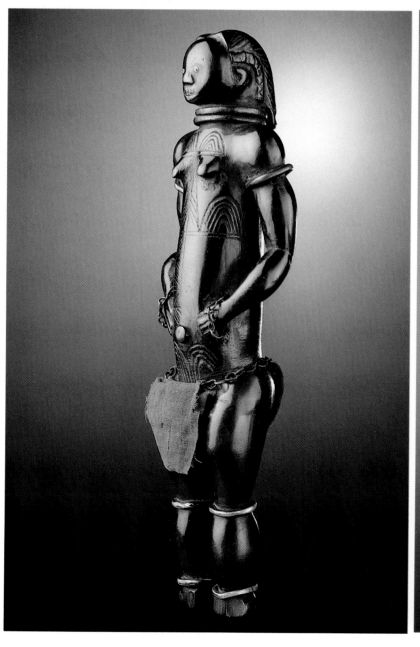

203

FANG
H. 19 cm.

204

FANG
H. 23 cm.

205

FANG
H. 17 cm.

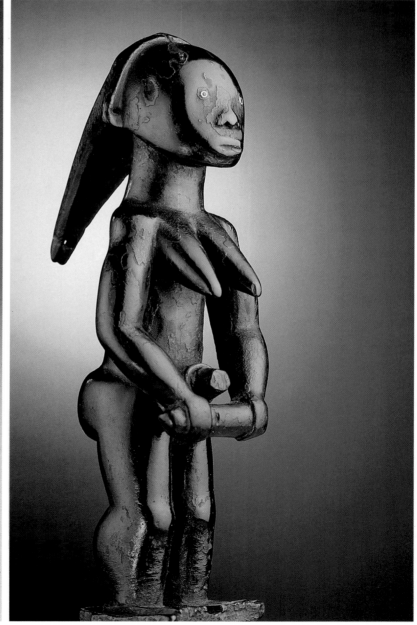

206

FANG
H. 50 cm.

207

FANG
H. 61 cm.

208

FANG
H. 41 cm.

209

KUYU
H. 30 cm.

210

AMBETE
H. 62,5 cm.

211

AMBETE
H. 80 cm.

212

TEKE
H. 80 cm.

213

BEMBE
H. 22 cm.

214

BEMBE
H. 18 cm.

215

BEMBE
H. 22 cm.

216

B'WENDE
H. 21,5 cm.

VILI
H. 22,5 cm.

VILI
H. 28 cm.

219

YOMBE
H. 25,5 cm.

220

VILI
H. 29 cm.

221

KONGO
H. 35 cm.

222

KONGO
H. 37,5 cm.

223

SUKU
H. 39 cm.

224

BAKWA-NDOLO
H. 45 cm.

225

BENA-LULUWA
H. 51 cm.

226

KONGO
L. 65 cm.

227

KONGO
H. 91 cm.

230

LUBA
H. 36 cm.

231

LUBA
H. 44 cm.

232

HEMBA
H. 35 cm.

233

SONGYE
H. 95 cm.

234a, 234b

TABWA
H. 38 cm.

235
TSHOKWE
H. 46 cm.

236
TSHOKWE
H. 49 cm.

237
TSHOKWE
H. 35,5 cm.

238

M'BOLE
H. 87 cm.

239

M'BOLE
H. 104 cm.

240

M'BOLE
H. 41,5 cm.

241

LEGA
H. 29 cm.

242
ZULU
H. 28 cm.

243
KAMBA
H. 26,5 cm.

244

BARA

H. 107 cm.

ENVIRONMENT
ALLTAGSGEGENSTANDE

245

M'BUNDA
H. 15 cm.

246

TSHOKWE
H. 14 cm.

247

KUBA
H. 18,3 cm.

248

TSHOKWE
H. 24,5 cm.

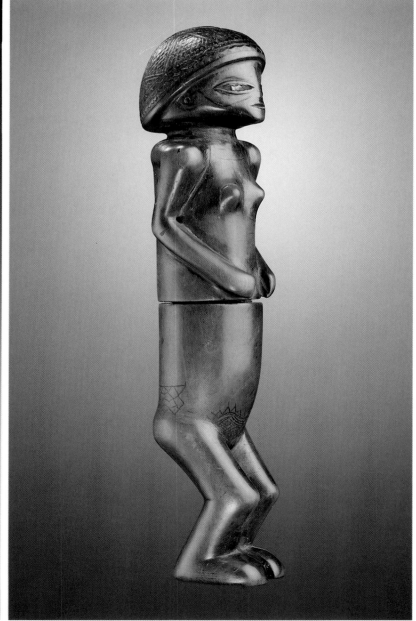

249

KUBA
H. 20 cm.

250

KUBA
H. 19 cm.

251

VILI
H. 20 cm.

252/254

VILI
H. 19 - 17 - 16 cm.

255

LUMBO
H. 15 cm.

256

VILI
H. 20 cm.

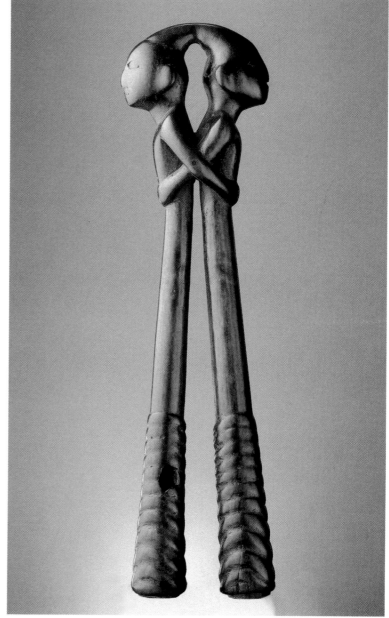

257

BAULE
H. 26 cm.

258

GURO
H. 17,5 cm.

259

GURO
H. 18,5 cm.

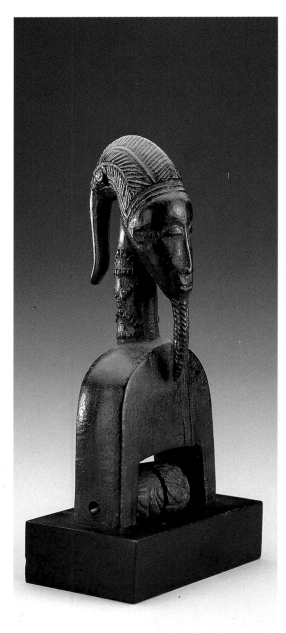

260

SENUFO
H. 16 cm.

261

DOGON
H. 18 cm.

HUNGANA
H. 31 cm.

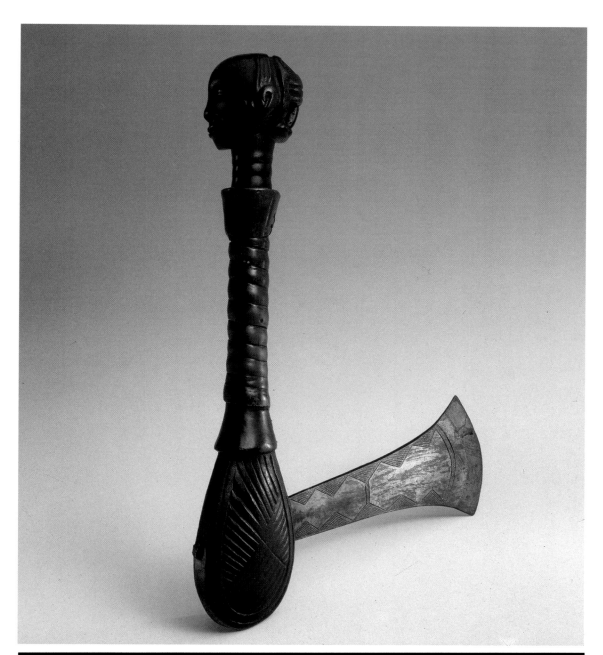

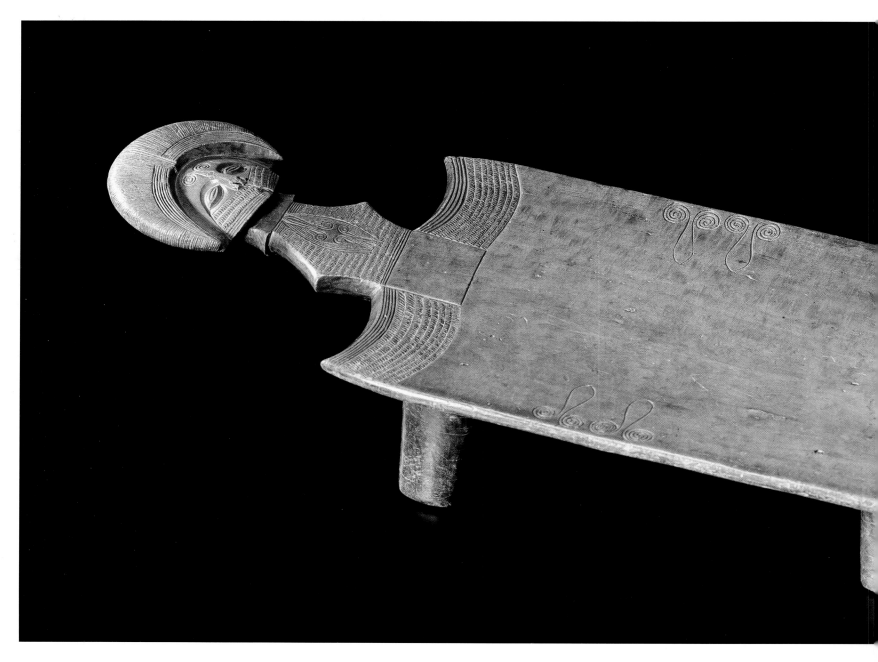

265

TSHOKWE
L. 131 cm.

266

BAMBARA/BAMANA
H. 53 cm.

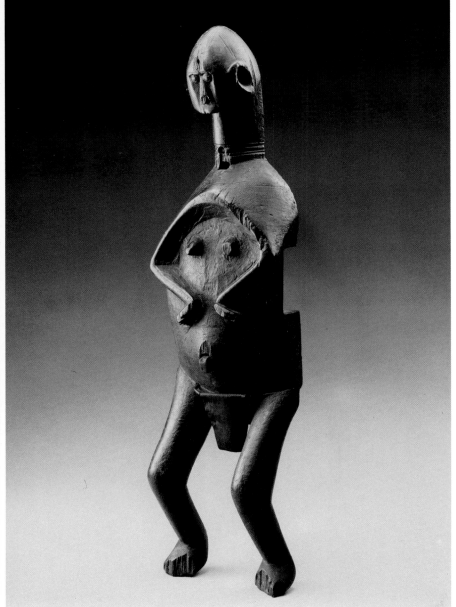

DAN
H. 53 cm.

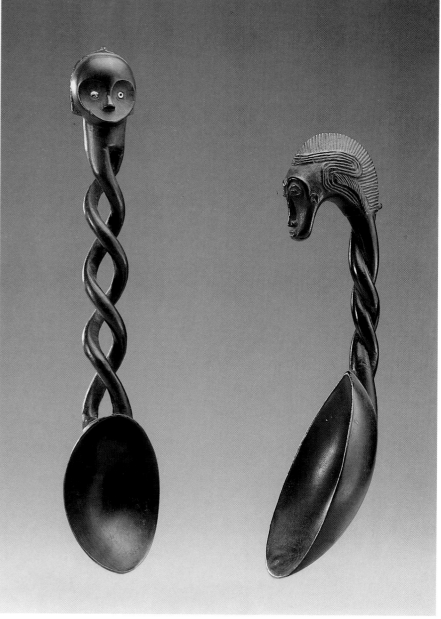

271

DAN
H. 59,5 cm.

272

GIO
H. 45,5 cm.

273

KULANGO
H. 32 cm.

274

DAN
H. 63 cm.

275

MANGBETU
H. 69 cm.

276

AMBETE
H. 45,5 cm.

277

BAULE
H. 26,5 cm.

278

KONGO
H. 22 cm.

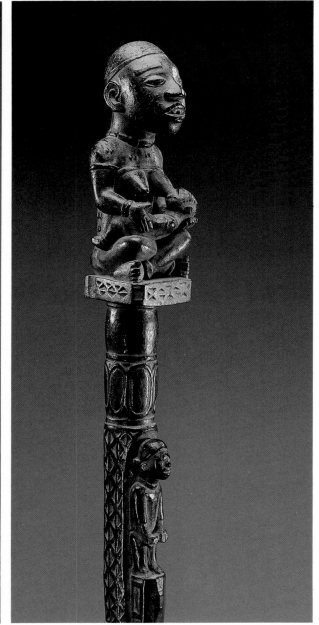

281

SENUFO
H. 138 cm.

282

ZULU
H. 153 cm.

283

MAKONDE
H. 118 cm.

284

LUBA
H. 80 cm.

285

LUBA
H. 85,5 cm.

286

LUBA
H. 160 cm.

287

LUBA
H. 164 cm.

288

ETHIOPIE
H. 71 cm.

289

KIKUYU
H. 59 cm.

297

ZULU
H. 15,5 cm.

298

ZULU
H. 11,5 cm.

299

SHONA
H. 13,5 cm.

300
KALANGA
H. 21 cm.

NOTES

TERRA COTTA

1/ Terra cotta head, with central cavity communicating with the eyes (numerous quartz inclusions). NOK culture. Nigeria. Height: 28 cm. Thermoluminescence tested by the Laboratory of Haigerloch, West Germany: 2,000 years old ± 25 %.

THERMOLUMINESCENCE TESTS
These tests, to which we make frequent reference, are a recent scientific method that allows us to determine the age of pottery (and also of bronze objects, if they still contain fragments of the clay around which they were cast). To carry out this test a drill is used to take a sample of about 50 milligrammes of terra cotta powder from the object to be examined. This powder, heated to 500° C emits a measurable light corresponding to the release of the energy produced by the effect of radioactivity and slowly stored by the pottery since its last baking (which had then reduced its energy content to zero).
One can thus deduce the time that has passed since its last baking with a margin of error of ± 10 % or sometimes higher.
The dating achieved should be corrected according to the characteristics of the environment measured on the spot of the finding; place often unknown to the owners of the object.

2/ Hollow terra cotta head with pierced pupils, with a double-shelled cap, a band of pearls on the top of the forehead and another at the nape of the neck.
The lower part of the jaw is missing. Thermoluminescence tested in Oxford: 1,500 to 1,900 years old. NOK, Nigeria. Height: 21 cm.

3/ Terra cotta mask 1 to 2 cm thick. Traces of red paint. Interior Delta of the Niger. Mali. Height: 22 cm. Thermoluminescence tested in Oxford: 500 to 800 years old.

4a, 4b/ Terra cotta head. Probably a copy of a commemorative bronze head, realistically crafted, showing the exact details of the headdress, the tribal scars on the forehead and the high necklet of coral pearls. BENIN. Nigeria. Height: 24 cm. Thermoluminescence tested in Oxford: 230 to 350 years old.

5/ Commemorative funeral head, or Mma, this specimen is characteristic with its outsized forehead prolonging the face. This is the portrait of a woman, as evidenced by the orifice piercing the ears and the particularly exuberant hairstyle, with 'curly' locks and high set chignons. Thermoluminescence dating of these heads has shown ages ranging between the XVIIth and the XVIIIth centuries.
These kinds of heads were created by a female modeller to accompany the head of a dead chief. They were placed side by side with the heads of other men, members of the family, or servants sacrificed during the first funeral ceremonies. They were not placed on the dead person's tomb, but in a shelter in a grove, or Mmaso. Ritual vases stood nearby, sometimes Abebudie with reliefs evoking proverbs. These were stuffed with hair shaved from the mourners, thus symbolising the unity of the female line clan. On the occasion of the second funeral rites celebrated each year, these heads were cleaned, then coated with Eto (a mash of yam and palm oil) or with egg yolk. HEMANG-TWIFO ethnic group. ASHANTI. Ghana. Height: 30 cm.

6/ Woman carrying a rolled up mat (?). Interior Delta of the Niger. Mali. Height: 30 cm.

7/ Seated man circled by a snake. Interior Delta of the Niger. Mali. Height: 40 cm. Width: 18 cm. Thermoluminescence tested in Oxford: 780 years old ± 120 years. This dignitary (photograph 7) was apparently found in a tomb flanked by two women, the one in photograph 6 and another, not illustrated here, holding a fan.

8/ Warrior lying down or injured (?) wearing a lot of jewellery and a dagger attached to the left arm. Interior Delta of the Niger. Mali. Height: 20 cm. Length: 19 cm. Thermoluminescence tested in Clamart: 680 years old.

9/ Seated man, legs sticking out to the sides, holding a stick. He is wearing two pairs of bracelets and a necklet. Terra cotta. BANKONI. Bamako region. Mali. Height: 52 cm. Width: 33 cm. Thermoluminescence tested in Oxford: about 600 years old.

10/ Extremely thin seated man, covered with snakes. His head lies on his crossed arms and his cheeks bear tribal scars. Terra cotta, traces of colour. Interior Delta of the Niger. Mali. Height: 36 cm. Length: 23 cm. Depth: 33 cm. (To be compared with similar Pre-Columbian statues from the region of Colima in Mexico.) Thermoluminescence tested in Oxford: between 800 and 1,000 years old.

11/ Kneeling dignitary holding shackles. Terra cotta. Interior Delta of the Niger. Mali. Height: 48 cm. Thermoluminescence tested in Oxford: 625 years old ± 95 years.

12/ Woman sitting cross-legged, holding a child at each breast with a third holding on to her back. Terra cotta. Interior Delta of the Niger. Mali. Height: 39 cm. Thermoluminescence tested in Oxford: 470 years old ± 75 years.

13/ Horseman with majestic carriage, well trimmed beard and sumptuous, finely moulded jewellery. The horse's harness is also of great refinement. Note the bell under the neck. Terra cotta, red motifs. Interior Delta of the Niger. Mali. Height: 58.5 cm. Thermoluminescence tested in Oxford: 300 to 500 years old.

14/ Mounted horseman with short stirrups. Terra cotta. BANKONI. Bamako region. Mali. Height: 50 cm. Thermoluminescence tested in Oxford: between 600 and 700 years old.

15/ Bust displaying the vestimentary elegance of the Djenne. Note the crocodile head dagger sheath on the right arm and official staff at the shoulder. Terra cotta. Interior Delta of the Niger. Mali. Height: 38 cm.

16/ Male bust, probably that of a horseman. To be compared with the bust on the same page. Terra cotta. BANKONI. Mali. Height: 48 cm. Thermoluminescence tested in Oxford: between 450 and 650 years old.

17/ Terra cotta mask of an unusual size and outstanding craftsmanship, in the style known as 'multiple eyelids'. This work is made up of five separate pieces fitting together like a jigsaw, with three holes in the forehead perhaps allowing them to be linked together. Lofty forehead, protruding almond-shaped eyes surrounded by the fine lines of the eyelids. Tribal markings on the temples added later. Round, engraved ears. Straight nose with a sharp bridge. Mouth with prominent lips revealing the teeth. The oblong skull is covered with a cap with geometrical designs. Interior Delta of the Niger. Mali. Height: 55 cm. Thermoluminescence tested in Haigerloch, West Germany: between 700 and 800 years old.

METALS

18/ Bull. Mali. In bronze with green patina. Numerous chalky concretions. Height: 22.5 cm. Length: 32.5 cm. Probably XIVth or XVth century.

19 to 25/ Seven small bronze horsemen. Timbuctoo region. Mali. Their heights are between 4 and 6 cm.

26/ Bronze plaque showing a warrior clad in a padded, scaled costume holding a spear and a sword. On either side, an escort of two men holding shields. All three are wearing leopard's tooth necklaces and a bell on the chest. Between them, two small musicians with horn and sistrum, but without the ferocious look of the warriors. BENIN. Nigeria. XVIIth century. Museum für Völkerkunde, No. 64717, Vienna, Austria. Height: 39 cm. Width: 39 cm.

27/ Commemorative head. Cast in bronze with iron inlays. Height: 22 cm. BENIN. Nigeria. XVth-XVIth centuries. National Museum of African Art, NMAFA 82-5-Z, Washington.

28/ Woman found with her feet in two kinds of bracelets (?) of inappropriate size. In bronze. Mali. Height: 25 cm.

29/ Horseman with saddle and shield, of outstanding stylisation. In bronze. Mali. Height: 23 cm.

30/ Articulated brass necklet. These necklets, like the small brass figures and horsemen, with slender bodies and limbs (Nos. 19 to 25), were buried in small terra cotta vases near the burial grounds towards Niafounke, in the Ke Macina region. This culture was different from that of the Djenne but just as ancient. The purity and rhythm of the lines of this piece of jewellery are truly outstanding. Mali. Height: 20 cm. Width: 24 cm. Thickness: 2.5 cm.

31/ Decorative bronze plaque. Here the subject is a chief wearing the emblems of his position: headdress with high necklet of coral pearls, leopard's tooth necklet, bracelets and leggings, yet he is not the Oba, for on his chest hangs a bell to ward off conflict but also to signal victory, an emblem not worn by the king. The leopard's head adorning the war robe was intended to frighten the enemy. The chief is flanked by two warriors playing the horn or the double bells, and by a naked servant carrying his ceremonial sword. These three figures are smaller than the chief although close to him, indicating a sort of 'conventional perspective' linked to their lesser importance. The representation of the Portuguese, with their plumed helmets, long hair, small beards and buttoned jackets, means we can date this plaque to the Oba, Esegie. In 1515, this Oba was given military aid by Portugal when war opposed him to the Ata of the Igala. The four-leaf motif engraved in the background is known as Owen Iba Ede Ku (the sun never forgets a day), and is associated with Olokun, god of the waters. These plaques in their hundreds decorated the great rectangular cut pillars that bore canopies over the various courtyards of the Oba of Benin's palace. Their layout corresponded to complex themes. BENIN. XVIth century. Nigeria. Height: 45.7 cm. National Museum of African Art, Washington. NMAFA 82-5-3.

32/ Commemorative brass Oba head. According to folk legend, the last king of the mythical Ogiso dynasty reigning in Benin before the arrival of the Yoruba was dethroned following a revolt. He was replaced by an Ife prince, Oranmiyan, son of the Oni of Oduduwa. Ever since this period, custom required that the Oba of Benin be beheaded after death, so that his skull could be sent to Ife to be buried in the sacred Orun Oba Ado enclosure, and in exchange, a commemorative brass head be sent to Benin to be displayed on the altar of the royal ancestors. At the end of the XIVth century, the sixth Oba, Oguola, apparently suggested that an Ife smelter should come to Benin to teach local artists. The Oni is said to have sent Iguehae. This perhaps mythical master is still venerated today as the founding patron of the Iguneromwon corporation of smelters, and has his own sanctuary. This commemorative head is that of an Oba, the male sex being indicated by the three vertical reliefs on the forehead above each eye (four for women). It corresponds to the so-called middle period, stretching from the middle of the XVIth century to the end of the XVIIth century. The vertical iron inlays of the first period have disappeared, the neck and chin are concealed under a pile of twenty coral necklaces, and the face has lost all realism. The greater thickness may be put down to the smelting technique, definitely less strict than in the XIVth and XVth centuries, yet it has its use since by increasing the weight of the heads, it allowed them to serve as better plinths for the sculpted tips of tusks that were traditionally inserted through the circular opening in the headdress. BENIN. Mid XVth to end XVIIth century. Nigeria. Height: 23 cm.

33/ Bronze warrior carrying a sabre and a bow. SENUFO. Ivory Coast. Height: 9.8 cm.

34/ Mounted warrior with helmet and lance. In bronze. KULANGO. Ivory Coast. Height: 8 cm. Length: 9.5 cm.

35/ Pewter Kpelie mask. This was cast by the lost wax method using poor native pewter. The item was found during excavations with the Tiembala fraction of the Senufo, one of the first to migrate, coming from the north-east between the XIth and XIIIth centuries. The three forehead bands and chin strap have given rise to the idea that it could well be a funeral mask, like those used by the Ashanti. The long straight nose, jugular scars and peripheral horned ornaments might perhaps be the forerunners of the current Senufo Kpelie wood masks. The sub-labial vertical strip is a labret comparable to those used by the Dogon and the 'Djenne', present and former occupants of a region neighbouring their initial point of departure. SENUFO. Ivory Coast. Height: 28 cm.

36/ Bronze mask, clearly displaying tribal scars, tufted hairstyle and short twisted beard. BAULE. Ivory Coast. Height: 5.5 cm.

37/ Bronze weight. ATIE. Ivory Coast. Height: 3.1. cm.

38/ Bronze mask, cast with great precision. BAULE. Ivory Coast. Height: 6 cm.

39/ Mask that was worn at the waist. Bronze. BENIN. Nigeria. XVIIth century. Height: 9.3 cm.

40/ Bronze head with sunken eyes, the pupils in relief. Numerous tribal scars and highly original representation of the headdress. Lower Niger. Length: 18 cm.

41-42-43-44/ Four brass rings representing horsemen. Dogon (?). Heights between 4.9 and 6.8 cm.

45/ Elegantly made pendant with a spiral twist. In brass. SENUFO. Ivory Coast. Height: 5.2 cm.

46/ Fantastical horseman. In brass. AKAN group. Ivory Coast. Ghana. Height: 7 cm. Length: 9 cm.

47/ Erotic couple. In brass. ASHANTI. Ghana. Height: 8 cm.

48-49-50/ Three gold masks. BAULE. Ivory Coast. Heights: 6.2, 5.4 and 3.6 cm.

51/ Animal-shaped figure with arms crossed, carrying an anklet (?). In bronze. Mali. Height: 12.5 cm.

52/ Seated figure with a long beard and a lot of jewellery. In bronze. AKAN Group. Ivory Coast and Ghana. Height: 8 cm.

53/ Seated figure with regal tiara and a beard tressed into a necklet, holding a sceptre. In bronze. YORUBA. Nigeria. Height: 28.5 cm.

54/ 'Edan' statuette used within the 'Ogboni' initiation society. Kneeling figure holding its breast. In brass finished with an iron stem. YORUBA. Nigeria. Height: 30.5 cm.

55/ Bronze pendant representing twins. Mali. Height: 6.5 cm.

56/ Two gazelles emerging from the same stem. In iron (?). BAMANA. Mali. Length: 16 cm.

57-58-59/ Brass pendants. These charms were worn at the neck on a leather strap that passed through the double ring that the arched abdomen forms with the elbows thrust backwards. This is a well-known model that always includes a triangular face with ears sticking out and a square goatee beard. There is the familiar long extended neck, forming an angle with the head and the body, that can be seen on certain wooden statues. The feet are always indicated by a trapezium where the toes are simply grooves. This rhythmical play of angles and counter-angles creates a high level of tension, worthy of the most modern works. There are also Janus specimens or those including several figures lined up side by side. This kind of pendant is also to be found with the Abron. KULANGO. Ivory Coast. Heights: 5.5, 7.5 and 9.5 cm.

60/ Large flat lizard holding a snake in its jaws. This is an applique bronze item. Nigeria, exact origin undetermined. Length: 44 cm.

IVORY

61/ Head from the Zimba ethnic subgroup. Intended as an emblem of the Bwani secret society. In ivory with dark patina. Found in 1947 in the province of Maniema. LEGA. Zaïre. Height: 10 cm. Depth: 10 cm.

62/ Head on a plinth, with red patina. Its eyes are inlaid with cowries. LEGA. Zaïre. Height: 15 cm.

63/ Female figure in ivory. Note the accentuation of the navel and the knees, and the way in which the arms are held away from the torso. LEGA. Zaïre. Height: 30 cm.

64/ Ivory whistle pendant. YAKA. South-West Zaïre. Height: 18.5 cm.

65/ Ivory pendant representing a figure with a halo. LUBA-TABWA. East Zaïre. Height: 7.2 cm.

66/ Double-holed hunting whistle pendant. Ivory. PENDE. Zaïre. Height: 11.5 cm.

67/ Ivory pendant representing two figures, perhaps twins. LEGA. Zaïre. Height: 8.5 cm.

68/ Ivory sceptre, representing a man sitting above a prisoner. KONGO. Mouth of the Zaïre river. Height: 22 cm.

69/ Ivory tip of a trunk with pewter inlays. YOMBE. Republic of the Congo. Length of the trunk: 38.5 cm.

70/ Female statue. LEGA. Zaïre. Height: 24.5 cm.

This object (like those shown in photographs 61, 62, 63 and 70) played a role in the Lutumbo Iwa Kindi acceptance rites, that awarded the highest Kindi grade, of the most powerful dignitaries of the Bwani secret society. It was taken from the classical basket along with other wooden, ivory or bone, anthropomorphic or animal-shaped figures and maquettes summarizing man's knowledge and linked to his social, political and religious training. The candidate had to interpret their esoteric meaning, taking into account the manner in which they were laid out on the ground or held in the hand. Here we see the plastic characteristics common to all Lega art: the pure style of the heart-shaped face and the protruding almond shape of the eyes, shown picked out in cowrie shells on the head on a plinth. Nevertheless each statuette retained the style of its own workshop, sometimes keeping close to realism with its tribal markings, or sometimes being expressionist. Note in photograph 70 the arms sketched out, barely separated from the body.

71-72/ Ivory pendants. These two figures clearly display the stylistic characteristics of this small, little known people, living in the Kwilu valley. The face, oversized compared to the body, is marked by hair in parallel crests. The hands are held at the chin. The figure is kneeling, its knees together. The style is close to that of its neighbours, the Suku and Mbala. The precise meaning of these pendants has so far not been established. HUNGANA. Zaïre. Height: 5.8 and 5.5 cm.

73/ Anthropomorphic ivory spoon. LEGA. Zaïre. Height: 18.6 cm.

74/ Ornamental anthropomorphic hairpin. ZANDE. North Zaïre. Height: 19 cm.

75/ Ivory horn decorated with four bearded faces. Ring for suspending and plug closure. ATIE. Ivory Coast. Length: 19 cm.

76/ This amazing ivory horn was undoubtedly a tobacco case, closed by a wooden lid. The two-faced Janus figure, with stylised figuration of the jutting backbone, the ribs simply engraved, buttocks and thighs marked with circles, is a truly astonishing piece of work. We know of three other comparable animal horns, their tips sculpted in a head crowned with a loftier cap, but also having a flat base. One of them represents a mother figure. NYAMWEZI. Tanzania. Height: 8.5 cm.

77/ Ivory knob of walking stick, kneeling woman holding a child in her arms. Eyes inlaid with metal. Necklet representing cowrie shells. VILI. Republic of the Congo. Height: 14 cm.

78/ Two figures back to back, one male and the other female, adorned with copper bracelets, eyes inlaid with copper, form the handle of this leather fan. FANG. Gabon. Overall length: 34.5 cm. Height of the handle: 15.5 cm.

MASKS

79/ Animal-shaped helmet crest representing a bird prolonged by antelope horns. Known as 'Poningo' mask. In wood with crusted patina. SENUFO. Ivory Coast. Height: 39 cm.

80/ Anthropomorphic 'Kpelie' mask representing a harmonious female face crowned with ram's horns. Beneath the ears emerge representations of legs. In wood with patina. SENUFO. Ivory Coast. Height: 29 cm.

81/ Lacework oval mask, topped by an elaborate headdress. In light wood inlaid with nails and copper plates. YAURE. Ivory Coast. Height: 35 cm.

82/ Unicorn mask representing a bird. In heavy wood with highly polished black patina. Detail highlighted in ivory paint and blue bands. This is one of the Do masks used by the Muslim community of Ligbi. KULANGO. Ivory Coast. Height: 29 cm.

83/ Dege mask, known as the black monkey. This model, with its very geometrical style, is similar to the specimen in the Musée de l'Homme (Paris) of Bandiagaran origin. It is characterised by the triangular eyes and many-sided shape. A fibre necklet went under the throat and behind the head, draped on the shoulders of the wearer. It was associated with other animal-shaped masks representing the animals sent from heaven in Nommo's ark, which danced with the anthropomorphic mask during the funeral rites of an initiate of the Awa mask society, and also at the end of mourning, or Dama, marking the departure of the Nyama of the deceased leaving the world of the living. Naturally they also appeared during the great national Dogon festival of Sigi, which every 50 years commemorated universal death. DOGON. Mali. Height: 29.5 cm.

84/ Kore mask. BAMANA. Mali. Height: 42 cm. Width: 14.5 cm.

85/ Kore mask. BAMANA. Mali. Height: 42 cm. Width: 17 cm.

86/ Kore-Dugaw masks. The three masks in photographs 84, 85 and 86 correspond to the second stage of initiation into the Kore societies. Contrary to the two further stages (Dyaraw and Karaw) here the wearers were highly agitated: they ran, jumped, kicked out, sometimes straddled a stick topped by a small horse's head. Specimen 85 is a black horse mask, probably coming from the Dioila region, whose jutting forehead, seat of wisdom, has in its centre a horny protuberance where animal blood was poured during the sacred rites. Mask 86, sculpted surface by surface, is less characteristic and may well correspond to a hyena. Its impressive mouth has an outsized upper lip, no doubt used as a handle. BAMANA. Mali. Height: 39 cm.

87/ 'Comb' mask with six horns influenced by the Malinke, known as 'N'tomo'. In light wood with black patina. BAMANA. Mali. Height: 45 cm. Width: 11.5 cm.

88-89/ Segouni Koun dance helmet crests of the Tyi-Wara society. The Tyi-Wara was a strictly agricultural society, responsible for fertility rites and appeasement of the earth spirits disturbed by man's activity. Each ceremony was accompanied by dances performed by couples with sisal caps topped by these crests. The wearers were masked with red hoods and cloaked in fibre garments. The curious graphic appearance of these sculptures is quite exceptional in Negro art. The purity and refinement of the lines and the intricate play of the curves of the neck, mane and horns make it one of the glories of BAMANA statuary. This vertical type corresponds to the style of the Segou region. The male specimen represents a large antelope (also known as antelope-horse), remarkable for its highly worked mane. The female crest always carries its fawn on its back, its straight horns and small ears being those of another animal, the oryx. BAMANA. Mali. Heights: 87 and 66 cm.

90/ Nimba dance bust.
This sculpture is the most impressive specimen of Baga art, and perhaps of African art, reaching 140 cm in height and weighing over 50 kg. The voluminous head was designed above all to be seen in profile, with its overall semi-circular shape in which the face only accounts for a tiny proportion. Whereas the nose is huge and hooked, the mouth is reduced to a tiny cylinder. The same morphological features, with an arrow-shaped crest, are to be found in the small statuettes connected with the warriors' associations. The cylindrical neck always had a small protrusion at the back to fix a liana hoop bearing a fibre dress. The bust has the shape of a four-footed chasuble from which spread ample breasts with large nipples on either side of two central sight holes. The whole is decorated with carved geometric de-

signs and picked out with rows of upholsterer's nails. It is above all a fertility symbol, the common property of the male Simo association. A new Nimba had to be properly enthroned, while the old one, rejected, remained hanging on the tree were maize was dried. It carried out the Kipissie Ka Nimba dance to a slow rhythm in the centre of a circle of women beating on gourds and throwing handfuls of rice, and a wider circle of men beating drums. Is was brought out at the end of the rainy season during rice sowing, and in the middle of the dry season, before reaping. BAGA. Guinea. Height: 134 cm.

91/ Kaissi swordfish mask. This composite mask is made of a real swordfish sword embedded at the top of the wooden triangle that forms the head. Fringes of palm leaves and raffia fibres hang at its base. It was placed vertically on a wooden plinth that the dancer carried on his head, bending forward so that the fish he represented seemed to be swimming horizontally. Furthermore, the young Kabaro initiate held a wooden fin attached with lianas to his back. This kind of mask, representing the heads of cattle (vaca bruto), hippopotamus (egomore), pelican (kaiogouna), or shark (kaboro) depending on the island, appeared every ten years at the time of the Manrat Che initiation festivals. BIDYOGO. Bissagos archipelago. Height: 66 cm.

92/ Expressionist and fantastical mask, designed to frighten. In wood, with metal, fibre and cowrie incrustations. GUERE. Liberia and Ivory Coast. Height: 32 cm. Width: 52 cm.

93/ Mask of surrealistic appearance. In

wood with brown patina, brass nails, fibres. BETE. Ivory Coast. Height: 44 cm.

94/ Dancer's mask of a masculine type called Gle. The Bete made fantastical masks that were more or less ugly, virtually entirely limited to the groups in the west who were neighbours of the Miabwa, and thus indirectly inspired by the Guere. They were usually implanted with symmetrical appendices and decorated with upholsterer's copper nails. These appendices were subjected to the wildest and most incredible deformations and strains, yet certain constant factors remained. The sides of the nose spread sideways like drawn out moustaches, and there were also lateral hooks folded back over the face, and even linking up and blending together, as in the specimen shown. These appendices could also point up or down, or less commonly, outwards. The forehead always had the shape of a round half-helmet cleanly cut off horizontally at eye level, sometimes with a discreet crest. The mouth was slit across the whole width of the mask. The eye, sometimes cylindrical but more often like a half lentil and slit like that of a Guere mask, was rarely pierced, the dancer guiding himself rather by means of underlying holes or a discreet slit. The drawn out moustache is the main distinguishing feature of Bete masks. Such a detail never appeared in Niabwa models, whose general shape, although very similar, was also more rectangular. This was purely a dancer's mask. Formerly it represented the spirit of war, appearing during battles or intervening in the establishment of peace between two villages. Today, it has lost its identity and has become a sort of jester, appearing during official feasts

and important funerals. BETE. Ivory Coast. Height: 32 cm.

95/ Male mask with half-closed eyes and a pointed, slightly turned up nose. The high bulging forehead is divided vertically by a ridge sculpted in relief. Some teeth in wood. Cross-shaped scars on the cheeks. Cap in vegetable fibre and beard in human hair. In wood with shiny, black patina. DAN. Liberia. Height: 25 cm.

96/ Idealised portrait of an ancestor. Mask known as the 'brush runner', used by young men during the ceremonies marking the end of the rainy season. In shiny, black patina. DAN. Liberia and Ivory Coast. Height: 23 cm. Width: 14.5 cm.

97/ Mask with half-closed eyes, adorned with tribal scars engraved above the eyebrows, and obliquely on the cheeks. These masks representing attractive young girls were probably worn in the evening during the initiation period in the forest, when collecting food for the future young initiates among the mothers. They can also be considered as similar to the more classical Dan masks with slit eyes which were used during entertainment and pantomime dances. DAN. Ivory Coast and Liberia. Height: 24 cm. Width: 15 cm.

98/ Finely sculpted mask. Tribal markings on the temples, necklace-type beard and goatee. The tressed hair is crowned with three birds' heads. BAULE-YAURE. Ivory Coast. Height: 26 cm.

99/ Kpan mask. Dancing in duo, this kind of mask was used for the Goli dance, an innovation borrowed from the neighbour-

ing Ouan, who were Mande and not Akan. This was strictly a celebration dance, sometimes performed for men's funerals. The Kpan only acted exceptionally at the end of the dance, and only at night, after three other couples (Kple-Kple, Goli-Goulin, and Kpan-Pre). It is interesting to note that it combines masculine characteristics (an old man's knotted beard) with feminine features of beauty and youth (a long fine nose, half-closed eyes, headdress in the form of a crest and tufts, face painted red, the colour of life and revival). The wooden skullcap on which the face rests is representative of the north-west Baule style, in particular of the Kode and Goli fractions, very close to the Gouro and the Ouan. It was often heavy and bulky and larger than the face. The peripheral holes are few, intended only for fixing the mouth bar of the mask. An out-turned lip going round the shell was used to hold a taut cord to which a heavy raffia costume was attached from which a panther skin was suspended. The eyes were not perforated, only the mouth, hence these masks were guided by an acolyte who danced with them. They played an important role and wielded the dance whips, recognised emblems of the nobility. BAULE. Ivory Coast. Height: 46 cm.

100/ Mask. YAURE. Ivory Coast. Height: 31.5 cm.
Photographs 98 and 100 represent anthropomorphic masks of the Die society. The Yaure migrated to the Ivory Coast at the beginning of the XVIIIth century, after the split-up of the great Akan block. The Yaure formed the first wave, occupying the wooded hills of Central Western Ivory

Coast, a little before the Baule. Their masks combined the delicacy of the Guro models with the noble seriousness of those of the Baule. They are to be recognised by their trefoiled hair, their chin appendix, in this case a goatee beard in ringlets (but sometimes rectangular, triangular, diamond-shaped or cylindrical) and above all by the elegant lacework (sometimes in openwork) collarette that surrounds the face. In photograph 100 the two allegorical birds drinking out of a vase are fertility symbols, and the copper triangles fixed to the forehead and cheeks are religious emblems from the local pantheon. In specimen 98, the arches of the eyebrows carry on into the line of the facial contour, thus assimilating it to the most archaic Baule masks. The three cock heads emerging from the headdress are also male fertility symbols.

101/ Mask expressing dignity and serenity with an elegant headdress. Perhaps the portrait of an ancestor. BAULE. Ivory Coast. Height: 25 cm. Width: 17 cm.

102/ 'Gu' mask representing a king or chief of the royal line. Contrary to most African regions where sculpture was carried out by blacksmiths, Baule sculptures were the work of specialised, renowned artists working together in workshops. In light wood with brown patina. BAULE. Ivory Coast, Bonake region. Height: 32 cm. Width: 18 cm.

103/ Mask topped with antelope horns to which an upright figure is attached. In wood with brass inlays. YAURE. Ivory Coast. Height: 44 cm.

104/ Double-horned mask, two fine slits for the eyes. Beard in four tresses. In light wood with dark brown patina. BAULE. Ivory Coast. Height: 39 cm. Width: 18.5 cm.

105/ Mask with removable lower jaw from the Ekpo society, characterised by its four substantial tribal scars on the temples and the double ring round its forehead. In light wood, formerly red, black and white, covered over with a coating of soot. IBIBIO. Nigeria. Height: 27.5 cm. Width: 18 cm. Depth: 13.5 cm.

106/ 'Elu' female mask.
These masks are the equivalents of the Ibibio Mfon Ekpo masks, but were always much smaller: to be worn they required the adaptation of a conical facial headdress in raffia. They are recognisable by the light-handed touch of their construction, their small upturned noses and their articulated jaws with rush teeth; they can however prove difficult to distinguish from Ibibio masks. The specimen shown corresponds to a rare variety, with its half-moon eyes, like an Idiong mask from the Eket, the elongation of its jaws in the form of a bird's beak, and its strange flat nose, like a film peeling off the beak. OGONI. Nigeria. Height: 21.5 cm.

107/ Gelede cult mask.
Founded by the sorcerers of the Ketu region, the Gelede cult was limited to south west Yoruba country. The masks always danced in identical pairs, first by night (Olori Efe) then by day (Olori Ogberu), in honour of Iya-Nla, the ancestral mother of all women and all witches. There was also an annual dance intended to appease the evil forces of the sorcerers and to fend off many and varied calamities.

Naturally they reappeared for funerals of members of the society. They were worn obliquely on the head so that vision through the eye openings was possible, which in this case presented no difficulty given the exceptional openings of the face. This specimen is covered with a black patina, no doubt because it had not been danced with for a long time as the custom was to repaint them in bright colours before each dance. Here the extremely simple headdress is that of a married woman; this is the significant element of the mask, capable of infinite variation, often complex and even composite, evoking fruits, animals, various instruments and animated scenes. YORUBA. Republic of Benin. Height: 36 cm.

108a, 108b/ 'Izi' mask, a representation of the elephant spirit, the rear decorated with a realistic face. Worn horizontally on the top of the head. IGBO. North-East Nigeria. Length: 43 cm.

109/ Mask known as 'Ogoobo Enyi' or 'Wawa'.
These kinds of elephantine human masks were found mainly in the Abakaliki region, on the edges of the Izzi and Ezza ethnic sub-groups, and even further south, among the Ikwo, on the border of the Igbo, close to the Idoma and the Mbembe-Osopong. They apparently belonged to an initiation group worshipping the elephant, and probably danced during the festival of the new yams and for chiefs' funerals. The amazing plastic shape of this polychrome specimen (black, white, red) makes it a masterpiece of its kind. The harmonious vault of the forehead, curved back in a central lock evoking the elephant's trunk, per-

fectly balances the spread of the diamond-shaped mouth, armed with its geometrised tusks. IGBO. Nigeria. Height: 56 cm.

110/ White mask. These masks have the same sensitivity and fine eyes as the Okua kind. They too are burial masks but were only worn by the Idoma of the south and by the northern Igbo. Here the teeth are usually sculpted and impregnated with kaolin. IDOMA. Nigeria. Height: 23 cm.

111/ Mask of the Okua kind. This black model was used for funeral ceremonies by the Idoma of the south. It was also used by the Osokom clan of the Boki of Cross River and by the Idoma-Iyala. Its implanted teeth cut out of iron, or in bamboo, suggest a link with the Boki, whereas the prominent horizontal scars above the eyebrows on the contrary evoke the Idoma. According to Neyt, the stylistic heart of this art sprang from the Boki region, and then probably spread towards the west. IDOMA. Cross River. Nigeria. Height: 22.5 cm.

112/ Top of headdress representing a young girl with an elegant hairstyle, her face covered with white kaolin, metal teeth. IDOMA. Central Nigeria. Height: 36 cm.

113/ Kaolin coated Mwo helmet mask, top of headdress in three sections. Tribal scars in relief on the temples and the forehead, and in bas-relief on the cheeks. Teeth in metal. IGBO. Nigeria. Height: 54 cm.

114/ Mask called 'Mwo', representing the spirit of a young girl. IGBO. Nigeria. Height: 57 cm. Depth: 32 cm.

115/ Six-headed helmet crest termed 'ungulali'. These six faces deployed in quincunx might suggest the ubiquity of the mask's spirit. In natural wood and kaolin. Black nails on the skull. IDOMA. Nigeria. Height: 29.5 cm.

116/ Top of 'Ogbom' head-dress. A wickerwork basket held this sizable statuette on the head of the dancer. In wood with crusted smoked patina. EKET. South-East Nigeria. Height: 65 cm.

117/ Top of headdress. These statuettes (photographs Nos. 116 and 117), which were kept under the roofs of huts, are coated with a smoked patina. EKET. South-East Nigeria. Height: 61.5 cm.

118/ Mask representing a death's head. In wood with black, crusted patina, traces of paint on the teeth. EKET. OYO style. Delta of the Niger. Height: 27 cm. Length: 26.5 cm.

119/ Mask representing a gorilla head. In wood with black, crusted patina. EKET (?). Delta of the Niger. Height: 32.5 cm.
120/ Triple-faced mask. The lower mask is pierced with moon-shaped orifices. The eyes are represented by concentric circles and the three faces are surrounded by geometrical friezes. EKET. South-East Nigeria. Height: 34 cm.

121/ Helmet mask. See description below. IGALA. Nigeria. Height: 30 cm.

122/ Helmet masks with half-closed eyes perforated in half moons. Fine parallel and curved incisions on the face, which already existed in Ife sculptures. Egu cult, Ojuegu masks, royal court of the Ata of

Idha. IGALA. Nigeria. Height: 31 cm.

123/ Top of headdress with jutting jaw, rectangular mouth and parallel teeth. Mat patina and sheens on the prominent parts. In wood, skin, natural hair, wickerwork. EKOI. Nigeria. Height: 29 cm.

124/ Top of headdress mounted on a wickerwork circle. Antelope skin stretched over a wooden frame. Metal teeth, human hair and three horns. EKOI. Nigeria, Cross River region. Height: 36.5 cm.

125/ A 'Mabedike' type mask with four horns, used during nocturnal dances and also during funerals. In wood stained black and white. IGBO. Nigeria. Height: 75 cm (including beard).

126/ Okum mask. This leather-covered helmet mask belonged to the Ngbe society and corresponded to the highest Nkanda rank within the hierarchy. It has three faces, thus evoking the omniscience of the god, who was both bisexual and a prophet of the future and the past, the visible and the invisible. The male face is dark and has eye-holes through which the wearer could guide himself; its chin is garnished with human hair. The female face is lighter and blind, the eyes being represented by a piece of cast iron, with a nail forming the pupil; the skin could bear some of the 24 secret curvilinear pictograms, known as Nsidibi. The upper teeth are the only ones represented by means of a central incision: here they are made of metal, but they can also be bamboo or ivory. The tribal markings in the form of a target or pastille on the temples and the vertical temple lines of the male face may vary within a same group, and cannot thus be used to attribute an origin. There are holes on the top of the skull for feathers or porcupine quills. The dancer wore a long gown and a hood, the colour varying according to his rank in the society. The gown could be adorned with shells—evoking the human ear and the power of the mask to hear all. Each dancer was accompanied by two assistants bearing a whip or a branch of croton, symbolic of the power of the society. EKOI. Mid and Lower Cross River. South-East Nigeria. Height: 40 cm. Width: 31 cm.

127/ Ejagham dance helmet crest.
This female head with giant rolled tresses belongs to the Nsikpe society. The finest examples were sculpted at the end of the last century by an artist called Asam. Each horn was sculpted individually, then fixed to the skull before being garnished with leather. This form of headdress was worn by young maidens promised in marriage, during their reclusion for initiation and fattening up prior to the actual marriage. The tresses were formed by weaving extra locks into the hair, their form being sustained by a rigid framework and an earthernware shape. K. Nicklin points out that similar tressed heads were to be seen among the Etung of the Ikom region, and among the Annang-Ibibio, though the latter did not clad them in leather. EKOI. Cross River. Nigeria. Height: 54 cm. Depth: 59 cm.

128/ Ogbo society mask.
The Ijebu formed a Yoruba sub-group that embraced certain cults, such as the Ogboni Edan, imported by the people of Oyo or Ibadan seeking access to the sea.
As fishermen, they also completely adopt-ed the Ekine society of the Ijaw, which they named Ogbo. This mask represents a water spirit, the antelope Agira, recognisable by its cubist horns and ears, with two superposed Igodo fisher birds. However, one should note that the Ijebu also made anthropomorphic helmet masks akin to those of the Gelede. IJEBU. Nigeria. Height: 54 cm.

129/ Karikpo mask.
This cubist specimen is astounding in the simplicity of its line. The usual horn appendices here are simply suggested by the crest that extends the angle of the eyebrows. These masks were frequently accompanied by ugly models adopting savage postures and acting in a more or less fantastical manner. OGONI. Nigeria. Height: 38.5 cm.

130/ Mask representing simultaneously a man, a bird, and a ram. Worn horizontally on the head. IJO. South-East Nigeria. Height: 54 cm.

131/ Mask personifying a dead woman, in wood painted white for the face, dark brown for the headdress. Traces of red on the nine scale-shaped tattoos borne on the forehead and temples. PUNU. Gabon. Height: 28 cm. Width: 22 cm.

132/ Mask personifying a dead woman. Eyes very delicately slit. Double-shelled head-dress. Face painted black and white, tribal markings and surround of forehead orange. PUNU. Gabon. Height: 30.5 cm.

133/ White Okouyi masks. It is difficult to pin down the precise ethnic origin of these masks (Nos. 131, 132, 133) since a com-mon religious base united the Punu, Lumbu and Eshira tribes. The Okouyi are portraits of dead ancestors, hence their complexion whitened with Pembe kaolin. Formerly animating funeral ceremonies in the valleys of Ngounie and Nyanga, today they are simply celebration masks. The dancers, dressed in raffia trousers and a cotton fabric cape, swirled around on stilts, performing acrobatic feats and waving small wicker stem brooms.
Specimen 133 is of particularly good craftsmanship: its fine eyes are pierced with a slender slit, more arched towards the earlobe, the features are refined, in particular the realistic mouth with the groove under the nostrils. It has a so-called stabilising handle under the chin, indicative of its great antiquity and its middle Ngounie origin. The thick rear edge is for fixing the cotton wimple. The lack of skin marks shows that this is a male representation.
Masks 131 and 132 on the contrary correspond to female faces, as evidenced by the nine fish-scale projections grouped in diamond form on the forehead and in rectangles on the temples. The eyes are obliquely slanted in the Miso-Ma-Mighembe form and the hair, in arrow-shaped shells between two side tresses, corresponds to the ancient headdress of the Punu worn ceremonially. PUNU-LUMBU-ESHIRA. South Gabon. Height: 31.5 cm.

134/ Realistic, narrow-jawed mask. Pierced eyes. Band in studded cloth. KONGO. Zaïre. Height: 30 cm.

135/ Realistic mask with a kaolin coated face. Small beard in monkey hair. Teeth showing. KONGO. Zaïre. Height: 23 cm.

Width: 17.5 cm. Musée Royal de l'Afrique Centrale, Tervuren, Belgium.

136/ Flat, circular wooden mask, the top half slightly overlapping the bottom. Nose in relief. White symbolic decorations on an ochre background. TSAYE. Congo. Height: 30 cm. Length: 29 cm.

137/ Figure attached to a reliquary basket made of strips of skin and a leather bag containing a skull. In wood, copper, brass, earthenware button eyes. SANGO. Gabon. Height: 45 cm.

138/ Figure surmounting a reliquary. In wood, copper, brass. MAHONGWE. Gabon. Height: 55.8 cm. Width: 25 cm.

139/ Animal-shaped mask representing a gorilla skull. Widely hollowed out eyes under deep eyebrow arches. In wood with brown patina. KWELE. Republic of the Congo. Height: 38 cm. Length: 12.7 cm. Depth: 17.5 cm.

140/ Mask representing a gorilla skull. In wood with brown patina. On the forehead, a hollowed out triangle with traces of red colouring. KWELE. Republic of the Congo. Height: 24 cm.

141/ Mask known as 'Gon'. In wood with brown patina. KWELE. Republic of the Congo. Height: 37 cm.

142/ Mask with pointed chin and concave face. Eyes and mouth in high relief. MAHONGWE. Gabon. Height: 40 cm.

143/ Reliquary figure, base missing. Just as in the rest of Gabon, the Kota prac-

tised the cult of the skulls of male ancestors of the royal line, which they anointed with red camwood or adorned with metal, in particular those of former members of the brotherhood of hunters and warriors. They kept them religiously in a basket crowned by a reliquary figure. This was a flat core of wood with a concave profile, the rear side of which was plated with copper.
They were associated with propitiation rites, healing and soothsaying and were grouped together at the end of the Satsi initiation festivals, where all the assembled chiefs of the blood danced, clasping their Mboy baskets to their chests.
The face here is of a special concave-convex type, where the forehead bulges out and the face is concave, taking on, due to its eyebrows, the shape of a heart. The mouth is just suggested by a median strip. This Kota from the south probably comes from the Congolese sector, since it has the particularity of not having the crest in crescent form. In wood, copper, brass. NDASSA. KOTA. Congo. Height: 23.4 cm. Width: 17.8 cm.

144/ Convex style reliquary figure. One of the most realistic of Kota art. In wood, copper and brass. NDASSA. KOTA. Congo. Height: 57 cm. Width: 27 cm.

145/ Egg-shaped mask with prominent, straight nose. Eyes rectangularly pierced, prolonged by ridged scars. In wood with natural patina. Eyes, mouth, ears and hair picked out in hollowed out geometrical incisions highlighted in white. LWALWA. Central Zaïre. Height: 31 cm. Width: 21 cm.

146/ This specimen is a variant of the

mask on the same page. Brown, black and light beige. LWALWA. Height: 32 cm.

147/ Mask in light wood of natural colour. Zig-zag mosaic inlaid in brass. Top of the forehead painted black and white. Headdress of brown feathers. Small wickerwork beard finished off with a tassel. SALAMPASU. Zaïre. Height: 35 cm.

148/ Female mask. Half-closed eyes in concave orbits. In light wood with brown, white and orange pigments. Metal ring in the nose. BENA-LULUWA. Angola. Height: 21.5 cm. Width: 13.5 cm.

149/ Luluwa mask.
According to Cornet, this mask, similar to the one he published (1972, Fig. 78), would appear to have been altered by a Tshokwe user. A cross has been pricked out on the forehead and upholsterer's nails have been inset, which is not the custom of the Luluwa. Furthermore, the squared, cubist shape with multiperforated receding eyes is rather rare in this region where eyes are usually protuberant, and it makes a contrast with the particularly realistic and refined statue art. BENA-LULUWA. Zaïre. Height: 31 cm. Width: 18.5 cm.

150/ Helmet-mask, known as 'Bwoom', with prominent forehead and tribal scars on the forehead and nose. In wood with copper incrustations on the mouth and cheeks. Multicoloured pearls on the nose. KUBA. Central Zaïre. Height: 41 cm.

151/ 'Kifwebe' mask representing the spirits of the dead. In light wood with natural patina. Parallel and curved scoring enhanced in white. Traces of red on lips and lower eyelids. SONGYE. Zaïre. Height: 37 cm. (This mask is illustrated on the jacket.)

152/ Male 'Kifwebe' mask with an arrow-shaped crest, representing the spirits of the dead. SONGYE. Zaïre. Height: 38 cm.

153/ 'Cihongo' dance mask representing a male ancestor. It was formerly worn only by the chief or one of his sons and was the symbol of power and wealth. It could also be used to render justice. In wood, brass rings, feathered, wickerwork headdress (perhaps made later than the mask). TSHOKWE. Angola and Zaïre. Height: 24 cm.

154/ Pwo dance mask representing a female ancestor; also called 'Mwana Pwo', young woman. When procuring this mask, the dancer, who was always a man, had to give the sculptor a copper ring, a kind of money symbolising marriage binding him to the mask. In wood with tressed vegetable headdress and brass earrings. Southern TSHOKWE. North-East Angola. Height: 22 cm.

155/ Mask with lowered eyelids and two horns. Headdress and beard in monkey skin. LUBA. Zaïre. Height: 41 cm.

156/ Bwami mask. Tribal markings around the mouth. Eyes in conical relief with incrustations. Beard in vegetable fibres. LEGA. Zaïre. Height: 22 cm.

157/ Oval shaped mask with a concave face. The line of the nose follows on to the forehead. In wood and kaolin. LEGA. Zaïre. Height: 32 cm.

158/ Ogival Boa mask with ears sticking out. This Bantu people dwelled to the south of the Zande and to the south west of the Mangbetu. They shared the same aesthetic feeling and were once part of the Mangbetu empire. Just like the latter, they used decorative body art, coating themselves from head to foot with a rich ruby colour with white and black patches. Formerly, they dilated the centre of their outer ear and spread the edges out by inserting a metal ring or a wooden disk in the hole. It is this particularity, displayed on either side of the oval face, that one frequently observes on their war masks. They are moreover engraved with parallel bands and triangular, quadrangular or curvilinear patches, stained alternately white and black. The mouth always carried teeth either wooden, or sometimes human. The same particularities are to be seen on their rare geometrical statuettes, harp handles, and the covers of their cylindrical boxes. BOA. North Zaïre. Height: 36 cm.

159/ Elongated mask with half-closed eyes in concave orbits. Very unusual tribal scars; median scarring covering the forehead and the nose, lateral scarring running from the templates to the chin. In wood, copper inlays, human teeth. NGBAKA NGBANDI. Mongala region. North-East Zaïre. Height: 36 cm.

STATUARY

160/ A ritual statuette whose simplicity and harmony blend to perfection. Its mystic import is displayed by the chevron chiselling which, according to Griaule, symbolizes the vibration of light and water. In wood with black, crusted patina. SONINKE. Mali. Height: 69.8 cm.

161/ Head of a horseman, representing Amna, god of creation. He is mounted on a horse, a symbol of power and the emblem of the genie, Mommo. In heavy, hard wood with a dark reddish patina. (Note the similarities with the Djenne terra cotta horsemen.) DJENNE. Mali. Height of the rider: 65 cm. Pattern: 35 cm.

162/ Statuette of a kneeling hermaphrodite, its arms held down by its sides. In wood with sacrificial patina. SONINKE. Mali. Height: 29 cm.

163/ Statuette of a bearded hermaphrodite. Ear pendants and metal bracelets. In wood with sacrificial patina. DOGON. Mali. Height: 21 cm.

164/ Statuette with arms raised and hands clasped, with thick sacrificial patina. In the style of the Tellem, who preceded the Dogon. DOGON. Mali. Height: 58 cm.

165/ Statuette with arms raised and spread wide, pierced with symbolic triangles. In the style of the Tellem. DOGON. Mali. Height: 46 cm.

166/ Statuette of a seated woman in geometric style. Navel hernia accentuated by a vertical groove running the length of her body. In wood with black patina. BAMBANA. Mali. Height: 62 cm.

167/ Statue of a woman holding a gourd in her hands, sitting on a stool supported by five figures. In wood with black, crusted patina. DOGON. Mali. Height: 80.5 cm.

168/ Heavily scarified female statuette with prominent forms. In wood with black patina. BAMBANA. Mali. Height: 66 cm.

169/ These kinds of statuettes named Nieleni (photographs 168 and 169) were transported from village to village by young initiates of the Djo society, who accompanied them with songs. They dressed them in cotton fabrics and adorned them with pearls and copper rings. These Nieleni played a kind of, as yet, unclearly defined marital role. Their bomb-shaped breasts carried high and horizontally on an elongated, thin, geometrical torso, together with their prominent buttocks, characterised what was seen as feminine beauty. Here the head, sculpted surface by surface, with a small, slightly concave face and two tresses either side of a crested headdress, are clearly indicative of its southern origins, a style from the Bougouni district which is fairly close to that of the Malinkes. BAMANA. Mali. Height: 61 cm.

170/ Female statuette commemorating an ancestor, with crested headdress and dangling arms. In wood with natural patina. MOSSI. Burkina-Fasso. Height: 47 cm.

171/ Horseman representing an ancestor figure, probably used for divining. In wood with black patina. SENUFO. Ivory Coast. Height: 34.2 cm.

172/ Statuette of a woman representing Katielo, the mother goddess, sculpted in the style of the bronzes of the same region. In wood with crusted patina. Damaged feet. SENUFO. Ivory Coast. Height: 57 cm.

173/ Large fertility statue called 'deble', on a base with a stump with which young initiates struck the ground during 'poro' ceremonies to call up ancestors. SENUFO. Ivory Coast. Height: 108 cm.

174/ Animal-shaped 'gbekre' statue, half man/half ape, upright and carrying a begging bowl. Probably the protector of farmers. BAULE. Ivory Coast. Height: 82 cm.

175/ This female statuette was undoubtedly sculpted in the Issia or Daloa region, the only Bete zones where sculpture existed. The headdress is quite different from that of Dan or We effigies. The neck bears characteristic oblique tribal scars instead of being smooth or ringed. Despite the obvious femaleness, a certain virility can be distinguished, doubtless due to the movement sketched by the arms and by the way they are segmented. The same is true of the powerful shoulders thrusting forward and the relative leanness of the breasts. The plastic process by which the artist indicates the stylised rib cage is quite original.
Here, statuettes as well as masks were relative newcomers compared to the stylistic core of the We from which they evolved. It is possible that this statuette was linked in some way to a ceremony similar to the Ba-Nyon, the annual election of the strongest and most handsome boy in the village. BETE. Ivory Coast. Height: 64 cm.

176/ Figure seated on a stool. Tribal scars on the neck and face. A row of glass pearls around the neck holding a trophy of a brass head. In wood with brown patina, the face coated in a lighter shade. BAULE. Ivory Coast. Height: 37 cm. Width: 11 cm.

177/ Woman seated on a stool in the Akan style and breast-feeding a child. Her headdress is very elaborate, her ankles are adorned with rings. In wood with black shiny patina. BAULE. Ivory Coast. Height: 47 cm.

178/ Tall thin statuette in archaic style, with crusted patina. BAULE. Ivory Coast. Height: 28.5 cm.

179/ Unlike classical African statuary in which the head is proportionately the major element, here it accounts for only one-sixth of the statuette. The closer one gets to the feet, the more striking is the disproportion, the legs being far too large in comparison with the tiny arms. The worn patina has completely effaced the two horizontal features of the cheeks that should be apparent, as well as the fingers and the tribal markings on the abdomen — yet one can still see the typical coffee grain eyes. These kinds of statuettes were also to be seen among the Kulango, a closely related ethnic group situated further north, who nevertheless retained their own style. ABRON. Ivory Coast. Height: 36.5 cm.

180/ Magical statuette representing a man holding his beard. Representations of tribal markings and jewellery. Sophisticated headdress. BAULE. Ivory Coast. Height: 41 cm.

181/ Statuette of a man clasping his beard in one hand. Long tribal scars on the temples. Hair in scored crests. Nose line prolonged by the eyebrows. BAULE. Ivory Coast. Height: 45 cm.

182/ Standing woman with damaged feet. Numerous tribal scars and bracelets in relief. Heavy eyebrows. In wood with shiny patina. BAULE. Ivory Coast. Height: 45 cm.

183a/ 'Akwaba' dolls of abstract shape with ringed necks and disk-shaped faces. Attached to the backs of pregnant women, they were supposed to help give birth to fine, healthy children. ASHANTI. Ghana. Height: 30.5 cm.

183b/ The same Ashanti doll seen from behind.

184/ Iran male figure.
This statuette was the incarnation of the spirit of a dead ancestor belonging to the royal line. The spirit could only survive provided an Eraminho ceremony was carried out for him, and he could well have played evil tricks on the members of his own family if he was not duly honoured. This Iran was guarded by the priestess Oquinca, appointed by the tribal chief. It possessed agrarian powers, receiving blood sacrifices and offerings of eggs and wine before the clearing of the land and sowing. It was present at the harvest, receiving a portion of the grain in tribute. This statuette also played a role of prediction, answering questions dependent on whether a sacrificed red cock moved away or came closer in its death throes. Finally,

young maidens carried it in triumph before their marriage ceremony. This figure represents a man of high social rank, as shown by his stool. The geometric style of his face, with characteristically prominent forehead, cylindrical neck, sometimes ringed and of disproportionate length, and rectangular torso, are specific to the island of Carache.
(The arrival of this item in Europe was documented in around 1830). BIDYOGO. Bissagos Islands. Guinea-Bissau. Height: 37 cm.

185/ Female cup-bearer with a talisman around the neck. Remarkable headdress in cascading levels. YORUBA. Nigeria. Height: 49 cm.

186/ Female cup-bearer in realistic and fluid style. Its face is reminiscent of the 'Ibeji'. In wood with shiny, dark brown patina. YORUBA. Nigeria. Height: 50 cm.

187/ Statuette of a female cup-bearer. YORUBA. Nigeria. Height: 49 cm.
The three statuettes in photographs 185, 186, 187 are dedicated to Obatala, the Orisha cult of creativity.
They were usually graced by a white ornament, like the priests and faithful of this god, an iron bracelet, and here a necklet of white pearls with pendant. The bowl they hold above their bosoms is to receive the hommage of the snail's white blood, symbol of patience and calm. This is the female element of this Orisha, the male element being represented by a statuette carrying a fan and a fly-whisk. The figures in photographs 185 and 187 are probably by the same sculptor and the style seems to correspond to that of the Ekiti region, whereas the remaining figure, with rounder forms,

is more likely to come from the northern central Yoruba, i.e. from the Oshogbo region.
These cup-bearers should not be confused with the Olumeye, or kola vessels, sculpted as kneeling mother figures, which are much larger and hold a cup that often has a lid.

188/ Female 'Shango' statuette, god of Thunder and Fertility. Its headdress represents two stylised axes, symbols of the thunderbolt, and thus of rain. In wood with fine black patina. YORUBA. Nigeria. Height: 56.5 cm.

189/ 'Shango' statuette. Kneeling figure carrying a 'Shango' and a rattle. In wood with black patina. YORUBA. Nigeria. Height: 37.5 cm.

190/ Kneeling woman carrying a child on her back. Hair drawn back and swept into four loops. YORUBA. Nigeria. Height: 47 cm.

191/ Statue of a spirit or Edjo. This statue represents Edjo Re Akare, the spiritual founding hero of the village. It was placed against the back wall of a sanctuary called Oguan Redjo situated in the centre of the village. This statue was usually accompanied by lesser figures as an escort lined up along the wall. They were all daubed with white 'Pembe', and clad in white linen skirts, as this colour stood for religious purity in all the lower delta of the Niger. The Urhobo statues are recognisable by their bulky torso, with an exaggeratedly thrust out chest. The navel protrudes. The head is characteristic with its high swollen forehead striped with vertical tribal scares in relief, or Iwu, on either side of a longer median line, or Akpurusi. The nape follows through the neck and back in a concave vertical line, forming a right-angle with the shoulders. Sundry accessories reveal the social standing of this hero. A small medicine gourd, or Ukokorogho, hangs against its chest; this is a martial charm and a symbol of power which is also to be seen on Ijaw statuettes. Close to the neck is a large tubular pearl, or Ophara, indicating a high rank within the Ohonvworhin male society. A curved relief going from one shoulder to the other represents a second pearl necklet, signifying membership of this society. Quite frequently the leading theme is martial with the Edjo holding a knife, sword, club, spear or warning horn. URHOBO. Nigeria. Height: 124.5 cm.

192/ Large female statue with tribal markings on the abdomen typical of the ethnic group. It is coloured red and white. Necklet featuring panther's teeth. IGBO. Nigeria. Height: 108 cm.

193/ This statuette is a ceremonial cup for libations of palm wine. In wood with brown patina. KORO. Nigeria. Jos Plateau. Height: 44.5 cm.

194/ Statue of an ancestor with an enlarged abdomen. In his hands he is carrying what appear to be two horns. In deeply channelled hard wood. ORON. Cross River. Nigeria. Height: 81 cm.

195/ Figure of an ancestor. To be placed in front of large idiophonic slitted drums, these works were sculpted by the Mbembe-Obubra, one of the two known

Mbembe ethnic groups. They occupied the Mid Cross River, at the confluence of the Ewayon, whereas the Mbembe-Njari, with their different style, lived in the north-east Cameroon grasslands. These large drums, of Iroko, were used as altars on which were placed the heads of slain enemies, and at the foot of which human sacrifices were carried out by beheading. This very worn mother figure represents a wife of the Ovat, the traditional chief; she was no doubt sculpted during her lifetime, following a tradition still current in the Cameroon grasslands. MBEMBE. Nigeria. Height: 94 cm.

196/ These rare statues from the Djimetta region are all in channelled hard wood, proving their great age; one of them, subjected to the Carbon 14 process, is estimated to date back to 1470 ±90 years. They have a powerful, stiff torso set on oversized thighs and prolonged by a long upright neck, sometimes adorned with necklets, culminating in a disproportionately small head. The face, softened by wear, has a pointed beard, sometimes in lacework. MBOYE, Bauchi Plateau. Nigeria. Height: 108 cm.

197/ Standing male figure, the head jutting out in front of the body. In wood with heavily crusted patina. JUKUN. Nigeria. Height: 82 cm.

198/ These two statuettes, emerging from a single trunk with a single pair of legs, would appear to be magical objects to ward off the death of twins. Monoxyle wood. CHAMBA. Benue river. Nigeria. Height: 47 cm.

199/ This statuette is a variant of the previous one and would appear to serve the same purpose. CHAMBA. Benue river. Height: 61 cm.

200/ Reliquary figure, eyes inlaid with brass. Two brass rings at the top of the arms. Hands joined over the navel. FANG. Gabon. Height: 41.5 cm.

201/ Statuette in black wood with shiny patina. Eyes inlaid with ivory. Tribal scars on the back and the torso. Two copper necklets around the neck, one at the top of each arm, at the knees and round the ankles. BANE, ethnic sub-group. FANG. South Cameroon. Height: 23 cm.

202/ Statuette in dark brown wood with shiny patina. Four copper necklets around the neck, one at the top of the arms, and rings around the ankles. Its navel is inlaid with copper. FANG. Gabon. Height: 21.5 cm.

203/ Reliquary made of a wickerwork sphere filled with bones and magical substances, topped by a head. In wood with dark red patina. Ivory eyes. FANG. Gabon. Height: 19 cm.

204/ Female statuette with long falling headdress and protruding navel circled by a brass ring. In wood with black patina. Eyes inlaid with ivory. FANG. Gabon. Height: 23 cm.

205/ Top of 'Byeri' reliquary representing a woman's head with trefoiled headdress. Eyes formerly inlaid with metal. FANG. Gabon. Height: 17 cm.

206/ 'Byeri' statuette with realistic muscles. The eyes are inlaid. Hands carrying a horn. In hard wood with a black, greasy patina. FANG. Height: 50 cm.

207/ Female 'Byeri' statuette with rounded forms. Note the refined headdress, the eyes inlaid with metal and the cubist treatment of the legs. In wood with black patina. FANG. Gabon. Height 61 cm.

208/ This statuette corresponds to the style of the Okak ethnic sub-group, from the Rio Muni region. Here the face displays a tendency towards idealised realism, with its edged ears, visible nostrils, curved lips and carved teeth. However, there is an overall taste for well rounded shapes, in particular for the limbs. Just as the Ngoumba, certain copper decorations adorn the triple crested headdress, eyes and neck. The figure holds symmetrically a small, sculpted, protective gourd. FANG. Equatorial Guinea. Height (without base): 41 cm.

209/ Removable head of a statue. Great refinement in the headdress. Brightly coloured white, black, red and ochre wood. KUYU. Republic of the Congo. Height: 30 cm.

210/ Reliquary cover surrounded by wickerwork, carrying a head bearing a helmet crest. In wood with black patina. Brown face enhanced with black. Pupils and teeth in iron. Glass pearl pendants. AMBETE. Congo. Height: 62.5 cm. Diameter of the base: 24 cm.

211/ Impressive reliquary statue. Its back contains a cavity which was used to hold magical substances. In wood, pearls and cowries. AMBETE. Congo. Height: 80 cm.

212/ Standing male figure, the face entirely covered with tribal scars, with necklace-type beard finishing in a trapezoidal goatee. Headdress with crest. In wood coated with a dark brown crust. TEKE. Republic of the Congo. Height: 80 cm. Width: 18.5 cm.

213/ Figure of an ancestor seated on a kind of chest. Headdress crowned with a large crest. In wood. Eyes inlaid with ivory. BEMBE. Republic of the Congo. Height: 22 cm.

214/ Kneeling figure playing a drum, with the characteristic tribal markings of the ethnic group. BEMBE. Republic of the Congo. Height: 18 cm.

215/ Statuette with fine tribal scars. In hard wood with natural patina. Diamond-shaped eyes inlaid with ivory. BEMBE. Republic of the Congo. Height: 22 cm.

216/ Statuette of a heavily scarified man holding a gourd in each hand. In wood inlaid with copper nails and pearls. BWENDE. Republic of the Congo. Height: 21.5 cm.

217/ Statuette of a crouching woman holding a child in front of her by the arms. In wood with brown patina. Eyes inlaid with ivory. VILI. Republic of the Congo. Height: 22.5 cm.

218/ Kneeling mother figure. Hanging from her forehead is a basket carrying a tiny baby. On her abdomen, a reliquary box closed by a mirror. On her back there is a leather bag containing magical substances and she is carrying a 'load' between her legs. In wood, leather, fibre, fabrics, iron, ivory. VILI. Republic of the Congo. Height: 28 cm.

219/ These 'phemba' mother figures personified fertility. Necklet of leopard's teeth and bonnet with geometrical designs. In wood with natural patina. KONGO-YOMBE. Zaïre. Height: 25.5 cm.

220/ Figure seated in the lotus position with belt, necklet and bracelets in fabric. A reliquary covered with a round mirror emerges from its chest. An iron bell on a small chain hangs around its neck. In wood with yellow patina on the face and white patina with red spots on the body. Mirror eyes. VILI. Republic of the Congo. Height: 29 cm. Width: 15 cm.

221/ Figure seated on a barrel (?) with hands holding his chin. A reliquary on his forehead and another on his abdomen are closed by mirrors. Bell pendant. KONGO. Zaïre. Height: 35 cm.

222/ Figure covered with fabrics secured by chains and cords from which dangle shells. Feathered headdress. On its chest, a reliquary containing magical substances closed by a mirror. KONGO. Zaïre. Height: 37.5 cm - 46 cm with feathers.

223/ Male statuette carrying a horn. The style is very unusual. Note the stylisation of the neck, mouth and hair. In wood with crusted black patina. This statuette was probably suspended. SUKU. Zaïre. Height: 39 cm. Width: 10 cm.

224/ Statuette of a heavily scarified woman with conical headdress and decorated skirt. In wood with natural patina. BAKWANDOLO. Zaïre. Height: 45 cm.

225/ Statuette of a chief standing, wearing a loincloth, holding a stick in one hand and a gourd in the other. Prominent navel hernia. Numerous tribal scars, symbolising an iguana. In wood with very old patina. BENA-LULUWA. Zaïre. Height: 51 cm.

226/ Animal-shaped magical statuette with nails, called 'N'kondi'. Probably a double-headed dog. Used by a 'Nganga' to work both good and evil. In wood, metal and raffia. KONGO. Angola and Zaïre. Width: 65 cm. Museu de Figueira da Foz, Portugal.

227/ Magical 'N'kondi' statue with nails. Upright man brandishing a knife (missing on this specimen) and acting as a law enforcer. Recipient for magical items on its abdomen. In wood, metal and glass. KONGO. (YOMBE). Height: 91 cm. Museu de Faro, Portugal.

228/ Seat supported by a woman bowing in an elegant posture. Her forehead is circled by a diadem holding back her hair tied in the form of a cross. Tribal scars on the stomach and bracelet on the left arm. (The plinth of this statuette presents visible partial reconstruction.) HEMBA. Zaïre. Height: 46 cm.

229/ Figure of a male ancestor. A very so-

ber style emphasising the dignity and serenity of the figure with its closed eyelids. Ringed neck and diadem high on the forehead. HEMBA. Zaïre. Height: 64 cm.

230/ Seated woman holding a cup which contained kaolin and was used for soothsaying. Note the ringed neck, opulent headdress and very pronounced tribal markings. In light wood with very smooth, black patina. LUBA. Zaïre. Height: 36 cm. Width: 16 cm. Depth: 24 cm.

231/ Female cup-bearer known as 'Mboko' or also 'beggar'. This ancestral figure, when placed before the hut of a recently delivered mother, was also used to collect the gifts of friends. In wood with black patina. LUBA. Zaïre. Height: 44 cm.

232/ Monoxyle seat with female caryatid, whose legs are worn away. Note the tribal scars in relief and the quality of the bracelets. HEMBA. Zaïre. Height: 35 cm.

233/ Magical male statue whose function was that of guardian of the village. Note the horn emerging from its left eye. In wood, fibre and animal horn. SONGYE. Zaïre. Height: 95 cm.

234a/ Male statuette, with long cap hanging in tresses. Arms held away from the body. V-shaped tribal scars on the forehead, the line of the shoulders emphasised by a double row and breasts picked out with cross-shaped incisions. TABWA. East Zaïre. Height: 38 cm.

234b/ Back of the preceding statuette. Such statuettes were garnered in the royal treasure house, and were created to perpe-

tuate the ancestral family trees. The larger the figure, the greater the importance of the ancestor concerned. The plinth, not attached, here evokes the chief's seat.
This specimen comes from Central Tabwa, and corresponds to the first, and most glorious style. The face is typically triangular, with protuberant eyes. The elongated torso, with its geometricised shoulders, is marked by a long vertical scar line, both front and back, with two angles at the level of the nipples and the shoulder blades. This style centre is also characterised by the vertical tribal markings on the forehead. Note the particular detail in the sculpting of the headdress, reproducing the blackened, pearl-adorned braids that were part of the ancient way of dressing hair.

235/ Statuette of a chief sitting down saluting. In wood with beautiful black patina, brass, pearls. Fringe on forehead, eyelashes and beard in natural hair. TSHOKWE. Angola. Height: 46 cm. Museu da Sociedade de Geografia, Lisbon. (In the museum since before 1900).

236/ Statuette of a chief seated on a folding chair saluting. In wood stained dark brown, with shiny patina covering the chest, forearms and hands that would seem to come from ritual unctions. Brass, natural hair for the beard, and red seeds. TSHOKWE. Angola and Zaïre. Height: 49 cm. Museu do Instituto de Antropologia, Porto, Portugal.
These two Quioco statuettes represent chiefs sitting on folding chairs, which were inspired by those of the merchants who came from Europe in the XVIIIth century, and served as thrones. They are wearing

the ceremonial Cipe Nya Mutwe bonnet that displays their princely rank. Both are performing the Mwoyo salute, a sort of hand wave, to wish long life and fertility.

The first is not monoxyle, since the upper part of the body is joined at waist level to the rest, and the rear leg of the chair has been jointed on. It was made out of a different wood from the second.

Both were brought back at the beginning of the century.

Their realism and their painstaking and particularly careful craftsmanship correspond to the Origem style of the Moxico school.

237/ Statuette of a chief. In reddish wood, stained dark brown. TSHOKWE. Angola and Zaïre. Height: 35.5 cm. Museu de Etnologia, Lisbon.

238/ M'BOLE statue. North-East Zaïre. Height: 87 cm.

239/ M'BOLE statue. North-East Zaïre. Height: 103 cm.

240/ M'BOLE statue. North-East Zaïre. Height: 41.5 cm.

These three photographs 238, 239 and 240 represent statues of hanged men to be hung on the walls and were intended to enlighten initiates as to what might befall them should they reveal the secrets of their 'Lilwa' secret society.

241/ Standing figure of a man carved in a cubist manner, used in the 'Bwani' initiation society rites. In polished wood with natural patina. LEGA. North-East Zaïre. Height: 29 cm.

242/ Statuette (perhaps the top of a cane). Work typical of the Nguni peoples (who included the Zulus). A simple yet refined sculpture. In brown-red wood. ZULU (?). South Zambezi. Height: 28 cm.

243/ Elongated statuette. Eyes, navel and hair inlaid with metal. Numerous brass rings. In wood with natural, clear patina. KAMBA. Kenya. Height: 26.5 cm.

244/ 'Alualu' memorial statue.
This was erected when the body was not buried in the family tomb, or when the deceased left no male descendant. It was surrounded with a hedge of pickets bearing the horns of hump-backed oxen (zebus) sacrificed during the funeral rites. The strict rule demanded that it be a female representation that became the substitute for the deceased male, thus symbolising the element destined to ensure continuity. In hard camphor wood. BARA ethnic group. Ambusitra region, South-East Madagascar. Height: 107 cm.
(We have chosen to show you a statue from the island of Madagascar which is geographically part of the African continent. Art books tend to omit it, as the local art is a blend of Bantu and Indonesian elements. However, the item illustrated shows that the Negro influence of the Bantu people was very extensive.)

ENVIRONMENT

245/ Anthropomorphic cup. Statuette of a woman whose head has been transformed into a finely engraved cup. In wood with natural patina. M'BUNDA. Angola and Zambia. Height: 15 cm.

246/ Tobacco box with a female caryatid thrusting out her breasts. In wood stained chestnut brown. TSHOKWE. (Moxico style). Angola and Zaïre. Height: 14 cm. Casa Museu Teixeira Lopes, Vila Nova de Gaia, Portugal.

247/ Head-shaped ritual cup for drinking palm wine. It is inlaid with cowries around the neck and on the handle and with brass on the mouth, temples and back of the skull. KUBA. Central Zaïre. Height: 18.3 cm.

248/ Anthropomorphic tobacco box. Female figure. In wood with natural patina. Eyes inlaid with ivory. TSHOKWE. Angola. Height: 24.5 cm.

249/ Head-shaped wooden cup. The neck is adorned with an intertwined pattern that was much used by the KUBA. Central Zaïre. Height: 20 cm.

250/ Head-shaped cup in sculpted wood: headdress deeply cut back above the temples. Finely striped tattoos on the cheeks and concentric tattoos on the temples. A copper strip decorates the middle of the face and the eyebrows. Dark, shiny patina. KUBA. Central Zaïre. Height: 19 cm.

251/ Charm representing a person kneeling inside a pitchfork. In dark wood with shiny patina. VILI. Republic of the Congo. Height: 20 cm.

252, 253, 254/ Three magical whistles used by priests and hunters. Tips of antelope horns set into wooden statuettes. VILI. Republic of the Congo. Height: 19, 17 and 16 cm.

255/ Hook representing a person on horseback on a drum supported by interwoven wood imitating wickerwork. In wood with brown patina. LUMBO. Republic of the Congo. Height: 15 cm. Width: 5.5 cm.

256/ Double-barrelled whistle. In hard wood with natural, dark brown patina. VILI. Republic of the Congo. Height: 20 cm.

257/ Heddle pulley. BAULE. Ivory Coast. Height: 26 cm.

258/ Heddle pulley. GURO. Ivory Coast. Height: 17.5 cm.

259/ Heddle pulley. GURO. Ivory Coast. Height: 18.5 cm.

260/ Heddle pulley. SENUFO. Ivory Coast and Mali. Height: 16 cm.

261/ Heddle pulley. DOGON. Height: 18 cm.
These heddle pullies were hung from the weaving frame by the neck or by a hole in it; the pulley guided the rope which raised and lowered the heddles. This decorated system spread throughout all the Sudan cotton growing area: Mali, Burkina-Fasso, Ghana, the Ivory Coast, Guinea and even Casamance.

This specimen represents the Setien 'calao', whose stylisation gives greater importance to the beak, with elegant out-turned lips. The pullies could also represent the human Kpelie mask, impregnating, in both cases of ancestral rituals, the actions of the weaver. With the Senufo, they sometimes featured buffalo heads or human faces or, more rarely, a hand or a tortoise.

262/ Adze with hard wood shaft. The head of the half man/half lizard tool is prolonged by a curved iron blade. WANA. Zaïre. Overall length: 31 cm. Length of blade: 23 cm.
263/ Display weapon whose shaft, wrapped round in brass, is topped by a sculpted head. Chiselled iron blade. LUBA. Zaïre. Height: 37 cm.

264/ Display weapon. In wood, brass and iron. LUBA. Zaïre. Height: 38 cm. Length of blade: 26 cm.

265/ Ritual bed (?) with four feet, prolonged by a head with a very typical Tshokwe headdress. It is decorated with engravings that are reminiscent of the earrings known as 'Ukulungu' common to this ethnic group. In wood in natural patina. TSHOKWE. Angola and Zaïre. Length: 131 cm.

266/ Anthropomorphic lock: woman-guardian of a granary door. In wood with leather loincloth. BAMANA. Mali. Height: 53 cm.

267/ Spoon with a half man/half ram head. In hard wood with black patina. DAN. Liberia-Ivory Coast. Height: 53 cm.

268/ Spoon whose handle represents a man with his hands on his hips. In light wood with brown patina. GURO. Ivory Coast. Height: 28 cm.

269/ Twisted spoon in dark brown wood, eyes inlaid with pearls. FANG. Gabon. Height: 25.5 cm.

270/ Twisted spoon in very dark brown wood. GURO. Ivory Coast. Height: 21.5 cm.

271/ Anthropomorphic spade in light wood with black patina. DAN. Height: 59.5 cm.

272/ Spoon whose handle is decorated with four figures back to back, having a total of six legs. In wood with natural dark patina. GIO. Liberia. Height: 45.5 cm.

273/ Pestle-spoon of abstract shape, evoking a woman's body. KULANGO. Burkina-Fasso. Height: 32 cm.

274/ Ceremonial Mia or Wa Ke Mia spoon. These spoons were above all used by the Dan from the west, but also by the Kran who called them Minatu. The Wobe sometimes used spoons of Dan origin that they called Poh. The owner, or Wunkirle, was always a woman of high rank named by her predecessor who passed on the spoon before her death. This Wunkirle organised feasts in which she danced and paraded dressed as a man, waving the spoon filled with rice in her right hand. Acolytes followed her, holding her by the edges of her garments and distributing peanuts and titbits to the guests. She herself had to serve the food to all the participants with the aid, it is said, of the spirit that inhabited the spoon.

These large spoons look more like spades and were sometimes doubled. Their backs were engraved with geometrical patterns, and sometimes sculpted in animal forms in relief. That which seems to be the handle (since handling mainly took place using the edges) is the main decorative element; it nearly always represented a female face with an elaborate headdress, sometimes enhanced with fibres. It could also be a pair of legs with a rough sketch of the body, a closed fist, a tiny bowl of rice evoking the collective meal, or a ram's head, recalling the animal that was sacrificed on such occasions. These spoons were hung up in the hut, often hidden under the thatch above the entry, and it was forbidden to touch them under penalty of having to organise at one's own expense the feast where they would be exhibited.
DAN. Ivory Coast. Height: 63 cm.

275/ Top of a five-stringed harp. Female head with ivory inlaid eyes. MANGBETU. Zaïre. Height: 69 cm.

276/ Eight-stringed harp crowned with a stylised face. In wood, skin and nails. AMBETE. Gabon. Height: 45.5 cm.

277/ Music hammer. Statuette of a woman topped by a striking head decorated with a gazelle's head. BAULE. Ivory Coast and Ghana. Height: 26.5 cm.

278/ Wooden bell with clapper known as 'Madibu'. Used to attract the spirits of ancestors. Handle made of a seated man. Monoxyle wood with natural patina. KONGO. Republic of the Congo. Height: 22 cm.

279/ Top of walking stick bearing a Janus figure with a woman's body. LOBI. Burkina-Fasso. Overall length: 102 cm.

280/ Walking stick knob adorned with a woman sitting cross-legged breast-feeding a child. In wood with crusted patina. YOMBE. Zaïre. Overall length: 70 cm.

281/ Female statuette with black and crusted patina topping a light wood walking stick clad in leather, sewn at the front. SENUFO. Ivory Coast. Overall length: 138 cm.

282/ Anthropomorphic abstract motif crowning a walking stick. In wood with black patina. Small ivory necklet. ZULU. (?) South Zambezi. Length: 153 cm. Motif: 30 cm.

283/ Two-faced soothsayer's stick with special scarifications. In polished wood in natural tones. MAKONDE. Mozambique. Overall length: 118 cm.

284/ Top of walking stick bearing a scarified woman, her hands on her shoulders. LUBA. Zaïre. Overall length: 80 cm.

285/ Spear shaft. Scarified woman with a fine headdress. LUBA. Zaïre. Overall length: 85.5 cm.

286/ Top of walking stick. Statuette of a scarified woman with a pearl necklet. LUBA. Zaïre. Overall length: 160 cm.

287/ Top of ceremonial walking stick. Head decorated with a huge headdress crowned by two figures holding each other by their waists. LUBA. South Zaïre. Overall length: 164 cm.

288/ Leather shield, embossed to create a frightening face. Its outer surface around the embossing is covered with fine notches. Rhinoceros hide. South Ethiopia. Height: 71 cm. Width: 64 cm.

289/ Oval-shaped wooden shield. To be worn on the forearm, thus leaving the hand free. A central aperture allows the warrior to look through. KIKUYU. Kenya. Length: 59 cm.

290/ Anthropomorphic water pipe. Made of a blend of wood, coconut, bamboo and terra cotta. MAVIA ethnic sub-group. MAKONDE. North-East Mozambique. Height: 27 cm.

291/ Anthropomorphic pipe representing the graceful body of a woman. In light polished wood. ZULU. South Africa. Height: 30 cm.

292/ Pipe made of a statuette of a man whose abdomen, circled by a brass wire, forms the bowl, the whole being held by an open hand. In wood with shiny black patina. TSHOKWE. Angola. Height: 25 cm.

293/ Stool with caryatid.
In the mid XIXth century a territorial expansion by the Tshokwe towards the north brought about a political change and expelled the court art which till then had seen chiefs' seats based on copies of Louis XIII chairs. This kind of stool, undoubtedly due to some influence of the Luba, began to emerge, with heads frequently appearing on the top surface or on its rear

edges. In this specimen, the luxurious headdress with its upturned edges is more suggestive of the Lwena, a very close ethnic group located more to the east. LWENA. Angola- Zaïre. Height: 50 cm.

294/ Seat with female caryatid. In wood with dark patina, eyes inlaid with cowries, multi-coloured pearls. LUBA. Zaïre. Height: 42.5 cm. Museu de Etnologia, Lisbon.

295/ Door of a dignitary's house or sanctuary. The central panel shows the solar navel with four rays spreading out. The lower and upper panels are decorated with stylised animals: a tortoise between two 'calao' birds, benevolent animals. Heavy crusted patina. SENUFO. Ivory Coast. Height: 132 cm. Width: 72 cm.

296/ Degue Dan granary door. Frequently made out of two planks joined by iron clasps, given the rarity of large trees in this region. These sculpted doors are the privilege of the initiated religious chiefs. Four Yurugu specimens are shown here, the fourth supposed to have been created by the god Amma; he is hiding his face, having transgressed the laws of nature by committing incest with his mother. It was following this unnatural deed that Amma decided to create man; among them figures Diongou Serou, the witness of Yurugu, who always takes up the same pose. DOGON. Mali. Height: 45 cm.

297/ Neck rest on six small columns. In brown, monoxyle wood. ZULU. South Africa. Height: 15.5 cm.

298/ Neck rest in dark, heavy, polished wood. Both feet are pierced which means it could be carried slung over the shoulders. NGUNI (ZULU?). South Africa. Height: 11.5 cm. Width: 22.5 cm.

299/ Elegant neck rest sculpted from a single piece of wood ornamented by a scroll bearing two breasts. In hard wood with light, natural patina. SHONA. Zimbabwe. Height: 13.5 cm. Width: 15 cm.

300/ Two old women seated with knees apart holding their faces. They are holding up the neck rest on their heads. In wood with black, slightly crusted patina. BAKALANGA. East Zaïre, near Lake Tanganyika. Height: 21 cm. Width: 23 cm.

BIBLIOGRAPHY

TERRA COTTA

BALLARINI, Roberto, 1985 *Djenne' Terracotta Statuettes Mali.* Milan.

CISSOKO, S.M., 1975 *Tombouctou et l'empire Songhay.* Dakar.

EVRARD, J., 1977 'Archéologie ouest-africaine. Les figurines en terre cuite du Mali'. Mémoire de Licence. Louvain-La-Neuve.

FAGG, Bernard, 1977 *Nokterracottas. The Nigerian Museum.* Lagos.

FAGG, William & PICTON, John, 1970 *The Potter's Art in Africa.* London (British Museum).

GHANA MUSEUM & MONUMENT BOARD *Clay used in Funeral Ceremonies.* Accra (s.d.).

de GRUNNE, Bernard, 1980 *Terres cuites anciennes de l'Ouest Africain.* Louvain-La-Neuve.

de GRUNNE, Bernard, 1981 *Ancient Treasures in Terra Cotta of Mali and Ghana.* New York (The African-American Institute).

de GRUNNE, Bernard, 1982 *La statuaire en terre cuite du delta intérieur du Niger au Mali.* München (Galerie Biedermann/Fred Jahn).

de GRUNNE, Bernard, 1983 *La poterie ancienne du Mali: quelques remarques préliminaires.* München (Galerie Biedermann/Fred Jahn).

JACOB, Alain & de HEECKEREN, Axel, 1977 *Poteries-Ivoires de l'Afrique noire.* Paris (A.B.C. Décor, Hors Série n° 33).

LEBEUF, Jean-Paul & Annie, 1977 *Les arts des Sao: Cameroun, Tchad, Nigeria.* Paris.

MONTEIL, Ch., 1972 *Une cité soudanaise, Djenné, Métropole du delta central du Niger.* Paris.

SCHAEDLER, Karl-Ferdinand, 1985 *Céramiques de l'Afrique noire et d'Amérique Précolombienne: La collection Hans Wolf.* Zürich.

STÖSSEL, Arnulf, 1981 *Keramik aus Westafrika. Einführung in Herstellung und Gebrauch.* München (Galerie Biedermann/Fred Jahn).

STÖSSEL, Arnulf, 1981 *Nupe Kakanda Basa-Nge. Gefässkeramik aus Zentral-Nigeria.* München.

BRONZE & IRON

BRINCARD, M.-Th., Ed., 1982 *The Art of the Metal in Africa.* The African-American Institute. New York.

DARK, Philip J.C., 1964 *Cire-perdue Casting: Some Technical and Aesthetic Considerations.* Ethnologica.

FAGG, William B., 1959 *Cire-Perdue Casting. 7 Metals of Africa.*

JACOB, Alain, 1974 *Bronzes de l'Afrique noire.* Paris (A.B.C. Décor, Hors-Série).

LEBEUF, Jean-Paul & MASSON-DETOURBET, A., 1950 *La civilisation du Tchad suivi d'une étude sur les bronzes Sao.* Paris.

LIPPMANN, M., 1940 *Westafrikanische Bronzen.* Frankfurt-am-Main.

UNDERWOOD, Leon, 1949 *Bronzes of West Africa.* London.

IVORY

CURNOW, Kathy 1983 'The Afro-Portuguese Ivories: Classification and Stylistic Analysis of a Hybrid Art Form'. 2 vols. Ph. D. dissertation, Indiana University.

EZRA, Kate, 1984 *African Ivories.* New York (The Metropolitan Museum).

FAGG, William Buller, 1959 *Afro-Portuguese Ivories.* London.

HEAGER, F., 1899 *Alte Elfenbeinarbeiten aus Afrika in der Wiener Sammlungen.* Wien.

JACOB, Alain & de HEECKEREN, Axel, 1977 *Poteries-ivoires de l'Afrique noire*. Paris (A.B.C. Décor Hors-Série n° 33).

MALGRAS, G.-J., 1972 *Les Ivoires*. Paris (A.B.C. Décor, numéro spécial).

PENNIMAN, T.K. 1952 *Pictures of Ivory and Other Animal Teeth, Bone and Antler*. Occasional Papers on Technology, 5. Oxford (Pitt-Rivers Museum).

SCHONFELD, W.L., 1976 *Benin Ivory Anthropomorphic Masks*. M.A. thesis, Columbia University.

TARDY, 1977 *Les Ivoires, 2ème partie: Antiquité, Islam, Inde, Chine, Japon, Afrique noire, Régions polaires, Amérique*. Paris.

TONG, Raymond, 1958 *Figures in Ivory*. London.

GENERAL WORKS & MISCELLANEOUS

* ADAM, Leonhard, 1963 *Primitive Art*. London.

ANDERSSON, E., 1954/74 *Contribution à l'éthnographie des Kuta*. Studia Ethnographica Upsaliensia VI & XXXVIII. Uppsala.

* BASCOM, William Russel, 1973 *African Art in Cultural Perspective*. New York.

* BASLER, Adolphe 1929 *L'Art chez les peuples primitifs*. Paris.

* BASTIN, M.-L., 1984 *Introduction aux Arts d'Afrique noire*. Arnouville.

BEN-AMOS, Paula, 1980 *The Art of Benin*. London.

BIEBUYCK, Daniel, 1973 *Lega Culture*. Berkeley.

* BOAS, F., 1955 *Primitive Art*. New York.

BOLZ, I., 1966 *Zur Kunst in Gabon*. Ethnologica, neue Folge, Band 3. Köln.

* BOSSERT, Helmuth Th., 1955 *Folk Art of Primitive Peoples*. London.

* BURAUD, Georges, 1961 *Les Masques*. Paris.

* BRAVMANN, R., 1973 *Open Frontiers: The Mobility of Art in Black Africa*. Seattle.

CHAFFIN, A. & Fr., 1979 *L'Art Kota, les figures de reliquaires*. Meudon.

CHAUVET, St., 1933 *L'Art funéraire au Gabon*. Paris.

* CHRISTENSEN, Erwin O., 1955 *Primitive Art*. New York.

* CLOUZOT, H. & LEVEL, A., 1926 *Sculptures africaines et océaniennes*. Paris.

* d'AZEVEDO, Warren L., ed., 1973 *The Traditional Artist in African Societies*. Bloomington.

DAVIS, Charles B., 1981 *Animal Motif in Bamana Art*. New Orleans (Davis Gallery).

* DELANGE, Jacqueline, 1974 *The Art and Peoples of Black Africa*. New York.

DEMOTT, Barbara, 1982 *Dogon Masks: A Structural Study of Form and Meaning*. Ann Arbor.

* De RACHEWILTZ, Boris, 1966 *Introduction to African Art*. London.

* COLE, Herbert M., 1985 *I Am Not Myself: The Art of African Masquerade*. Los Angeles (UCLA).

DREWAL, Henry John, 1977 *Traditional Art of the Nigerian Peoples: The Milton D. Ratner Family Collection*. Washington (Museum of African Art).

* EINSTEIN, Carl, 1915 *Negerplastik*. Leipzig.

* EINSTEIN, Carl, 1921 *Afrikanische Plastik*. Berlin.

* ELISOFON, E. & FAGG, W., 1958 *The Sculpture of Africa*. New York.

* FAGG, William Buller & PLASS, Margaret, 1964 *African Sculpture: An An-*

thology. London & New York.

FAGG, William Buller, 1981 *African Majesty From Grassland and Forest*. Toronto (Art Gallery of Ontario).

FAGG, William Buller, 1982 *Yoruba: Sculpture of West Africa*. New York.

* FORGE, Anthony, ed., 1973 *Primitive Art & Society*. London & New York.

* FRASER, Douglas, 1962 *Primitive Art*. New York.

* FRASER, Douglas & COLE, Herbert M., ed., 1972 *African Art & Leadership*. Madison (Wisconsin) & London.

* FRASER, Douglas, ed., 1974 *African Art As Philosophy*. New York.

* GILLON, Werner, 1985 *A Short History of African Art*. New York.

* GLÜCK, Julius F. & NOSKe, Margot, 1956 *Afrikanische Masken*. Baden-Baden.

GOLDWATER, Robert, 1960 *Bambara Sculpture From the Western Sudan*. New York (Museum of Primitive Art).

GOLDWATER, Robert, 1964 *Senufo Sculpture From West Africa*. New York (Museum of Primitive Art).

HARTER, Pierre, 1986 *Arts anciens du Cameroun*. Arnouville.

* HIMMELHEBER, H., 1960 *Negerkunst und Negerkünstler*. Braunsweig.

* HIRSCHBERG, W., ed., 1962 *Monumenta-Ethnographica. Vol. 1: Schwarz-Afrika*. Graz.

* HUET, Michel, 1978 *The Dance. Art and Ritual of Africa*. Text by Jean-Louis Paudrat. New York.

* JOPLING, Carol F., 1971 *Art and Aesthetics in Primitive Societies: A Critical Anthology*. New York.

* LAUDE, Jean, 1971 *The Arts of Black Africa*. Berkeley.

LAUDE, Jean, 1973 *African Art of the Dogon: The Myths of the Cliff Dwellers*. New York.

* LEIRIS, Michel & DELANGE, Jacqueline, 1968 *African Art*. New York.

* LEUZINGER, E., 1977 *The Art of Black Africa*. New York.

* McCALL, Daniel F. & BAY, Edna G., ed., 1975 *African Images: Essays in African Iconology*. New York.

* MEAUZE, P., 1967 *L'Art nègre: sculpture*. Paris.

* MURDOCK, George Peter, 1959 *Africa: Its Peoples and Their Culture History*. New York.

* MURRAY, Jocelyn, ed., 1981 *Cultural Atlas of Africa*. New York.

* OTTENBERG, Simon & Phoebe, 1960 *Cultures and Societies of Africa*. New York.

PERROIS, L., 1972 *Statuaire Fan, Gabon*. Paris.

PERROIS, L., 1979 *Arts du Gabon, les arts plastiques du bassin de l'Ogooué*. Arnouville.

PERROIS, L., 1985 *Art ancestral du Gabon dans les collections du musée Barbier-Mueller*. Genève.

* PRICE, Lorna, ed. 1984 *Praise Poems: The Katherine White Collection*. Seattle. (The Seattle Art Museum).

* RASMUSSEN, René, 1951 *Art nègre: ou le salut par les sauvages*. Paris.

* RATTON, Charles, ed., 1951 *L'Art Nègre*. Paris (Présence Africaine 10-11).

* RATZEL, F., 1894/95 *Völkerkunde*, ed. rev., 2 vol. Leipzig & Wien.

* RIVIERE, M., 1975 *Les Chefs-d'œuvre africains des collections privées françaises*. Paris.

* ROY, Claude, 1957 *Arts sauvages*. Paris.

* RUBIN, A., 1974 *Power and Display, African Accumulative Sculptures.* New York.

* RUBIN, W., 1984 *'Privitivism' in 20th Century Art: Affinity of the Tribal and the Modern.* 2 vol. New York (The museum of Modern Art).

* SANNES, G.W., 1970 *African 'Primitives': Function and Form in African Masks and Figures.* London.

* SCHMALENBACH, W., 1953 *L'Art Nègre.* Paris.

* SCHNEIDER, I.L., 1951 *Masques primitifs.* Paris.

* SYDOW, Eckart von, 1923 *Die Kunst der Naturvölker und der Vorzeit.* Berlin.

* SYDOW, Eckart von, 1954 *Afrikanische Plastik.* Aus dem Nachlass heraugeg. von Gerdt Kutscher. Berlin.

TAMARA, Norhten, 1984 *The Art of Cameroon.* Washington (Smithsonian Institution).

* TERRISSE, André, 1965 *L'Afrique de l'Ouest berceau de l'Art Nègre.* Paris.

* THOMPSON, Robert Farris, 1974 *African Art in Motion: Icon and Act in The Collection of Katherine Coryton White.* Los Angeles (UCLA).

THOMPSON, Robert Farris, 1976 *Black Gods and Kings: Yoruba Art At UCLA.* Bloomington (Reprint of the 1971 ed.).

THOMPSON, Robert Farris & CORNET, Joseph, 1981 *The Four Moments of The Sun: Kongo Art in Two Worlds.* Washington (National Gallery of Art).

* THOMPSON, Robert Farris, 1983 *Flash Of The Spirit: African and Afro-American Art and Philosophy.* New York.

* TROWELL, Margaret & NEVERMANN, Hans, 1968 *African and Oceanic Art.* New York.

* UNDERWOOD, Leon, 1964 (First edition 1947) *Figures in Wood of West Africa = Statuettes en bois de l'Afrique Occidentale.* London.

* UNDERWOOD, Leon, 1964 (First edition 1948) *Masks of West Africa = Masques de l'Afrique Occidentale.* London.

VANSINA, Jan, 1978 *The Children of Woot: A History of the Kuba Peoples.* Madison.

* VANSINA, Jan, 1984 *Art History in Africa: An Introduction to Method.* London.

* VOGEL, Susan, ed., 1981 *For Spirits and Kings: African Art From the Paul and Ruth Tishman Collection.* New York (The Metropolitan Museum of Art).

* VOGEL, Susan & N'DIAYE, Francine, 1985 *African Masterpieces From The Musée de l'Homme.* New York (The Center For African Art).

* WILLET, Frank, 1971 *African Art: An Introduction.* New York.

ZAHAN, Dominique, 1980 *Antilopes du Soleil: Arts et rites agraires.* Vienne.

* ZAYAS, M. de, 1916 *African Negro Art.* New York.

* General Works.

Gérald Berjonneau, ARTS 135, Paris
Cover photograph
1, 5, 9, 18, 19, 20, 21, 22, 23, 24, 25, 30, 33, 34, 35, 36, 37, 38, 40,
41, 42, 43, 44, 45, 46, 47, 48, 49, 50, 51, 52, 54, 55, 56, 57, 58, 59,
63, 68, 69, 70, 71, 72, 74, 75, 76, 78, 81, 82, 84, 85, 86, 87, 88, 89,
92, 93, 96, 97, 98, 99, 100, 102, 104, 106, 107, 108, 109, 110, 111,
112, 115, 116, 118, 119, 120, 121, 122, 124, 125, 126, 127, 128,
129, 131, 132, 133, 136, 137, 139, 141, 142, 143, 144, 145, 147,
149, 151, 161, 162, 163, 164, 165, 172, 174, 175, 176, 177, 178,
179, 180, 183, 188, 189, 194, 195, 197, 201, 202, 203, 204, 206,
208, 209, 210, 211, 212, 213, 215, 216, 217, 220, 222, 230, 231,
232, 241, 244, 247, 248, 249, 250, 251, 252, 253, 254, 255, 256,
257, 258, 259, 262, 265, 267, 268, 269, 270, 271, 272, 273, 274,
275, 276, 279, 280, 281, 282, 283, 285, 287, 292, 296, 297, 298,
299, 300

Bruno Albertoni, ARTS 135, Paris:
17, 168, 169, 288, 295

Hughes Dubois, Brussels:
12, 28, 29, 39, 53, 60, 62, 64, 65, 66, 67, 73, 79, 80, 83, 90, 91, 94,
101, 103, 117, 123, 130, 134, 135, 138, 140, 148, 150, 152, 153,
155, 156, 157, 166, 167, 170, 173, 181, 182, 184, 185, 187, 193,
198, 199, 200, 205, 218, 224, 225, 228, 229, 238, 239, 243, 245,
260, 261, 266, 277, 278, 284, 286, 289, 293

Roger Asselberghs, Brussels:
2, 4, 6, 7, 8, 11, 14, 77, 192, 196, 214, 240, 264

Maurice Aeschiman, Switzerland:
10, 207, 263

Carlos Ladeira, National Museum of Ethnology. Lisbon:
226, 227, 235, 236, 237, 246, 294

Daniel Fauchon, Paris:
16, 105, 158

N.M.A.A., Washington:
27, 31

Florin Dragu, Paris:
95

Fritz Mandl, Museum für Volkerkunde. Vienna:
26

Paul Macamia, Seattle:
32

Horst Kolo, London:
160

Sato, New York:
186

Werner Forman archive, London:
13, 190, 219

Marc Léonard:
61, 154, 159, 233, 290

John Taylor, New York:
171

Courtesy of L. Entwistle, London:
15, 191

Courtesy of L. Kahan, New York:
114

EDITING STAFF

ARTS 135, 135 rue d'Aguesseau, 92100 Boulogne, France

Lay-out: Gérard Pestarque, Paris

Photo-engraving: Digamma, Fontenay-sous-Bois, France

Printing and binding: Lannoo, Tielt, Belgium

ACKNOWLEDGEMENTS

First of all we address our warmest thanks to the Dapper Foundation. This book would never have seen the light of day had it not been for its support and advice.

We thank the members of our selection committee, who throughout two years dedicated a significant amount of their time to us, and helped us by their knowledge and their vast experience in selecting items.

We thank those collectors for their great generosity and openness in lending us their masterpieces.

We thank the Museum Curators who gave us permission to delve into their reserve stores to select unpublished items.

We thank Henri Lopes, former Prime Minister of the Congo, for his preface.

1828

De luxe edition numbered from 1 to 2000
ISBN 2-905 351-06-3
Printed in Belgium 1987